Finding Bobby Fischer

Dirk Jan ten Geuzendam

Finding Bobby Fischer

Chess interviews

New In Chess 2015

© 2015 New In Chess
First published in 1994
www.newinchess.com

Photos: New In Chess Archives, unless indicated otherwise.

Cover design: Volken Beck

ISBN: 978-90-5691-572-8

Contents

Foreword

Modern chess is going through difficult times; it is in the throes of professionalization in which the game, in all its many facets, will have to adapt to a professional world.

What we need now is a body of truly professional chess players who are aware of their duties and responsibilities towards their fellow-players. What we need is new organizers, able to set up professional tournaments with due regard to the interests of chess players, the public and the press. And finally, for a truly professional approach to chess events, we need professional arbiters.

It is unfortunate that for many years (indeed, decades) chess was under a permanent ideological cloud. This was largely the result of the overall dominance of Soviet chess players. The ruling Soviet bodies used chess as an ideological weapon in their struggle against the West. International discord and internal squabbling within FIDE were further negative influences on world chess events.

In any case the politicization of the chess world always prevented its representatives from making the correct business decisions for radically widening its appeal. And it is here that Dirk Jan's work in the past several years has been of the utmost importance. I regard Dirk Jan as one of the few professional chess observers capable of providing news and summaries sufficiently honestly and impartially to allow both chess specialists and chess amateurs to find out what is really going on. He observes and reports without fear or favour and steers clear of political bias, limiting himself to factual, blow-by-blow accounts of chess events.

I believe that the format of lengthy interviews as adopted by New In Chess constituted a serious step in the right direction. It provides well-known chess players with a platform to air their feelings, and helps interested readers to draw their own conclusions, while taking account of the players' view on what is happening in the chess world.

I cannot stress enough that this approach is exactly what we need at the moment. Too often we run up against points of view, with authors prejudging events and making it impossible for their readers to discern the wheat of today's realities between the political chaff.

I gave my first long interview to New In Chess in 1989, when I met Dirk Jan after the tournament in Tilburg. Since then we have had several long and sincere talks, which I invariably enjoy.

I hope that the long series of interviews which you will find in this book will help you better to realize the complicated and often conflicting processes which chess has been going through lately. After reading the different points of view, you will be able to form your own picture of what is going on.

I firmly believe that this is Dirk Jan's greatest service to chess. Maybe he, too, had pressure put on him by different people from different sides. But having taken a sober and unbiased look at things – as a journalist should – he was able to come up with a strictly factual account, thus proving that he is rightly considered to be one of the finest chess journalists of the day. Professional chess has an awful lot to thank him for.

I hope that when reading the book, you will not only agree with me on this and enjoy it, but that you will also come away with a clearer idea of the direction chess has been moving into over the last few years.

Moscow, September 1994
Garry Kasparov

Note to the 2015 edition

Finding Bobby Fischer appeared in 1994, two years after my meeting with Bobby Fischer in Sveti Stefan, where the reclusive American resurfaced from his 'wilderness years' for a controversial second match against Boris Spassky. The book was well received and second-hand copies became sought after when it was no longer available. I am happy that my first interview collection has finally been reprinted. Apart from a number of minor corrections, additional footnotes and a different photo selection, this reprint is identical to the original edition.

The Hague, June 2015
Dirk Jan ten Geuzendam

Bibles of the Best

'If you think this is in the interest of chess, I will gladly do so.' The voice of the 81-year-old gentleman at the other end of the line sounded creaky in an aristocratic manner. We made an appointment and as I rang off I felt delighted. In the early months of 1986 I had sent Dr Meindert Niemeijer, founder of the Van der Linde-Niemeijeriana collection, a letter asking for an interview and he had raised no objections. Funnily, in the years to come I would interview dozens of people related to chess, but never again did I approach them by letter. Until more than six years later, when I directed one to the man who gave this book its title.

With hindsight it is only too appropriate that I had my first interview with the man who gave the Netherlands one of the biggest chess libraries in the world. My true passion for chess was sparked off by the Fischer-Spassky Match of the Century in Reykjavik in 1972. Yet, my devotion to the game underwent a fundamental change when I started to frequent the Van der Linde-Niemeijeriana collection in the Royal Library in The Hague in the early eighties. Treasure trove would be an understatement to describe the wealth of information I found there collected in some 25.000 volumes. The moves I learned from my father and Euwe's highly instructive *Volledige Handleiding tot het Schaakspel* (Complete Guide to Chess), but as the English put it so aptly, I was educated at the Van der Linde-Niemeijeriana collection. There I discovered what a splendid chess heritage has accumulated over the centuries. Delving into volumes of the *Wiener Schachzeitung*, the *American Chess Quarterly*, the *British Chess Magazine*, and any other magazine or book that cross references would lead me to, I entered a world rich in stories and full of romanticism.

Living a three-hour train journey away from The Hague, I aimed for one visit per month. At the end of the journey I would be welcomed by the indispensable Rob Verhoeven, who was always an invaluable source of information and a tireless help. I must have made thousands of photocopies, resulting in marvellous files on out-of-the-way subjects as the Rice Gambit, or more useful ones on the great champions. After my interviews had become a regular feature in New In Chess, the Royal Library remained my first source of information whenever I prepared.

As I made my visits to The Hague, the enigmatic person of Dr Niemeijer always loomed in the background. Occasionally I prodded Rob Verhoeven for some information about this remarkable man, but except for the fact that he still tried to fill gaps in the collection, I only learned that he hardly ever visited the library. I still regard my decision to have my first interview with him as a fortunate choice. Rereading the interview, I still feel the same inspiration that his drive and his wish to share his love of books gave me then.

The interview with Tim Krabbé is also a good illustration of the fascination that drew me into the world of chess. Again I was talking to a passionate collector, in this case an unparalleled collection of chess curiosities. Although Krabbé has converted to the boons of the computer in the meantime, the bulk of his immense curiosity collection is still stored in an extensive loose-leaf archive. Two memories from my visit to his Amsterdam home will always stick to mind. The piercing look with which he related his passion for the 'odder side of chess' and his mentioning the curious fact that he had been born exactly twenty years before Garry Kasparov. According to his strict guidelines I am sure Krabbé would not count this as a chess curiosity, but he still crossed out a false birth date on one of the books he presented me with. Before I could leave the premises he had taken a pen and changed it to the correct date: April 13th.

Not surprisingly, my interest in chess books and the rich and diversified history of the game kept playing a prominent role when I went on to interview leading grandmasters of past and present. However, more often than not the questions related to their literary interests did not make it into the final version of the interview. Mostly they were not integrated in the subjects we discussed, but rather added to satisfy the personal curiosity of the interviewer. Often as I asked grandmasters about their literary preferences, we rarely elaborated on the subject. Until, that is, I had the idea to start a special series in New In Chess, 'Check your Library', in which I asked leading chess authors about their recommended reading. I agree with John Nunn that sometimes these lists became a bit tiresome and slightly predictable. Frequently they would start with Alekhine's *Selected Games* and automatically lead to Bronstein's *Zurich 1953* both, of course, admirable books in themselves. Yet, apart from these inevitable shared favourites, there were a lot of sparkling and startling moments. Anatoly Karpov, who complained about the level of today's chess literature and used the occasion to slate the merits of Kasparov's widely acclaimed books. Or Garry Kasparov himself, the author of my personal favourite at the time, *The Test of Time*, who appealed for a more objective assessment of the mediocre quality of most of the older scribes. And of course the stern and inimitable Mikhail Moiseyevich Botvinnik. No longer friends with him, he also managed to skip Kasparov's brainchildren. Botvinnik's words of praise were saved for champions that are no longer with us, like Capablanca and Alekhine. With one notable exception. During our talk in Brussels the inevitable conclusion had been in the air for quite some time, but I still feel my heart jump when I recall the moment The Patriarch confessed, 'This may not sound modest, but I think that the first three books of my collected games are required reading.'

Dr. Meindert Niemeijer

Broek in Waterland, March 1986

'Your foremost urge should be love for the book'

'What should one do, leave or sell one's collection to a public institution or make it possible for private individuals to take the same delight in it that it has given me? I have carefully weighed these two considerations against each other and chosen to disadvantage the private person: I have deprived them of the pleasure it has given me, because to me the importance of there being a facility to which these same private individuals can turn to keep themselves informed, came first.' In 1948 Dr. Meindert Niemeijer decided to donate his chess-library, which at that moment contained some seven thousand volumes, to the State of the Netherlands. Among his conditions was the stipulation that his collection be amalgamated with the more than eight hundred chess books which the Royal Library in The Hague had acquired in the 19th century from the eccentric chess-historian Antonius van der Linde, and that the entire collection be named the Bibliotheca Van der Linde-Niemeijeriana. The Royal Library, henceforth, was to acquire mainly new publications, while Dr. Niemeijer continued his unremitting efforts to trace older publications still missing and out-of-the-way chess books. This constant supply of books has resulted in the Royal Library now boasting approximately 24,000 books on chess and about four thousand on draughts, and rivalling the Cleveland John G. White collection's reputation of being the largest chess library in the world.

Some months ago, Dr. Niemeijer, who has now reached the venerable age of 84, moved from Wassenaar, near The Hague, to Broek in Waterland, a friendly village so close to Amsterdam that the proximity of the metropolis never fails to surprise[1]. On the morning of the interview spring has laid tender siege to it. Delicious scents of trees and shrubs and flowers waft on the gentle air, and in the first street I enter I see a woman scrubbing her doorstep in the bracing early morning sunlight.

Somewhat further on into the village, in an even quieter byway, Dr. Niemeijer resides. There is nothing in the house to betray the fact that he moved in only recently but one cannot help noticing the paucity of books in his living room.

Dr. Niemeijer passed away one and a half years later, on October 5, 1987, at the age of 85.

Apart from works of reference like Van der Linde's *Geschichte und Litteratur des Schachspiels* (History and Literature of Chess), *Das erste Jahrtausend der Schachlitteratur* (The first Millenium of the Literature of Chess) by the same author, and Sacharov's Russian bibliography, his only chess books are exchange-copies.

'I don't even have my own chess books, the ones that I authored, here, so you can see I can also leave the whole thing alone when I want to. That, I think, is something that one ought to always do or one is lost.

'As a boy one quite naturally starts collecting all kinds of things, for instance marbles, matchboxes and God knows what else. Then one becomes devoted to one subject, really, in my case chess, and then this innate collecting mania focuses itself on that. I have got it from my parents, I come from tainted stock. It runs in the family. My mother, who was born in 1864, collected postage stamps. For a girl that was quite a rarity in those days, of course. My father did the same, amongst other things. A sister of mine has made a collection on the subject of Atlantis.

'Chess books were not the only thing I collected; there were various other things, chessmen, for instance. I had acquired about a hundred sets and, well, there was no room for them in the house, which meant that they had to be stored in cigar boxes. Well, those I sold and for the money I bought more chess books. Then I have also collected picture postcards, especially those with topographical views of Holland of which I gathered some fifty thousand. And silver birth spoons. Of these I had only around two hundred which you could hardly call a collection. But I have disposed of all of them. I find it not at all difficult to part with something I have collected, no problem at all. Only the subject that I thought I would be able to achieve real success in, i.e. the bibliography of the game, I have kept on. Of that I thought, I can really get to the forefront here.'

At twenty-two years of age Dr. Niemeijer, encouraged and supported by Mr Oskam LLD, who, in those years, was a great promotor of chess in the Netherlands, started collecting chess books seriously. He built up his collection at great speed and by the end of nine years had acquired twenty-four hundred volumes. Nowadays this would be all but impossible, but how simple was it in those days?

'Dead simple. At auctions people did not even bid on them; I was the only person interested. Oh well, there was the occasional bid, of course, but the books were knocked down at what I would now call rock-bottom prices. Nowadays there is a great demand for older books, but in my early years it was exactly the other way around; it was the old books which were easy to get. That is just as well for otherwise I would not have been able to build up this collection. I was fortunate enough to have started at a time when prices were still manageable. If I had to do it all over again, the same collection, it would cost tens, if not hundreds of thousands of guilders. Also, in those days people were not all that interested in the value of the books. That is a bit unfortunate these days. People do not collect just because they like to have the book or because of what it contains, but imagine they have found a good way of investing money. That is most regrettable, as it tilts collecting away from the level it ought to be on. Love for the book should be the first consideration, and if the value increases so much the better, but that should not be one's starting-point. I have never allowed myself to be led by that consideration, otherwise I would never have given it away, of course. It has never been my intention to profit from it, and what's more, I have lost an awful amount of money on it, as you will understand.'

Despite the heightened commercialisation of the chess book trade, Niemeijer has stuck to his original principles. For many years now he has sent book-lists to all corners of the world, offering to sell, or preferably to exchange his extra copies and listing the titles he is looking for. He recently sent off number 134. His prices have always remained reasonable and are therefore way below those of the real dealers. He cares too much for his contacts, particularly the other major collectors.

'The number of collectors is increasing, although Holland does not have too many of them, not at all. There are only a few that stand out. A major collector should have at least a few thousand volumes, otherwise he does not count, he would be small fry. Well, such collectors do not exactly grow on the bushes here in Holland. I know a couple of them that have perhaps two or three thousand books but that is all. Other countries have more of them. Take a man like Lothar Schmid, he has a magnificent collection, the largest private collection in the world. Which is why I regularly have dealings with him. The number of major collectors is so small that somehow they never fail to find one another. There is rivalry, of course, that is inevitable. Some collectors are very secretive and refuse to say where they found something and what they have, but that, I think, is nonsense. One should help one another a little. Therefore, when I find a rare book that is already in our collection I make no bones about telling someone else about it. I could say, of course, now I shall make a point of not doing this, but that attitude seems to me to be rather small-minded.'

Openness and accessibility have always been important characteristics of Dr. Niemeijer's collection. Apart from the many book-lists he has sent all over the world, he has also published, often at his own expense, about collecting chess literature. A much sought after book of his is *Schaakbibliotheken. Een boek over verzamelaars en verzamelingen* (Chess-libraries. A Book about Collectors and Collections), dating from 1948, in which he offers a survey of the world's most important chess book collections. Showing great knowledge and insight, Niemeijer paints an absorbing picture of the nature and makeup of those libraries. Much of this knowledge was gleaned from the catalogues and inventories of these libraries, and from very early on he, too, made every effort to take stock of his collection. In 1930 he first published a mimeographed catalogue, to which he added supplements in 1932 and 1933. In 1939 he published a printed catalogue: *Catalogus van de Schaakboekerij van Dr. Niemeijer* (Catalogue of the Niemeijer Chess Library). Despite their undeniable usefulness, however, the drawback of these catalogues is that they date rather quickly, as Dr. Niemeijer collects with great speed.

'Only recently I bought a Yugoslav library. It belonged to someone who knew that I was a collector. Devotees of chess with the same interest usually know this, and sometimes such a person offers his entire collection for sale. I do not remember the exact number of libraries I have acquired but it should be about twenty-five. The libraries themselves vary from some hundreds of books to four thousand volumes. That big one belonged to Da Motta from Brasil, a truly magnificent library.'

Although a lot of newly acquired books, especially when they come in batches, end up on the exchange lists, the collection grew by leaps and bounds. For this reason Dr. Niemeijer, on making his donation in 1948, also made it conditional on the Royal Library publishing a catalogue within the next few years. This catalogue took until 1955 to appear and is still avidly consulted by collectors the world over. The year 1974 saw the publication of Volume One of a completely new catalogue, featuring Bibliography and History, but so far there has not been any sign of Volume Two.

Whenever the extent of the Van der Linde-Niemeijeriana collection comes up for discussion there is bound to be a comparison with the John G. White collection in Cleveland, Ohio, which for decades has been considered to be the world's largest. Thanks to a more active purchasing policy of modern chess books the The Hague collection now seems to have succeeded to that title.

'I am pleased, of course, that it is the largest collection at the moment, but that is not the most important point. To me the most important consideration is content, and I believe that in this respect White's collection comes an easy first. He, you see, was still in a position to acquire manuscripts. These are unique specimens, and once they have found a home they will never be on the market again. So far as that is concerned we are out of the race, but with regard to keeping up with new publications we probably have the edge over Cleveland. Pressure of work has always prevented me from visiting the Cleveland collection, but they have a catalogue as you know, and although it has grown a lot since, I have a fair idea of its contents. I have never seen Lothar Schmid's collection either, but he has been a visitor to my house. I have always been like that, everybody was welcome to see my collection, also in the time when I still had it at home. If I could be of assistance to somebody I would gladly do it. I see this as a common purpose. From the position one occupies and the circumstances one finds oneself in, one tries to do something for the game of chess, which is near to my heart, that is of use to all people sharing this interest.

'As a rule I am most interested in books from before the twentieth century. This is a somewhat limited field but what I like about it is the rarity of those works, tracking them down, looking for them, and comparing the copies. One examines the state they are in, whether they have an ex libris, preferably one with a chess motif. I take more pleasure in that than in the books which are now rolling of the presses in their thousands.

'I have for instance aimed at acquiring all the sixteenth century editions of Damiano. Lothar Schmid, has the full complement as well, but no other collection that I know of has the complete set. But one attempts to do these things only in very special cases. The Royal Library has a different policy; they try to acquire all editions of all Dutch publications. So if a book by Euwe has gone through thirteen printings, they want them all. For me personally that would go too far, even though I applaud the effort, and I must say that I enjoy it when I can help them out with a missing edition.

'You know that in 1881 Van der Linde published a bibliography, *Das erste Jahrtausend der Schachlitteratur*, which he thought contained practically everything that had been published in the field of chess up to that time. A very silly thought, of course, for such comprehensiveness is the nearest thing to impossible. I take some little pleasure in the fact that I have managed to unearth a few hundred books before 1881 that he has not included. That is more than I would ever have imagined there would be, especially since Schmid and Meissenburg[2] also have a couple of hundred of them. All in all I think there would be about a thousand.'

Asked what qualities he reckoned to be indispensable for a collector, Dr. Niemeijer some years ago mentioned, among other things, 'One has to be prepared to sit down on a rainy Sunday afternoon and send off a couple of hundred letters to all corners of the world.' Consequently he is not in the least inclined to romanticise the art of book collecting. Which does not mean that all acquisitions are effected in the same prosaic manner.

'At times, of course, one gets a nice surprise. Damiano was succeeded by a man called Porto, who in 1606 and 1607 published two booklets with contents practically identical to Damiano's publications. One day an Italian sent me both booklets for a song. He wrote, "Just send me something in return, never mind what; I do not collect this and you do, so you have an interest." It goes without saying that I sent him back a good parcel, but this is, of course, not the way these things are usually done. As I mentioned before, my main interest is in the chess literature of before 1900, but within that field I have a special predilection for the first authors, the sixteenth and seventeenth century writers. Where that is concerned I have no business in this country, as no one was writing about chess in those days. The first original chess book in Holland is by Van Zuylen van Nijevelt, published in 1792, which is very late. Of that book we have a French and a Dutch edition. These old books have nearly all been acquired, so they do not give me any more work. Of course, one can always say, like for instance Schmid, then I want two or three copies of it, but that strikes me as a useless exercise. Whenever

---

2 A collector whose chess library contains some ten thousand volumes.

Dr. Meindert Niemeijer, chess book collector *extraordinaire*, in 1951.

a second copy comes to hand one keeps the best one and disposes of the other. Schmid does not do that, so he has several Damiano's and so on. A magnificent catch was a Greco manuscript from 1625, written partly by himself, partly by a copyist. Of Ponziani I have been able to buy a whole series of manuscripts. They were offered for sale in an ordinary Italian catalogue. I was beside myself when I saw it, because you understand I wanted to have them. Now I can read Italian and understand it, especially if it is about chess, but I cannot speak it. Taking into account the amount of time it takes for a letter to reach Italy I thought that perhaps I had better telephone. At first the telephone was not answered, and when I finally got through I tried English, German and French, but to no avail. So I shouted some words like *scacchi* through the telephone, followed by the catalogue number, and immediately sent off a telegram, and so I got them. Those manuscripts had always remained in the possession of the Ponziani heirs and this was the first time that they had come on the market. Those are real coups, which leave me euphoric for a week. But these things happen very rarely, of course.

'Such a manuscript is really the height of perfection for me. If written in the author's hand it also contains a human element. I look at the handwriting for it can teach you a lot. It can be a hand that repels me, or one that attracts me. The same goes for books with an inscription.'

It could be called an ironic coincidence for an amiable and courteous person like Dr. Niemeijer to have amalgamated his collection with that of Antonius van der Linde (1833-1897), an almost demonic fault-finder who was at loggerheads with nearly everyone. After some initial activity in Dutch dissident religious circles he later departed to Germany. He not only wrote standard works on the bibliography of chess but also published, besides a number of other scholarly works on a wide variety of subjects, a treatise proving that the art of printing was not invented by the Dutchman Coster but by the German Gutenberg thus taking revenge on all his compatriots, with whom he had fallen out.

'That was a character that the world has never seen the likes of. He was impossible to live with, of course. He was simply incapable of sounding an objective note; his opinion was the only one that counted. The rest of the world consisted of nincompoops whom he constantly abused. That is not done, of course. The man was knowledgeable, and his contributions to the bibliography of chess are invaluable, but as a human being he was impossible. Now you could say the same thing about me perhaps, but I'm not that bad.'

Van der Linde's magazine *De Schaakwerld* (The Chess World) (the spelling of the title is in itself a manifestation of the author's pigheadedness), which survived only one year (1875), occupies a special place in the history of chess because of Van der Linde's recalcitrance.

'I find a magazine like *De Schaakwerld* amusing to read but there are dozens of that kind. My interest in that domain is so broad that I have not focused on one field. I always like to read about chess, provided it is not too dry. Among the historical magazines a few are special to me. They are *Le Palamède*, the *Deutsche Schachzeitung*, to which Von der Lasa has contributed a lot, and the *Chess Player's Chronicle*, that's about it. In our own country we had *Sissa* in those days. That was utterly worthless, and Mr Verbeek hadn't a clue, but heaven be praised that it was there because it is a goldmine of really invaluable information, for instance about clubs. There was, for example, the *Kalender van het Noordelijk Schaakbond* (Calender of the Northern Chess Federation), which went through nine volumes and from which I learned that in the eighties and nineties of the 19th century people in the north of Holland still played as follows: White started by advancing his d- and e-pawns two squares, to which Black invariably answered with d7-d5 and e7-e5. That is the way my father taught me to play, and he had been taught by his father, who was a protestant minister in Sneek. That did not come out of a book because in those days nobody played like that anymore, and there I was, reading that they played like that in the north of the country. Those things really fascinate me, that one hundred years ago chess in our country had *regional* variants. These are the things I like. I set them down and it is nice for later researchers to find them, otherwise the knowledge might have been lost. Unless such persons went and worked their way through all those thousands of books.'

These notes, together with particulars from Niemeijer's numerous scrapbooks, in which he sticks every item from newspapers and magazines having to do with chess, have given rise to a number of amusing booklets over the years, published, as nearly always, at his own expense. They contain not only historical finds like the one mentioned above but also notes like: 'Among the officially protected plants in Germany we also find the early (March/April) flowering, snake's head-like

Schachblume (chess flower) 'sehr selten in feuchten Wiesen and der Kocher, am Main und auf der Baar'.

'The collecting mania has of course subsided over the years. At my age one cannot raise the enthusiasm one had at thirty or forty. That goes for all things. One's nature grows more contemplative, one's enthusiasm does not gush over so easily anymore, but there are still some sparks left, indeed there are.

'I have always regretted refusing an item on the ground of it being too expensive. Five or ten years later I would always think, how stupid of me to have let such a chance slip. It has happened that I was offered a manuscript or a rare edition, and that I turned it down, because it did not fit into my plans of that moment, or I thought the asking price too steep. I cannot give you examples. I know them alright but I am still hoping to lay my hands on a few of them some day, so it would not do to say too much about it now.'

Tim Krabbé

Amsterdam, February 1987

The King of Chess Curiosities

For Tim Krabbé (1943) writing, cycling and chess have more in common than would seem at first sight. His love of numbers brought him under the spell of these seemingly so different activities, and he eventually managed to score successes in all three fields as a writer and a journalist.

As a novelist he broke through to a wider audience with his latest short novel *Het Gouden Ei* (The Golden Egg), which was very favourably received and sold well. The film rights have been sold and in September shooting will start in France and Holland. This is not his first novel that was turned into a film, nor will it be the last as far as he is concerned, for the novel he is currently writing, he assures me, might even be more suitable[3].

At thirty, Tim Krabbé decided to make a boy's dream come true and started a career as an amateur cyclist which, during the next eight years, would take him from one race to the other. The experience and impressions he garnered on and around the roads he described in numerous newspaper articles, as well as in his magnificent book *De Renner* (The Cyclist), which found an enthusiastic reception both within and without the world of cycling. A prominent sports journalist called it '...not only a literary masterpiece... but at the same time the best sports book in the Dutch language'.

In the world of chess, however, Tim Krabbé is mainly known as the king of chess curiosities. Although his merits as a player were not at all bad, and he twice got through to the finals of the Dutch championship, he was well aware of the limits of his talent. Driven by his great love of the bizarre and the beautiful in chess, a restless search for what he was later to call chess curiosities, became his main chess activity. His many contributions on this subject in *Chess Life*, *Schaakbulletin* and *New In Chess* were highly appreciated and led to a few books initially only in Dutch. In 1985 the English-language *Chess Curiosities* (published by George Allen and Unwin)

---

3 The film rights of The Golden Egg were later sold to Hollywood, which resulted in The Vanishing in 1993. At the cost of a loss of artistic merit this new adaptation reached a broader audience, but nevertheless highly displeased the author.

appeared and immediately met with recognition when the readers of the journal *Chess Notes* voted it Book of the Year.

Anyone familiar with his books will have an idea of the witty enthusiasm and infectious single-mindedness with which Tim Krabbé treats subjects like Nimzowitsch' gratis move, the Babson task, remarkable coincidences, or 46.0-0 in the game Bobotsov-Ivkov. Even his dreams, another hobby of his, are haunted by his 'disastrous craving for completeness', and he frequently dreams about castlings at move 79 not yet in his collection. A recurrent daydream he hopes to realise one day is a thousand-page tome entitled *All Chess Curiosities*.

What caused this love of chess curiosities?
'I have always had this interest, I don't know why, in the odder side of chess. I vividly remember my first look at the game Edward Lasker against Janowski from New York 1924, which ends with an utterly crazy endgame of two knights and three connected passed pawns on the seventh rank against a queen, with Black having a passed pawn as well. I could look at that final diagram for hours. Another strong memory is a game Spassky-Polugaevsky from the 1960 or 1961 Soviet championship, in which Spassky has his king stroll across a full board to g5 and could have won if he had pushed on to f6. I got *Chess Archives* containing that game with this diagram full of pieces and the white king on g5, and showed it to a chess friend who happened to call. We were standing there with the diagram in our hands, "Gee, how is this possible?" when my brother came in and asked, "Why are you laughing." When he saw it was a chess diagram, he looked at us with a face that said, "Those two are stark raving mad."

'He is not a chess player, but there were also chess players who reacted that way. I do not know why such a king on g5 moves my soul. I started chess like everybody else, I wanted to become champion, no matter of what, but by twenty I had long realised that I wasn't world champion, or even master, material. Eventually my ambition had shrunk to reaching the Dutch championship final, which was at least feasible. I belonged to the top twenty players of Holland for a few years, but never to the top ten. I did not fancy to go on playing chess at that level for the rest of my life. So at thirty when I took up cycling, I just called it a day. Being number twenty or thereabouts made me feel so old. So I stopped playing serious chess for ten years, and now that I have really become an old man, I can play my pathetic old man's game without too much self-reproach.'

But you never lost sight of the curiosities?
'No, that continued. Around 1970 I started taking notes. My first chess pieces appeared in Wouter van Rhoon's *Schaakrevue*, a kind of precursor of *Schaakbulletin*. That was in 1967. But this went broke, and shortly afterwards Wim Andriessen started up *Schaakbulletin*, with which I was involved fairly from the beginning. What I wanted to show as a chess writer was a mixture of beauty and the bizarre, but

always within chess itself. Never outside it. If a certain tournament had attracted three one-legged players I would not have been in the least interested. That tends towards a German kind of humour that doesn't agree with me at all. People sometimes associate me with this, and that I find insulting. "I know about a tournament for you where in round three all White's were bald and all Black's wore glasses." I'm not interested in that kind of thing.'

But writing about coincidences in chess you joyfully report the symmetrical game played by Weiss and Schwarz in Nüremberg 1883.
'I have my weak moments. If there is a funny game of Weiss with White against Schwarz with Black I cannot help noticing it, might even think it's wildly funny, and would probably publish it. But my interest has shifted. The purely bizarre I found far more fascinating in the beginning than now. Collecting all this material I have come across such an unbelievable number of beautiful things that my interest has shifted towards pure technical beauty.'

How do you go about garnering your material. What are your bibles?
'My bibles are chess magazines. I subscribe to about ten of them at the moment, and when they arrive I leaf through them and take notes of everything that rouses my interest. That is a rather cursory job. I look at all diagrams and if, for example, the magazine has endgame studies I try to have a glance at what they are about, that is, if they give the solution with the diagram. So I make these notes, which I sort in folders, and in the course of nearly twenty years this has grown into a system of nearly fifty loose-leaf files of about two hundred pages each, with about ten notes on each page. That makes some hundred thousand notes of sources, under some five hundred different headings. Now and then I start a new category when I see something very nice, but that's a rarity these days. The headings are mainly technical, and some of them have grown impractically large. Categories like for instance "Practical Stalemate", would have to be subdivided.

'In all those books on chess tactics the same few examples keep cropping up for ages, because nobody does the necessary research. Always the Lazdies-Zemetis stalemate, however stale it has grown. I am possibly unique in that I am not satisfied with one or ten examples of something. I want them all. I keep track of everything. Only, the computer age has made my archives rather obsolete. It should all be on computer, so you could call it up with a few strokes.'

You have no intention of doing this retrospectively?
'I have. The normal course of events with archives like mine is that, when the maker dies, they end up on the rubbish dump. Mine would fit into one refuse bag, if stuffed carefully. That would be a pity, however. It should be computerized and saved, and if I were five persons instead of one, one of me would gladly do that. But as it is, I think I should be subsidized to have this done.

Tim Krabbé: 'I have come across such an unbelievable number of beautiful things that my interest has shifted towards pure technical beauty.'

'I think my archives are interesting and worth preserving. When I study my predecessors in chess literature, Kurt Richter, Assiac, Chernev, Reinfeld, I can see they had far less complete archives than me. They had to rely on rather loose notes. None of them has ever collected as much as me, or suffered from the same *Gründlichkeit*, thoroughness.'

Is the difference that you, as you put it yourself, suffer from this disastrous craving for completeness?
'That's one difference, yes. When I have sixty examples of, say, the Zwickmühle, it is clear I cannot publish them all. I have to sort out the best ones. But with ten or fifteen examples, I have the problem that I cannot keep from publishing them all. Now, there is a typical combination where queenside castling checks a king on d8 and wins a rook on b2. You will find this combination in each and every book on tactics, but always the same, Feuer-O'Kelly, Liège 1934, which in itself is a good example. In *Chess Curiosities*, I have given twelve or thirteen examples, including one from an endgame study. Too many of course, but in such a situation I cannot resist to give them all, out of pure joy that I am the only person in the world who has collected so many.'

Have you any other sources besides the magazines?
'Yes, an enormous number of books, too. I leaf through lots of them, including the classics. *300 Schachpartien* by Tarrasch was my bedside book for a long time, and I also like writers like Nimzowitsch, Polugaevsky and Kmoch. A very important standard work is *De Schaakstudie* by Rueb. It is the study Bible, arranged according to themes. It only goes as far as 1950 and has a very peculiar style, he must have been a very peculiar gentleman. But that's a fantastic work, it goes back to the Arabs.'

During the thorough treatment of all kinds of phenomena you regularly surprise the reader with little historical facts. I found it very nice, for example, to read a short history of the underpromotion in the chapter of that name, and to learn that until about 1900 the rule was that a pawn could only promote to a piece which had already been captured, so that one side could never have two queens or three knights. One chess set sufficed. Do you do historical research to unearth such facts?

'Well, no, one has one's sources for that. I am no historian. In the White Christmas Series you have The Theory of Pawn Promotion. White has done that research for me, and he also refers to other articles. A man who has been invaluable to me is Rob Verhoeven of the chess department of the Royal Library in The Hague, who traces such things for me. Without someone like him life would be much more difficult, although I am often able to find my own way. Tracing back this history of the promotion you come across tremendously interesting things. For instance, that the first official international tournaments were still played with the rule that a pawn could remain a pawn upon reaching the other side, so that you had a choice of five promotions.'

This rule was on the books as late as Vienna 1873.

'Yes, Vienna 1873 was probably the last tournament in which it was used. The rules of the game had not been laid down so well, yet. There was no international chess federation. Rules often differed from village to village. Several grandmasters even now tell you they learned to play chess with very odd rules. Sosonko once told me that he had learned chess from his mother, who taught him White always begins with d2-d4 and e2-e4 as a double first move. I myself have learned chess with the rule that if you got your king to the other side you were allowed to choose five new pieces.'

The standardization of the rules of underpromotion may have taken so long because of its relative rareness.

'In the entire history of chess, only around ten real and relevant underpromotions, that is promotion to rook or bishop, have occurred in games. But there are millions of perfectly natural positions in which this could occur. Every week in my magazines I encounter new natural underpromotions which could quite easily have happened in games.'

Writing about underpromotions you say, 'promotion to knight is a fairly frequent occurrence, but of course this is not a real underpromotion: the knight covers squares that could not otherwise be covered.' How important a part do such quibbles play within your work?

'Such sophistries? Well, they do play a part, I do take some pleasure in discovering odd lacunae in the chess rules. I wrote about the difference between static and dynamic identity when this difference still went unnoticed and unacknowledged in the rules. These are properties of a position that you cannot photograph; can White still castle and to which side, can he capture en passant? This matters in the repetition rule, which has now been adjusted in that respect. It was nicely illustrated in the recent Interpolis tournament, in Karpov-Miles. When it was pointed out to Karpov, he was aware that the position in which he claimed a draw, had been repeated three times only statically and not dynamically. What he did not know was that wrongly claiming a draw carries a five minute penalty.

'These things interest me. Say you have this position: White king f2, pawn b7; Black king h1, and you want to promote your pawn on b8. You put it beside the board, take a queen from among your captured pieces, put that on the board, and holding on to it, you cry "Oh no", throw away the queen, and put a rook in its place. That is mate in two, whereas otherwise it would have been stalemate. The rules are not clear on this, they say nothing about it. Whether the *pièce touchée* rule applies to pieces outside the board is, to say the least, fuzzy. I like that.'

They are rather absurd things which may have a certain amount of relevance.
'This could certainly be relevant as it is a very natural game situation.'

A serious person might say, 'This is all very nice but to occupy your time with that...'
'But that's where I am different. A serious person, to me, is someone who wants to become chess champion of the world. Which leaves open the question of how serious that is. Isn't it the height of absurdity to want to become chess champion of the world? That is, in the eyes of a Uruguayan soccer star, or an Eskimo chieftain, the answer is that such things have value in themselves. This is a moralistic problem I have written about in *Chess Curiosities*. Take for instance the typical preface in problem and endgame study books. An over-the-board grandmaster is seduced to write a sympathetic word, saying how much the tournament player can benefit from studying endgame studies or even problems. But in general chess books, an authority figure from a larger world, this time a politician or a scientist, utters the well-known nonsense about chess developing such desirable character traits in people. So it seems always an excuse is needed, although never more than one pretence upwards. I have never looked for excuses. I like to quote Hans Ree, here, who simply said, "Chess is beautiful enough to waste your life for." To me, that sums it up. Once you start looking for excuses, you will end up needing an excuse for being happy.'

But you don't mind moralising yourself either.
'Not at all. I react against a morality that is often false, because those people who ask for a preface to their little problem book often do not subscribe to that view at all themselves.'

Do you, as a rule, get a lot of reactions on your articles and books?
'Yes, a lot. After that record article[4] I got at least twenty letters from all over the world from people who had improvements or liked it, as well as requests from

4 New In Chess 1985/4 and 1985/11.

foreign magazines to write something. I have several permanent correspondents, some of whom roughly know what I collect, and when they see something I will like they send it on. *Chess Curiosities* wouldn't have been what it is without people like Rob Verhoeven or René Olthof, who keeps me informed of late castlings, games of over 150 moves, the excelsior theme in games, and many other things. I do need help, it's hard enough to keep up with the magazines. But the bulk of the work has to be done by myself.'

In Chess Curiosities you offer a fortune to anyone able to send you a copy of the Dziennik Poznanski which is supposed to contain the game Tylkowski-Wojciechowski, a game which featured the same miraculous combination in 1931 as Ortueta-Sanz, Madrid 1933. Did you ever get a reaction to that?
'No. But through Litmanowicz I did track down a Mr Rozanski, who was still living in Poznan and had witnessed this unique game. I wrote him a letter, and a long time later I got a reply, but it did not say anything, really. Some people are simply impervious to these things. Yes, once a very nice combination occurred at the club, and it seems something like it occurred a few years later, in another club. Big deal. Even Harold Lommer, not someone to spurn the bizarre in chess, was not so impressed by this coincidence. He was a strange character, a nightclub owner of German descent in London, who later lived in Valencia. He was a composer and collector of endgame studies, and published two famous standard works on them. He was also a fanatic of tasks, and he composed the first AUW in a study. He seems to have been an extremely nice man. He sent me entire manuscripts about utterly obscure tasks, and also occupied himself with the eightfold promotion. There are eight pawns on the seventh rank, and if the problem is correct, it can only be solved if they are all promoted to the same piece, one after another, all eight of them. With rooks, Lommer managed that, I think Chéron did that too. It's a matter of taste, but that sort of thing does not appeal to me.'

Does it come too close to Fairy Chess or analysing endgames with four knights against queen?
'Yes, but when I imagine Troitzky in his Siberian forest, surrounded by howling wolves, analysing night after night whether king plus four knights can always beat king plus queen (laughs exuberantly), that is great. That is what chess is all about, only you have to be a chess player to appreciate it. How can you explain to a non-chess player that within chess there is a little world of endgame studies within which you have the even tinier world of theoretical major minor endgames, within which there is a micro-cosmos populated by utter madmen analysing four knights against queen? Or try to explain the significance of this Mr Veitch, an Englishman who seems to have lived on one of the canals here in Amsterdam, but who was otherwise untraceable, and whose reason of existence in chess was the cooking of endgame studies? (Bursting out in a loud laugh again)'

But Troitzky is certainly a man you admire.
'He was one of the greatest artists chess has ever produced. He discovered a great many brilliant manoeuvres, most of them in rather natural positions. He was a pioneer, and he towered far above his contemporary Rinck. Rinck definitely lacked the artistic touch. There was deadly rivalry between them, that is, from Rinck's point of view. Lommer once wrote me a very amusing letter about how he was in Barcelona and wanted to pay Rinck a visit, but Rinck refused to see him because Lommer had published an endgame collection containing one more study of Troitzky's than of his. Rinck's son apologised for his father not wanting to see Lommer, and ended up taking him to the zoo.'

A high point in your career of curiosities are your articles about the Babson task and the bibliophilic little book on the same subject, De man die de Babson task wilde maken *(The Man Who Wanted to Make the Babson Task), which opens with the telling sentence, 'Anyone not familiar with the story of Drumare knows nothing about chess'.*
'Yes, the greatest of all tasks is the Babson task, and the finding of it makes one of the most dramatic chess stories that can be told. No one in his right mind had ever thought it could really be done, Drumare spent half his life trying it, and suddenly this unknown Russian pops up and does it as if it never took him more than an hour.'

It does seem incredible when you compare those cluttered and artificial positions of Drumare's with that normal looking position of Yarosh.
'Yes, incredible. And if this Drumare had been the only one occupying himself with it... That man clearly wasn't all that talented. But I have researched this intensively, and then one comes across eight or so names of really great composers who have spent time on it. People like Lommer, Chéron, Siers, Loshinsky, Pauly. When such great composers had given up, others could safely assume that it simply couldn't be done. Or so it seemed. I'm glad I never tried, I might have become the victim of my own perseverance.'

How did it affect you at the time, when you read that someone had succeeded in making the Babson task?
'Well, shivers down my spine. It was like picking up the newspaper and reading, "Purpose of Life Discovered", or something like that.'

Reading the history of the Babson task or, for example, the investigation into the Saavedra position, one cannot escape being gripped, not only by the technical beauty but also by the story. Have you, as a writer, never felt tempted to use these stories for literary purposes?
'No, because the beauty is in the position. The Babson task and the whole epic around it, Drumare's tragedy, fascinate me, but I am not really tempted at all to turn this into a story, because what fascinates me is the position. Yarosh' solutions, and those dreadful positions by Drumare are the story. As a storyteller, I can do things

with cycling. In chess, all that matters is what pieces can do on the board, whereas cycling is the description of it. Before TV, cycling would not even have existed had it not been written about; in chess there is always a concrete abstraction, a position or a game one can play over. So I write cycling stories, and I show chess positions.'

What are your future plans as regards publishing? Will there be a sequel to Chess Curiosities?
'Yes, but I need a new English publisher. I was a bit unlucky with George Allen and Unwin. I got the impression they were not really interested in chess. I had to write ten letters to get one answer, and now I am looking for an English chess publisher with whom this ratio could be brought back to one to one. I would love to have a curiosities book out every three or four years, and for a less ridiculously high price than *Chess Curiosities*. I don't expect to make money from it. I have once calculated my hourly wages for *Chess Curiosities*, and it was something like one guilder and twenty three cents. My dream is one tome of thousand pages entitled *All Chess Curiosities*. That can wait until I am sixty.'

Despite its hefty price Chess Curiosities *received a good deal of recognition. The readers of* Chess Notes *even awarded it the Book of the Year Prize. That must have pleased you a lot.*
'Yes, of course. Money-wise, that prize is very small; but it is a journal which is really only read by bibliophilic chess lovers, by experts, who judge all books appearing all over the world. I do not know how many readers it has but for such an international club to vote my book the best book of the year naturally gives me great satisfaction.'

What are the characteristics indispensable for a collector of chess curiosities?
'A great love of chess, a sense of beauty, and the neurosis of completeness.'

Are there connections between your main passions, chess, writing and cycling?
'I think it all comes from an initial love of numbers. Don't ask me where I got that from. I love lists with numbers. When I was little the fact that my parents had a typewriter was a great discovery, and in one of my books I describe how I started to type a list of all natural numbers, beginning with one. I got close to five thousand and I still have those sheets, they are the most harmonious and satisfying piece of writing I have ever done. What else is chess but lists of hieroglyphs? One of my earliest chess fantasies was that I was going to hectograph a 106 move game Bobotsov-Bohatirchuk I had found in the tournament book of the Amsterdam Olympiad 1954, and deliver it door to door in the neighbourhood. It would be something like: Chess Agency Tim Krabbé; this week presenting Bobotsov-Bohatirchuk. I never got around to it, but it's really what I'm doing now, isn't it.

'And with cycling, one reason to take up that was that if I did the same tour every day, and recorded my time, and seven intermediate times, I would eventually have created, just as in chess, new and beautiful lists with numbers.'

Looking back on twenty years of chess curiosities, what high points do you see?
'A few things. The Babson task is unbeatable. And the coincidence Wojciechowski
-Sanz. Another remarkable coincidence is one concerning Kurt Richter. Somewhere
around 1910, a combination appeared in a magazine, which was very clearly a
plagiarised version of a combination Schiffers had once missed against Chigorin.
Now, this was plagiarised under the name of Kurt Richter. Only, it couldn't have
been *the* Kurt Richter, as he was only five or ten years old at the time. Ten year olds
have been known to murder, but not to plagiarise, so it must have been someone
else. That he should have chosen a name which was later to become almost synon-
ymous with combinations in chess, that's most extraordinary. And of course the
things which were the beginning of my love of curiosities, like that nearly winning
king's march of Spassky's against Polugaevsky, which later, when one has collected
so many other things, turns out not to have been so terribly special after all. But
it is still a milestone to me, like that endgame Janowski-Lasker, New York 1924.
The kind of thing that gives you an afterglow for a day. But I still think that there is
nothing to top the Babson task story.

'I am also very proud of having personally discovered the latest castling, in
Bobotsov-Ivkov, on move 46. It is very rare to find something like that in a primary
source, but I did pick this one right out of the tournament bulletin myself. Not
immediately realising how special it was, this was before my curiosity hunting had
really started. I remember seeing 46.0-0, and thinking, "Isn't that a bit late?" And
then it turned out to have been the latest ever.

'This has become a recurring dream which must be typical of me. In that dream,
I am playing over a game, and I gradually become aware that White castles at move
57, and Black at move 80. And I think, "Gee, that's a good one for my collection!"
I have this dream at least once in every two months. It varies, of course. It may be
that both players castle at move 79. In an old famous game! And I think, "How is it
possible I always overlooked this?" And at the same time there is the immense joy
that such a game exists. Well, this dream has taken the place of an older recurring
dream about soccer results of 12-11 and so.'

But again numbers.
'Numbers, yes. So in a way you could say that, through the detour of chess, my love
has returned to its source.'

Garry Kasparov

Tilburg, October 1989

'The duty of a World Champion is not only to play games, but also to explain to the public why he is winning'

Following the credo of his teacher Botvinnik, Garry Kasparov has enriched chess literature with several magnificent modern classics. His absolute masterpiece so far is *The Test of Time*, one of the best chess books ever written. But his accounts of the 1985 and 1986 World Championship matches are equally sublime samples of analytical expertise. Kasparov co-authored a number of highly successful theoretical works, and in 1987 published his controversial autobiography *Child of Change*, written together with Donald Trelford. And there is more in store. 'After the next World Championship match I will dedicate myself to the rebuilding of the world of chess literature.'

'We had no chess books at home. I think one of the first books I got was by Maizelis, an old Soviet author, a book for beginners. The second book was Panov and Estrin's book on openings. The first edition. A very old copy which was in a terrible state. The first book my father bought for me was Bronstein's *200 Open Games*. Then I gradually got more books and I studied them all. I was an avid reader. I'm not sure about the quality of these first books, but I liked getting this chess information. Just to read and then create something new.

'When I was nine I was given Fischer's *My Sixty Memorable Games* as a present. The Russian edition, with a dedication from one of my relatives that I had to become World Champion (laughs). That was in 1972, I was nine and I had to become World Champion. Two other books that made quite an impression on me were two volumes from the black Russian series of monographs. I had got the ones on Fischer and Larsen and was much impressed. Bronstein's book on the 1953 Candidates' tournament in Zurich I also liked very much. And then there is one other book I should not forget to mention, Alekhine's *300 Best Games*. The way he explained things was simple and straightforward. Our styles had much in common. I have to admit that this book made a very strong impression on me.'

To what extent were you interested in the history of the game? Did you also study the games of the pioneers of chess?

'Yes, I read for example this Tarrasch book, *300 Games*, and I liked it very much. This was when I was fifteen or sixteen, when I was already a strong player. I read with great interest about this dispute between Tarrasch and Nimzowitsch. Of course, both were dogmatists. I, for one, prefer Tarrasch. I think he did many things in the right way. Maybe I prefer Tarrasch because I like isolated pawns in the centre, who knows. I found these discussions very enjoyable. I like to read about the masters of the past, but the games, you know, the quality of these games... They are... (searching for a polite expression)... sorry, they are horrible. Look at Morphy's games where he gave odds of pawn and move and won in twenty moves. These are games from simuls, you cannot take them seriously. There are better games from his matches, but still... Even Steinitz-Zukertort, Steinitz-Lasker, (groans)... Of course, it's interesting to understand Steinitz's way of thinking, because he was ahead of his time, but for me these games are... I enjoy reading old chess magazines, and occasionally you may come across an interesting, well, not really an idea, but some moves. Because of their ignorance they thought something was very good, and now you can improve on this from the point of view of the end of the twentieth century.'

You never adopted some ancient continuation like Fischer did when he reintroduced Steinitz's Knight h3 in the Two Knights Defence?

'No, Knight h3, this is a very bad move. I can't imagine that it's a very good move. Short played several games with it that he won. I never play...e5, except for a couple of games against Timman, but if Short guarantees that he will play this line I am ready to play the position with Black. Knight h3, something is wrong. I'm very sorry, but if somebody doesn't understand that this is wrong... It may be playable, but it's wrong. OK, I have a knight on a5, but still..., a knight on h3, pfff.'

What kind of books did Botvinnik advise you to read when you started working with him?

'He was concerned about my chess education in the broadest possible sense. He tried to cover everything. Understanding that I am very strong in complicated tactical positions he wanted to give me some positional feeling for the game and to improve my technique. That's why I studied games of Petrosian, for example, and other players like Botvinnik himself and Smyslov.'

Which books do you think every student of chess should read?

'That's very difficult to say. For beginners the two books written by Lasker and Capablanca are very good, *Manual of Chess* and *Chess Fundamentals*. Also Alekhine's *300 Best Games* is a very good book for beginners. (Thinks) Bronstein's book on Zurich '53 is very good. And Keres's book of his games and his book on the 1948 World Championship tournament. I think we can include Timman's *The Art of Analysis*. And I think we have to include my book, *The Test of Time*. But now we're already talking about serious level chess books. I think Polugaevsky's book on his variation is a very interesting book, *The Birth of a Variation*5. That's more or less a list. As an introduction I can also recommend, although it's not of very high quality, I will improve it, *24 Lessons* by Garry Kasparov. I wrote it together with Nikitin and it provides a clear introduction for the adult beginner.'

The depth and accuracy of your analyses in The Test of Time *have met with wide acclaim. How did this book come about?*
'Actually I never started to write this book. In 1981 I began contributing analyses of my games to our chess periodical *Shakhmaty* in Azerbaijan, in Baku. I wanted to support them and I like analysing my games. I did this for several years and then I got an idea. OK, I had analysed these games and spent a lot of time on them, mostly burning the midnight oil. Now it seemed like a very good idea to take these analyses, to improve them, and to publish these original analyses together with the improvements in a book. This would show how the mind of the grandmaster works. It would show how my own ideas and understanding of chess developed, how modern theory develops. It would open the laboratory of my preparation. This was the idea of the book. And I'm proud of my analyses. Of course, there are many mistakes, but still it's very good and very deep analysis. Very often I use them for homework for my pupils. I'm very happy when they can find something. It means that life hasn't stopped. There are still things to be worked out. For a new edition of *The Test of Time* I will need time. I think that when I will seriously start my new magazine, after the next World Championship match, I will dedicate myself to the rebuilding of the world of chess literature.'

You have often stated that your winning the World Championship signalled the end of a dark period. Did you have a similar idea when you started publishing your chess books?
'Yes, more or less. I realized that the duty of a World Champion is not only to play games, but also to explain his games, to explain to the public why he is winning. Karpov had not been able to do this. Not because he was lazy, but because he was unable to. Either you can write or you can't. If somebody else writes instead of you, like I'm sure it was done for him, or if somebody corrects you like Trelford did for me, this is very bad. You have to express yourself. Another point is that it was impossible for him to explain how he was winning. Zero point zero chance. Because he won naturally, by his feeling. This is not something you can explain. You can explain your moves when you make the best moves, but you cannot explain them if you play just to win the game, having this unique talent to find weaknesses, using probably not the best move, but just lulling your opponent to sleep. That's why all attempts to monkey Karpov's style fail. My style, on the other hand, you can try to imitate, just by using my weapons. They are understandable. My style is based

---

5 Grandmaster Preparation is an updated version of this Russian edition.

on giving energy and creating. Karpov's style is something that is probably taking energy from his opponent. You can't explain it.'

You just mentioned Donald Trelford, the ghost-writer of your controversial autobiography Child of Change. What are your views on this now?
'I have now finished (emphatically) my real autobiography, written by me, in Russian, and it is called *Unlimited Challenge*. It is based on *Child of Change*, but about ninety per cent is new stuff. It is more or less a complete story, because I could draw a final conclusion. The final conclusion is that there is an unlimited challenge, the fight will continue. During the last few years many things have happened, many masks have fallen, and it was easier now to give everyone his role. About this book I'm very happy. This is the real Kasparov, without any English editors. I deserved the critical reception of *Child of Change*. I was too light-hearted, I did it just in between, which was very bad. I think that from a historical point of view the book was absolutely right, but the way it was presented was very bad. That was a mistake, which we can rectify. But the idea of the book I'm going to defend till the end. The only way to understand it better for people in the West is to go and live in the Soviet Union for a couple of years.'

You also wrote a number of highly popular opening books...
'Opening books are very difficult. Theory is developing so fast and the classical opening book doesn't work anymore. You need the computer industry to cover everything. Together with two of my coaches I did the second edition of BCO6 which is very good. One year ago it was absolutely the best, and now it's...(sighs). It's still a very good book for first category club players, but that's not enough.'

Don't you think that it must be very discouraging for the average amateur player to see opening theory take such an upward surge?
'Chess will protect itself. If we can't cope with this enormous amount of information, some solution will be found. Don't worry. I believe in chess. I believe that a protection against this wealth of information will be found.'

What should I be thinking of?
'I don't know, but I repeat that something will be found.'

What books are you planning to write in the near future?
'First of all I want to write a book on my World Championship matches against Karpov, these four or five matches. I have so many impressions and it is very important for the chess world to read the impressions of the World Champion. I think that if I will write this book it will be very interesting not only for professionals,

---

6 Batsford Chess Openings

but also for amateurs. And a book of my best games. Something different from *The Test of Time*, that's another story. But my best games should be available to the public. The best samples of Kasparov's genius.'

One final question. Do you think that chess literature still has a future in this computerized world?
'Come on, this is an important question and I'm not ready to answer it yet. That's why I told you that I will have to re-establish the standard. I think I will be able to do this. I think it's very important to preserve chess literature, the chess language, and to integrate the role of the computer. You have to combine the two. This is the task for the future and I feel that I'm able to perform this task. I have many ideas on this, but that may be the subject of our next talk.'

Lev Polugaevsky

Moscow, June 1990

'Ninety per cent of all chess books you can open at page one and then immediately close again for ever'

A frank conversation with Botvinnik in 1969 marked the beginning of Lev Polu-gaevsky's career as a chess author. Polugaevsky's place among the strongest players in the world was undisputed, but as yet he had not shown any writing ambitions. Botvinnik sternly condemned this omission and rebuked him for his laziness. 'It's the duty of every grandmaster to write books.' Heeding his great example's admonition, Polugaevsky set to work and wrote *Grandmaster Preparation*, a book which was instantly acclaimed as a masterpiece by colleagues and critics alike. This debut was followed by *Grandmaster Performance*, a collection of his best games, and a string of opening books. At the end of this year Pergamon will publish his new book, *In the Sicilian Labyrinth*, which again promises to be a treat not to be missed.

'When I was young, I had very few books. I lived in Kuybyshev, a city of about one million inhabitants on the river Volga. Kuybyshev didn't have a chess tradition, and, of course, at that time I didn't have any seconds to train with, nor any strong opponents. I studied chess at home and we didn't have many chess books. But there were three books that were very important for me. First of all there was a collection of Chigorin's games. In those days Chigorin was very popular in the Soviet Union. I got this book as a present from Romanovsky[7], a very famous player then, who was one of the founders of chess life in the Soviet Union. He gave it to me after I had taken first prize in a young boys' competition, saying "Please, this is for you. You must carefully study this book." It was a very big book with many games. It appealed to me very much, because it made me familiar with the style of the old players. I still think that young players should study and know the masters of the past, because if you've never seen the games of Chigorin, Schlechter, Gunsberg or Tarrasch, you cannot become a really strong player.

Then there were Kotov's books on Alekhine, which I studied diligently, and Botvinnik's *64 Best Games*, one of his earlier books. This book by Botvinnik I studied very fanatically. I even read it before I went to sleep and tried to remember posi-

---

7 Peter Arsenyevich Romanovsky (18921964).

tions. Even now, if you would open this book at random and show me a diagram, I could still tell you the number of the page and of the game. Botvinnik's style suited me down to the ground. I never met many people who said that Botvinnik was their favourite author, but to me he was. To me the logic of chess is very important. I always liked to see Botvinnik's games. Also later, when I went to watch his matches against Smyslov and Petrosian.

'In 1969 I played together with Botvinnik in Belgrade. This was his last tournament. One day we went for a walk together and Botvinnik asked me, "Have you already tried to write a book?" I said, "No, I haven't". And he told me, "You are very lazy. You should do so." During the remaining days of the tournament I immediately tried to think of what I could write about. I got a very nice idea and started to write my first book. In Russian it was called *The Birth of a Variation* and in English *Grandmaster Preparation*. I think it's my best book. It's not only about my opening, the Polugaevsky Variation, it's also about chess in general. I always say that in every position you should try to find the single best move. Not only in the opening, but also in adjourned games. So, I wrote about my work on my opening, about adjourned games and about how you should prepare for a specific opponent. Everything I wrote in this book derived from my opening preparation and my general preparation between 1960 and 1970. I worked on this book for eight years and it was published in 1977. After this book I published a collection of my best games[8] and many volumes for the opening series of the East German Sportverlag.

'Right now I've just finished my magnum opus, on which I have been working for the past two and a half years. Two volumes, five hundred pages altogether, called *In the Sicilian Labyrinth*. This book deals with all possible aspects of the Sicilian opening. I talk to the reader about my understanding of this opening. I discuss middle game positions, endings. It can be anything as long as it comes within the framework of the Sicilian, both from White's view point and Black's. I talk about good and bad squares, good and bad bishops, about psychological problems, my conclusions about certain positions, anything. I try to explain why, for instance, a square is strong or weak. Not simply to state, as so many authors do, "This square is weak", but explain why this is so. While it's a book about Sicilian variations, it is at the same time a book about all openings. Because certain problems apply to all openings. I give many examples from my own experience and practice. What happened in my match against Karpov? What happened in my match against Tal? How did I prepare for these matches and what did I think while preparing? What did I think my opponent would think?

'I try to write books that are different from the majority of books you see. Most books you come across are about openings. Only moves and nothing else. After one month you can throw away these books because they have lost their value. My books are more complicated to write. When I'm playing in tournaments my oppo-

---

8 Published in English by Pergamon as Grandmaster Performance.

Lev Polugaevsky: 'If you insist on seeing chess as a perfect entity, like an egg, you will never find a way to improve your results.'

nents can often take advantage of my writing activities. These take up so much time that it often influences my play. But I want to write this kind of book or none at all. I do not understand grandmasters who produce one book after another. Ninety per cent of all chess books you can open at page one and then immediately close again for ever. Sometimes you see books that have been written in one month. I don't like that. You should take at least two years for a book, or not do it at all. I want to write books you keep opening and keep coming back to. To study them again and to try to understand chess. Of course, there also exist some very good books on openings. For example Sveshnikov's book on the Cheliabinsk Variation. There is no better book on this variation and no one can explain it better than Sveshnikov. Or Bagirov's book on the Alekhine Defence. This is an excellent book and nobody understands this opening better than he does. But then again there are many, many books without any significance at all.

'When I want to write a book, I take one month to find a suitable subject to write about. If I don't get an idea, I won't begin. The only person I have in mind is the reader, a player who wants to become a stronger chess player. That's all that matters to me. I prefer books in which an author's own, individual style is manifest. Books in which I can find something I've never seen before. One of the best such books I know is Keres' book on the 1948 World Championship Tournament. Yes, a fantastic book. Also Bronstein's book on the Candidates' Tournament in 1953. One of the best books I know. Another book I liked very much was Botvinnik's book on the revenge match Alekhine-Bogoljubow. High quality analysis. And everything Kasparov or Karpov publishes I read with great interest. When Kasparov published his book[9], I studied it very carefully.

---

9 The Test of Time

'No, I never thought about writing tournament books. I like to express myself and enter into a conversation with the reader. "Why was this a mistake?", "What was the alternative?", etcetera. Now, why have I always preferred this approach? You know, for many years I had a chess school here in Moscow. Also, I was often invited to holiday camps to give advice to young boys and girls. I always used this method with my pupils and already after a very short time I would see that this method worked and that they began to think differently. The idea that this was the right method was strengthened by the experiences I had with my seconds over the years. All players who were my seconds when I played matches in the World Championship cycle ten years ago, became stronger afterwards. Bagirov, Tseshkovsky, Sveshnikov. I also saw that Karpov became stronger after he had worked with me before his match with Kortchnoi. For example, Tseshkovsky became champion of our country, Bagirov became grandmaster, and Sveshnikov had big successes as well. I don't have an explanation, but maybe it's my chess intelligence that they like.

'My chess method is without formulas, without orthodox thinking, without any special schemes. My method is purely based on dynamic thinking. I always explain that chess is an art and that there are no definite judgements. I approach my pupils or the reader as a partner. I try to understand what they think and tell them, "Maybe this is so, maybe it isn't." But I never give any one hundred per cent guarantees. Sometimes something can be good, sometimes it's bad. I refuse to see chess as a computer science, although I know that some trainers have good results with this approach. I know that you can have good results with these exact methods with graphs and things, but I also know that you will never score really great results that way. Never. If you insist on seeing chess as a perfect entity, like an egg, you will never find a way to improve your results when something goes wrong and you have a bad result. This, in my opinion, is the reason why old players like Smyslov or Kortchnoi can still have very good results. They have never locked themselves up in this egg, but have tried to remain dynamic. Without formulas or unshakeable truths. Of course, it's important to work with computers. Of course, it's important to study openings. But this is not everything. Sometimes, please, allow yourself a little time to rest and to play chess in tournaments.'

Mikhail Botvinnik

Brussels, August 1991

'This may not sound modest, but the first three volumes of my collected games are required reading'

Few of this century's chess authors have been as influential as Mikhail Botvinnik. Generations of Soviet chess players devoured his books and top grandmasters like Ivanchuk, Kasparov and Timman have often expressed their indebtedness to the former World Champion's writings. From the very first 'Check Your Library' columns in New In Chess Botvinnik has been an ever-present guest on these pages, but so far we did not have the opportunity to ask the main founder of the Soviet chess school about his own literary tastes and preferences. During the Candidates' matches in Brussels the Patriarch satisfied our curiosity and talked freely about the books that influenced him, the books every serious chess student should read and the revolutionary impact his new chess program will have on chess literature.

Which were the chess books you grew up with?
'There was not much choice. After the Russian Revolution in 1917 there was civil war in Soviet Russia and times were not so easy. There weren't any new books being published. My first chess book I got from one of my chess friends in October 1923. A bound volume of Chigorin's *Shakhmatny Listok*, containing the years 1876 to 1877. In December of that same year the publication started of a series of small books on opening theory written by Grekov and Nenarokov. Grekov was the publisher of the chess magazine *Shakhmatny* and Nenarokov was a strong chess master. In 1924 the first comprehensive book on opening theory was published. But by that time I was already a strong player and did not have much use of this, because I knew more variations than there were in this book.

'These years also saw the publication of three books by World Champion Capablanca. The first one was the Russian translation of *Chess Fundamentals*. For me this was the most important book. The second one was a textbook written by Capablanca, but as with Grekov's and Nenarokov's book it wasn't of any use to me as I had already passed that stage. And thirdly his *My Chess Career*, which contained the earliest games of Capablanca. He wrote this book before the First World War to show the chess world that he was entitled to play a match against Lasker. Other books that were important for my development were the translation of Tartakower's *Die Hypermoderne Schachpartie* and two books by Tarrasch *300 Games* and another games collection with many games by famous players, some of which also appeared in the first book. These were really good books with deep analyses. Tarrasch's way of analysing had a strong influence on me and I took over his style. He explained a lot, gave many variations and analysed deeply. When I wrote my first chess book on the USSR championship in 1931, I adapted his style. Many words, many general ideas, deep analyses, and lots of advice to the readers.

'A few years later I met Capablanca personally and I saw how he wrote his analyses to his games. He made very brief comments, only pointing out the crucial moments and the essential variations. Capablanca's point of view was that he only wanted to show the reader in which direction he should think himself. After I had seen this I began to write in the same manner. What other books should I mention? Around this time Emanuel Lasker's *Lehrbuch des Schachspiels* was published in the Soviet Union. I didn't like this book very much. And in the twenties the publishers of the magazine *Shakhmatny Listok*[10] also produced chess books and on their list was Bogoljubow's book on the Queen's Gambit, a book that impressed me a lot. What else? In 1926 a match was played between teams from Leningrad and Stockholm. At that time I had been playing chess for three years and I played on fifth board. The president of the Swedish Chess Association was Ludvig Collijn, who published the well-known *Lärobook*. Collijn was not a strong chess player and could never have written such a book. In fact this book had been written by three famous chess players. Rubinstein, Réti and Spielmann . Collijn gave this book to me and to all the other Soviet players as a present. This book meant a lot to me.

'The first book in which I was involved as co-author was the book written by Romanovsky and Levenfish on the match Alekhine Capablanca in Buenos Aires in 1927. For this book they asked me to comment on four games from this match. After the match Alekhine wrote his analyses of all the games of the match. It was a great honour for me to find that in these four games that I analysed I had made no mistakes. I was only sixteen years old, but already a strong chess player. (With undisguised irony) Unfortunately the rest of the games which had been analysed by Romanovsky and Levenfish were full of mistakes.'

When did it become easier to get chess books in the Soviet Union?
'In the thirties it became easier when the Soviet Union started to publish more chess books. Our own books and translations of foreign books. But right now it's very difficult to publish any chess books in the Soviet Union, because there is a great shortage of paper. And chess books should not be very expensive. Most of

---

10 A Leningrad magazine that ran from 1922 to 1931 and which should not be confused with the magazine mentioned earlier in which Chigorin wrote.

the paper is used up by gutter press and other trivial publications that make easy money. (Not hiding his contempt) At that time we didn't have this competition which was created by perestroika.'

I was very surprised to read that only one month after you played a match against Flohr in 1933, your book on the match was published.
'That's right. I can explain you why. All chess players, all masters were against this match. The Chairman of the Chess Section was Krylenko and he was a great chess enthusiast. The chess players told him that Botvinnik would lose this match for sure, but Krylenko had faith in me and believed that I had a chance. He accepted Flohr's proposal to play this match and organized it. The first part took place in Moscow and the second half in Leningrad. In Moscow I played badly, but in Leningrad Flohr played badly. Krylenko was happy that he had not been wrong and that the match was tied and he asked me if I could immediately write the analyses of this match. I was young, but I remembered all that had been going on in the games and in ten days I wrote all the analyses. Thanks to Krylenko's directives the book was published within a month's time. Perhaps this was the first Soviet chess book to be printed on good paper.'

You have often stressed the importance of Chigorin's heritage for your development as a chess player.
'That's right. In the magazines of Chigorin I found a lot of analyses that greatly impressed me. From these magazines I learned how the top players in the previous century played. I was very lucky, because nowadays the young masters no longer know how they used to play in the old days. In 1936 I read a collection of 75 games of Lasker. It had not been published in Russian and I read it in German. This book also made a deep impression. (Again with typical Botvinnik irony) And then I wrote my own books. I wrote many books. The last and maybe the best books were my collected games in four volumes. The first three volumes contain 380 games and the fourth volume is a collection of the articles I wrote. Very good analysis. I'm very proud of these books. And Ivanchuk fully agrees on this (laughs). He studied them.'

He's not the only one. Your writings had a strong influence on many strong players, like Timman, Kasparov...
'Not on everyone. Those who like to read analyses and like to analyse themselves, for these players these books are very useful. (Sarcastically) But these are not the real professionals I'm afraid. The real professionals are too strong to bother with such books.'

Can you become World Champion or a very strong player without thoroughly analysing your games and publishing them?
'For example, Petrosian was such a champion. And Spassky too. Karpov didn't publish too much. Initially Kasparov used to, but not anymore.'

You think that he should write again?
'If he wants to raise his level in
chess, yes.'

So far you haven't mentioned the books
of Alekhine.
'The books of Alekhine were
not published in the Soviet
Union until later, because
he was an emigrant. For a
long time his books were not
available in the Soviet Union.
What is more, when Romanovsky and Levenfish wrote
their book about the match
Alekhine-Capablanca in 1927,
Krylenko asked Ilyin-Genevsky
to contribute a special preface
in order to explain to the
readers why the Soviet Union
published the games of this
match between Capablanca
and a Soviet emigrant. Ilyin-
Genevsky wrote that Alekhine

**Mikhail Botvinnik: 'Karpov didn't publish too much.
Initially Kasparov used to, but not anymore.'**

was an enemy of the Soviet Union, but that in politics he was only a midget.
However, in chess he was a giant. And therefore the Soviet chess players had to
know his games. Later on some of Alekhine's books were published, like the Russian
translation of My Best Games. And after that all his other books.'

When you wrote about the Soviet school of chess you did include Alekhine.
'Yes, I did. The name of Alekhine means a lot in chess. In the years before the
Revolution we had four top players in Russia. Alekhine, Bogoljubow, Rubinstein
and Nimzowitsch. Alekhine was the strongest of these four players. In Soviet Russia
Alekhine was very popular. And he appreciated this very much. He always carefully
studied Soviet chess magazines. He really read everything that was published in the
Soviet Union as I realized when I met him in Nottingham in 1936. He also studied
the bulletins from the major Soviet tournaments. Apart from the game scores these
bulletins also contained games comments. Alekhine studied them all. When we met
again in Amsterdam in 1938, at the Wereld AVRO Schaaktoernooi (Not without
pride pronounced in perfect Dutch), he immediately came up to me and very
excitedly explained that he had studied an analysis by Smyslov in one of the Soviet
magazines and had found a mistake. At that time Smyslov was only seventeen years

old and had just won the championship of Moscow. He had published one of his games with comments and Alekhine had found a mistake in it. Such an exchange of ideas between Alekhine and Soviet chess players was permanently going on.'

To Western readers this idea of the Soviet school of chess has always sounded a bit like propaganda.
'(Starts laughing) There's nothing wrong with propaganda when it's propaganda for chess. Any other kind of propaganda I never made. I believe that Karpov and Kasparov deny the existence of the Soviet Chess School, but it exists nevertheless and you cannot ignore it. The idea of the Soviet chess school is based on two factors. First of all, from 1924 onwards chess was supported by the government. This support didn't come out of the blue. Benjamin Franklin already wrote an essay called *Morals of Chess* in which he wrote that chess helped to mould one's personality. After the Revolution one of the first goals of the government was to raise the cultural and educational level of the people. Chess should help in accomplishing this goal. As a result chess became very popular.

'The second factor I am to blame for myself, I think. I started to study chess as a science and created a system that described how a chess player should prepare for a chess competition. The first time I put this system into practice was before my match with Flohr. I convincingly showed the importance of my system. I collected one hundred games by Flohr and by the time I played him I knew him very well. I elaborated the theory of this system for several years. In 1939 these ideas had been worked out sufficiently well and I published my findings in the tournament book of the Soviet Championship of 1939. In the following years I continued to work with this method. In the period between 1941 and 1948 I demonstrated the great merits of this method. My colleagues who played with me were forced to use this method as well, if they wanted to be successful. And indeed, many grandmasters were successful with this method, particularly grandmasters like Boleslavsky and Geller. You may safely say that they all used this method in one way or another. This resulted in the Soviet Chess School. So, no propaganda at all. That is simply how it was.

'But today's grandmasters no longer work or analyse that much. They play a lot. Nowadays there no longer is a big difference between the chess players in the West and the chess players in the Soviet Union. But young players who are starting out and are trying to reach the top, they still use this method. For example Ivanchuk, Shirov and Kramnik. But once they've become strong grandmasters they have no time and it's Soviet Chess School bye bye (laughs). Well, what can you do?'

What will be the influence of the computer on chess literature?
'For the moment none. Now the computer is a source of information, but nothing more. But in the future the situation will change. I hope that in a few months our chess program will be ready that was developed by my mathematicians in the Botvinnik laboratory. This is the only program in the world that

doesn't use brute force. Instead of using brute force our program "thinks" in a similar manner as a chess master thinks. Deep Thought analyses one hundred and fifty million positions in three minutes. They are working on a program that will look at two billion positions in three minutes. However, my program looks only at twenty or thirty positions, just as a chess master would do. This allows the computer to show the player with whom it is playing everything it's been analysing, because it only looks at a limited number of possibilities. Thus the opponent of the computer can learn to play chess while playing the computer. I hope that this program will be further improved in the future and that the computer will be able to make analyses. When that happens no one will publish analyses anymore without consulting the computer. This will drastically change chess literature.'

Which books would you select if you were to recommend five chess books to a young and talented player of let's say sixteen years old?
'A chess player cannot play chess if he hasn't read Capablanca's textbook. Furthermore I think, although this may not sound modest, that the first three volumes of my collected games are required reading. Then, Alekhine's *Best Games*. As for the endgame, I would recommend grandmaster Fine's book *Basic Chess Endings*, although I don't know if it's still available. It was written fifty years ago, but I think that it's still a very good book. Averbakh published many volumes on the endgame, but they are very difficult to understand for young players. Fine's book is not so elaborate but he explains very well how to play the endgame. What else? They should study Fischer's games. Let me see, who else would be offended if I didn't name him? The other day Smyslov finished a book with 320 collected games that contains deep analysis. We're looking for paper to publish it. I have not read Kasparov's books, so I cannot include them in my list.'

You didn't read Kasparov's books? Why didn't you?
'Because when they were published I was not playing chess anymore. He wrote very elaborate analyses like Tarrasch did and I didn't like that.'

Weren't you curious to see what you're pupil had written?
'I looked at the games he played for the World Championship. Without great pleasure. The games of the Quarter Finals here are more interesting, even though they contain mistakes because of time-trouble. It's not possible to make sixty moves in six hours. Two time-troubles in one session is too much. It has a damaging influence on the level of the games. Capablanca was in favour of quicker time-schedules, because he thought very quickly. But he proposed to increase the playing speed from fifteen moves in one hour to sixteen. And no more. On only one occasion did I play a faster time-limit. In Nottingham, where we played eighteen moves in one hour. I was young then and managed quite well.'

You say that you didn't watch Kasparov's matches with pleasure. Because of chess reasons or because of personal reasons?

'Only chess. I'm very objective in my assessments. I did like the first two Karpov-Kasparov matches. But the matches in Seville and in New York and Lyon were not interesting.'

Anatoly Karpov

Linares, March 1991

'I think that the quality of chess books was much better in former times'

Ever since he published his first analysis more than a quarter of a century ago, Anatoly Karpov has been a consistently productive chess author. In all probability the former World Champion will not go down in chess history as the writer of one particular outstanding book, but rather as the author of a steady flow of instructive and entertaining chess books that have made him one of the bestselling grandmasters of today. After several earlier attempts had come to naught we finally found an opportunity to ask Karpov about his literary practices and preferences. It will not come as a shock that Kasparov's books are not high on his list.

What prompted you when you first started to write about chess?
'Everything started from the work I did for magazines. I annotated my first game, I think, in 1966 when I became national master. I had just come back from a tournament that I had won and one of the Soviet magazines asked me to annotate two games. Soon after this I started to write for different magazines. So, when I became a grandmaster I already had a lot of work done. Then, in 1973 or '74 I was approached, first by a Soviet publishing house and immediately after this by Batsford, to write my first book.

'Actually, I believe that it is really hard to write a brand-new book starting from zero. When you don't have any material prepared. It takes a lot of work and a lot of time. Even when you write about your own games, as I did when I made a book called My 101 Games. I believe that if somebody finishes more than one game per day there are bound to be a lot of mistakes in the analyses. Let's just suppose you can finish one game a day, which I don't think you can. I might keep up that pace for two weeks and then my production would become slower and slower. I would annotate one game in two days, and from thereon even become slower. However, even ideally you would need at least one hundred days for one hundred games. Working every day for three and a half months. That's why you need to do a lot of preparatory work. For books on openings or strategy you also need examples. Games from other grandmasters that you saw during tournaments. Games that gave you some ideas. The notes you made on those occasions you can collect and turn into a book. But to start writing a book, let's say on positional play in the seventies, because you got a proposal from an editor, that would be impossible.'

Were there any examples you had in mind when you started writing these analyses?
'I liked several books which I studied. For instance there was this very nice book from the Candidates' tournament in '59 in Yugoslavia. I think it was written in Yugoslavia, but it was available in the Soviet Union. I was eight years old then and bought this book when I was playing somewhere in the province. I studied the games and liked the photos. Another book I liked was the one written by Boleslavsky and Bondarevsky on the match Spassky-Petrosian, in which they looked at the match from both sides. In general, I have a strong preference for tournament books and games collections of grandmasters.'

Which annotators used a method that according to you was the right method?
'I think that the quality of chess books was much better in former times. They were also more serious. These authors felt a greater responsibility than our present-day authors. Probably they had less to do, less to play, but I still like the books of Alekhine, Capablanca, Lasker and Tarrasch. I followed their examples. Not only to give variations, but to explain some ideas.

'To understand variations you have to be already quite a strong player, but in words a chess author can explain many more things. I like the psychological way of annotating games of Lasker. I like the variations of Alekhine. He was one of the best annotators. Capablanca had his own style which I also appreciate very much. And I like the humour of Tarrasch.'

Do you think that these books are more truthful than the books today?
'I think they accepted more responsibility when they gave notes. Now many people give notes without checking variations. Unfortunately we have this in magazines, we have this in the *Informant*. We even know of some respected names that make mistakes on purpose when commenting on the openings. Just to set some traps. I never had any respect for these people and this method. If I don't want to say something, I just keep silent. I won't give wrong information. I think this is very incorrect. I wouldn't like to name these names, but I know who they are. I think you should be honest. The people who buy these books want the truth and not traps. And some of them may not have the chess qualification to find these traps. They are following these analyses and then one very respected grandmaster writes that White is winning. But after one or two moves White is losing. That is absolutely incorrect. Probably these people wrongly understand the responsibility of the annotator. OK, you can make a mistake, but if it becomes clear to an editor or a publishing house that one of their authors keeps making such mistakes, they have to warn him or just stop working with him.'

I take it that you yourself never fell victim to any of these recommendations. 'No, no, I check everything. But in one of the Moscow international tournaments, I think it was in '76, somebody played a King's Gambit. According to one of the games in the Informant the assessment was that White was better. One grandmaster had quickly looked this up before the round, had had no time to check, played it and after a few moves he resigned.'

You just mentioned how much time it takes to write a book. Often busy champions are helped by others in writing their books. Were you often helped by others?
'Yes, yes, I was. There are several books which I wrote on my own, without any help. Most magazine work I do on my own. But when I have to

Anatoly Karpov: 'For the first steps in chess I would recommend the books of Lasker and Capablanca.'

write a book about strategy, for instance, I ask people with chess qualifications to select material. That's why I have co-authored books with people like Evgeny Gik or Matsukevich. We normally work according to the following procedure. They collect material. If I know the game, the tournament and the ideas, I give them the ideas, we may tape them, they work up this information and finally come back to me, so that I can check whether I agree or not. Of course that is easier for them. It's harder for them when I am not familiar with the material. They select, I say OK, but now they have to prepare your own ideas, or check the material that has been published. Then, finally, we check together. So, that takes less time from me. But it's tougher for them because they didn't have an original idea.'

Which of your books do you like best?
'My first book was very good. This annotated games collection. I think that in English it was called My Favourite Games or Selected Games. In German it was called Wie ich kämpfe und siege. This was a very very good book. And there was this book with 101 games which was also quite good. My most recent set of books has been very successful. This Opening Games in Action series. Closed Games in Action, Open Games in Action,

Semi-closed, Semi-open. They are being published in English and German. I have been told that this is the most successful series of chess books of the last years. They have also been translated into Italian and I just signed a contract to have them translated into Spanish. At least two of them will appear in French. They are not limited to my games, but mostly deal with openings that I know very well. For instance, in addition to this series I wrote a book called *How to beat the Grünfeld*. I did a lot of work for my matches with Kasparov and I believe I have a right to make a book on the Grünfeld and how to beat it. I had good results against this opening.'

Some time ago the new Russian chess encyclopedia was published, an event that quite some people had been looking forward to. You were the chief editor of this project. What did your work mainly consist of?
'This was a very tough and long enterprise. We started to work on this Encyclopedia in 1981. It was finished in 1989. The first copies I brought to the New York match in 1990. It took us a long time to finish this project. We wanted to correct all the mistakes which we knew and also those we didn't know of yet, to get the fullest information possible about different aspects of chess and chess history. We had many collaborators and a very good editorial staff. We had many staff meetings and tried to find the best authors for the different parts of the world. I honestly think that this is probably the best chess encyclopedia there has ever been. I think it will be translated into English. We already had this idea to translate it into English when we were working on the Russian edition. Originally we wanted to have it translated in our own country, but now with all the problems we have with publishing houses, with paper, etc., it will probably be translated outside Russia. Of course, there is a strong emphasis on Russia and therefore the English edition will be slightly abridged. It should be shortened because it is a tremendous volume of about one thousand pages. That is too much.

'I was the chief editor. Our first task was to make a plan. I led this editorial meeting. I will not talk about the production problems. It was still the old system, and in the beginning we got permission to use paper to make an encyclopedia of 26 quires. When we realised how much material we had, I managed to increase it to almost twice its size. Then we had to contact people to write specific sections and I also advised in that. But we also had a good staff, people who know about chess. Then there were some special problems which I had to solve. Now that everybody sees the final product, everything looks fantastic and nobody wonders how it all came about. The book was printed in 1990, but already in '82 we had to decide, for instance, to insert all the photos of the Soviet champions and to include the biography of Kortchnoi. Which at that time was very problematic. Of course, people don't pay attention now, because now this is all normal, but it wasn't normal then. I approached the people who decided on these matters and told them that if we wanted to make the best book we had to exclude all politics. We make a book only on chess. Without any politics. Then it will be the best book. If you want to make another book, I don't want to be involved. I don't want to be the chief of this. And actually they gave their consent and said, "OK, if you don't include any politics you can insert photos of grandmasters." And so, in Kortchnoi's biography we wrote that he emigrated from the Soviet Union in '76. And we also wrote that some others followed later. That was allowed, but no additional remarks. Just biographical information.'

Which are the chess books that anyone should read who wants to make some decent progress in chess?
'For the first steps in chess I would recommend the books of Lasker and Capablanca. Lasker's *Manual of Chess* and *Chess Fundamentals*. Very good books for beginners. In Russia we had this book by Averbakh and Beilin, called in translation *Voyages in the Kingdom of Chess*. This is a nicely presented book. From the more serious books I would recommend the book by Fischer and also Larsen wrote a good book. So, sixty memorable games of Fischer and fifty games of Larsen. I like the way Larsen does his annotations. And I already mentioned this book about the Candidates' tournament in '59 and the book about the Petrosian-Spassky match for the world title.

'But actually I must say that from '78 we have had very few serious books about the World Championship matches. Mostly they were done very shortly after the match and contain a lot of errors.'

The books that Kasparov wrote about the first matches were widely praised. Don't you think they were very good?
'No, I don't... So, as far as the matches are concerned he maybe did more himself. But as far as I know, the book on the last match was done by other people. Geller, Lein and Chepizhny. Kasparov just gave his name.'

I don't think that the English edition was misleading. As far as I can remember it was perfectly clear that the book was written by Geller, Lein and Chepizhny.
'And the previous books have been mostly written by Nikitin. And Kasparov gave his name. But Nikitin was in his team so he could do some parts. But actually I couldn't believe my eyes when I read the book by Kasparov and Nikitin about the Sicilian Defence, the Scheveningen, in which there are so many mistakes. Kasparov wasn't even World Champion yet. This book appeared in '82 or '83 and was translated into English and has a lot of mistakes. Like I said about the *Informant*. When we prepared for the first match against Kasparov, we analysed this and found a lot of mistakes. Some quite clear. So, after this I have no respect for the work of Kasparov. I think the World Champion should be more cautious with his name.

'Now Kasparov presents a series of lectures, how to study chess, in Spanish. You know that they publish this course of lectures in a Spanish chess magazine. But this is a disaster, because in the first lecture they give two positions and in both Kasparov recommends brilliant play. You must play this sacrifice and you win, but in reality the move loses. This is terrible. And in another diagram he gives a brilliant positional sacrifice of a pawn. You close the diagonal and you win. But in reality the bishop comes back on another diagonal and you lose. You cannot do this. The least you can do is check things. How can you do this? Of course, you can make mistakes in your comments. You can make mistakes during the game and repeat them in your annotations. But when you give lessons and you give two examples and both are wrong. What can you say then? Then it doesn't matter if you are a fan of Kasparov, or a fan of Karpov, or a fan of anybody. If I did something like this my fans should criticize me.'

I was rather talking about his books about the matches which I think were very good books.
'No, no, when you have such examples you don't read books by this person anymore. Because you have no respect anymore.'

Are there any other contemporary authors you do have respect for?
'As I told you the best books were written by Fischer and Larsen. Also Portisch is doing quite well, but he is not very productive.'

But Fischer and Larsen, these books were written more than twenty years ago.
'Yes, quite some time ago. Well, I respect the annotations of Timman. I remember his book *The Art of Chess Analysis*. This was a good book. Jan works seriously, but he makes books for pleasure. He is not doing it for money. That is a big difference. When you are doing something for pleasure, you try to avoid mistakes. When you do annotations in twenty minutes you do it just to earn money.'

Of course there are a lot of other authors who will never make a lot of money by the books they write, but still write good books.
'By writing books you cannot earn too much money. I can say I like the style of Hübner. It's respectful. He shows a lot of work. But when he gives very long annotations, of course there are holes. But he works seriously. I like people who do serious work.'

You yourself would never make such long analyses. This is not your way of analysing.
'No, I believe that this may be good for grandmasters, but for the general public it has little use. They don't go so deep in their analysis. For them it is better to explain things in words. To describe what you have in mind, what your plan should be, etcetera. When you give very long analysis you are bound to make mistakes. When I try to bring across to people my understanding of chess I try to avoid mistakes.'

Finally, is there a book that you would still like to write. A book that you've been thinking of for a long time?
'Actually, for a long time I have had the idea to write a book *How to learn chess?* Not for absolute beginners, but starting from a certain level. Like Capablanca did or Lasker.

I was even asked by several publishing houses. But this demands a lot of work and a lot of responsibility. And I think it is very difficult to beat Capablanca and Lasker. Because their books are very good (laughs). That's why I have been reluctant to write such a book. And maybe, but for the moment I have no time to do this, maybe I will write a book about all the matches I have played. With annotations of all the games. Perhaps with some remarks about the things around the matches, but not too much. But this is something for the distant future. This requires a lot of work and time.'

Jan Timman

Amsterdam, May 1991

'Kasparov's books are the best, as far as high level analyses are concerned'

The World Champion is not the only chess author to pledge allegiance to Botvinnik's principles. In his preface to *Het Groot Analyseboek*, the result of his first analytical endeavours, Jan Timman acknowledged his indebtedness to the *Patriarch's* advice to expose one's individual analysis to objective criticism. The subsequent translations of this modern classic (*The Art of Chess Analysis, Jan Timman analysiert Grossmeisterpartien*) established Timman's name internationally as one of today's leading annotators. His other books include *Schaakwerk I* (1983, 'Chess Work I', a selection of analyses and endgame studies). *Het Smalle Pad* (1988, 'The Narrow Path', about his experiences in the World Championship cycle) and *Schaakzaken* (1990, 'Chess Matters', a compilation of journalistic articles). Currently Jan Timman is adding the final touches to *Schaakwerk II*, which will first appear in a German edition.

'There were a number of books that influenced me in my younger years. The books we had at home my father had bought before the War. 300 *Schachpartien* by Tarrasch, an old games selection by Euwe with a blue cover, as well as nearly all opening books by Euwe from 1939. My father would often play through games from this games selection by Euwe, together with my elder brother. The games they had played through were marked with a pencil. But the book that made the deepest impression on me was Müller's book on Botvinnik, which my grandmother gave me as a present when I was staying with her in Amsterdam for a week. I was about eight years old at the time and one of the reasons why this book made such a profound impression was probably the fact that my room had a chess set with tin pieces representing Roman armies. With these pieces I played through these games and this made a deeper impression than the books I had seen at home in Delft. Although I must say that Euwe was a much better player than Botvinnik. Obviously he had selected games that he had won, but apart from that he did indeed hold a positive score against Botvinnik until the World Championship in 1948.

'In fact, these were the two players I grew up with, Euwe and Botvinnik. Another book, which I read when I was something like ten or eleven years old and which I liked very much, was *Oordeel en Plan* (*Judgement and Plan*) by Euwe. A very pleasant and instructive book. And again some time later *Die Kunst der Bauernführung* by Kmoch. But, for instance, one of the things I have never read is Nimzowitsch. Neither then nor later. Well, occasionally I have flicked through *Die Praxis meines Systems*, but *Mein System* (laughs)... I've always more or less taken the line that if you write about chess you should do so in a down-to-earth manner. It shouldn't be too philosophical.'

You've got quite a substantial chess library. How did you fill these shelves through the years?
'I'm not really a collector. The books I collect I want to read. I don't think collectors set themselves the task to go through everything they purchase. I do, in principle. The things I particularly look for are books on endgame studies, tournament books, biographies and books on matches. As you can see, I have arranged them according to these subjects. I don't really hunt for books and most of the more special books I have acquired quite accidentally or I got them as gifts. Of course, I do like to poke around in bookstalls. Even during my match against Speelman I was able to buy a number of books, from this likeable nutty Englishman who had a bookstall there. One of them was a tournament book in Russian on Venice 1950, which was probably only published because Kotov won that tournament. Of course, nowadays you have *Tournament Chess* and tournaments on computer disks, but I like having a substantial collection of games that were played in the past. I think that's very useful. For instance, I have the bulletins of most Olympiads. I prefer to have them as a book. I like the smell of books and they have all sorts of advantages. You can shut them whenever you like and you don't have to goggle at a screen. It's probably also better for the eyes.

'When I talk about my early days, I can only speak about books that appealed to me then, but later on, of course, I developed a certain taste that was closely linked with the progress I made. In general I'm not really a lover of theoretical opening books, as they tend to be rather transitory. I do take a keen interest in tournament books. In the old days there were many beautifully produced books, a tradition which hasn't really deteriorated that much. The tournament books of, say, Interpolis and SWIFT were excellent too. And, of course, the second Piatigorsky book is very good and Zürich '53. It wasn't only at the beginning of this century that they made fine books.'

Which modern classics have given you most pleasure?
'I have to say that Kasparov's books are the best, as far as high level analyses are concerned. As for the others, my view doesn't differ much from Kasparov's. The book by Polugaevsky he mentions is very good. I completely agree on that. The books Keres wrote are very good and so are Botvinnik's, but I believe that Keres was clearer and more lucid in his comments. And Karpov's book with fifty games I liked. And of course the books Larsen and Fischer wrote about their games, although in these books I enjoyed the reading bits most. Fischer, of course, is a more spectacular player to take note of and *My Sixty Memorable Games* is also very good from

BAS BEEKHUIZEN

**Jan Timman: 'I'm not really a collector.
The books I collect I want to read.'**

an analytical point of view. But what I liked best were his remarks and observations, the things he said about his Russian colleagues. Fischer had a very unrestrained and open-minded, but at the same time very professional view of the chess world, and this combination is very attractive.'

What about your own books? Your first books were wholly dedicated to technical analysis, whereas in your later works background stories began to occupy an increasingly important place. 'Yes, this is true, but this might very well change again. My first book, *The Art of Chess Analysis*, was in fact the result of many years of analytical work. From a technical point of view this is the best chess book I have written. It cannot really be compared to the books I wrote afterwards, because *Schaakwerk I*, which soon will appear in German, was nevertheless better as a book. The nice thing about a book like *The Art of Chess Analysis* was that with every new translation I could add something and make essential corrections. The English translation is better than the Dutch original, the German translation is better than the English one, and the French and Spanish editions again contain many improvements. I don't know which languages are still left, possibly Russian. Maybe I could do something special for a Russian edition.

'The book I am working on now, a sequel to *Schaakwerk I*, which I think I will finish in June, is again very analytical. This book will contain fourteen attacking games, games in which I played for attack from the very first moves, as well as a number of thematically arranged endgame studies. So that will be another real chess book, for my latest two books, *Het Smalle Pad* and *Schaakzaken*, which have only appeared in Dutch so far, deal for a large part with non-technical matters.'

What does the ideal Timman book look like?
'That is hard to say. Probably a book like the one I'm writing now is most to my liking. This combination of attacking games and endgame studies. What I would even like better is a complete selection of games arranged by theme. But then I

would arrive at about one hundred games, and thoroughly annotated these would make a very thick book. That's why I prefer to nibble off small chunks from time to time and in *Schaakwerk* I and II, I have already included two themes.'

From time to time there has been criticism that your analyses have become less thorough in recent years. Is Schaakwerk II a return to the kind of profound analyses that made your name as one of today's leading analysts?
'That wasn't my intention. I don't believe that my analyses have become superficial, they simply became less extensive. At a certain point I decided for myself that I only wanted to analyse games extensively if I though it helpful for myself. And although there are a lot of people who speak highly about these analyses I don't have the impression that many of them had a thorough look at them. If you don't do this for your own benefit your target group becomes so much smaller than the group of people for whom you can also write a different type of book. If you make your writings slightly more accessible people also find it easier to react. I've had quite a few reactions on my first book from various countries. And very constructive reactions at that. I'm very happy about this. I had a letter from two Germans who had studied a couple of analyses very thoroughly, and came up with very good variations. These must be tremendously fanatical chess players, who really spend days on their investigations. Nowadays I find it less useful to keep delving into games than I used to. Of course, this is connected with the experience you gain. You learn to realize that there are one or a few critical moments in a game and you explain a number of things about these moments.

'If you are a top player writing books, it is best to write books that the broadest possible public can appreciate. I also think that it's a misapprehension that someone who is a strong chess player is less capable of explaining what's going on on the board than someone who has, for example, certain didactical qualities. It seems to me that top-class players like Keres, Karpov, Kasparov or myself understand better than anyone else what the reader wants to see and what is understandable. The best commentators remain the players themselves. If you take, for instance, Cafferty's book on Spassky or Vasiliev's book on Petrosian, you will find that these are rather shallow, uninteresting books. Books written by the players themselves are much more fascinating. During my match in Antwerp, for example, I read through Lilienthal's *Schach war mein Leben*. Lilienthal was a strong player, even though he isn't so well-known, and this book makes very good reading, because of the way he writes about himself. Something that is lacking almost entirely from books written by a third party.'

Returning to your bookshelves I cannot fail to notice that a considerable part of your collection consists of books on endgame studies.
'Yes, and I also have a fair amount of theoretical endgame books. As far as endgame studies are concerned my collection is by no means complete, but these are books

I cherish. Books like *Sämtliche Studien* by Réti. Shortly before his death Réti gave the manuscript to Mandler[11] and from these notes Mandler put together this book. These are about the most famous studies there are. Or Troitzky's and Kasparyan's books, in fact indispensable for every lover of endgame studies. And, of course, Rinck's *1414 Fins de Parties*, a book I always wanted to have. I was very happy when Olms published a reprint. And other endgame composers. (Starts showing a stack of specialist goodies) Nadareishvili, Prokes, Kubbel, the brothers Platov, a bit disappointing, Liburkin, that's a really good one, Selesniev, Fritz. All these books I have acquired out of a general interest in endgame studies. As far as endgame theory is concerned there are, of course, the well-known standard works, but an unknown book is this one by Gawlikowski. An excellent theoretical book, but as far as I know there is only a Polish edition. Another less familiar book is this one about endgames with rooks and knights by Umnov.'

Do you think that now the financial conditions in the chess world are improving many top players will become reluctant to annotate their games or write books?
'I don't know. Kasparov is still very ambitious. Karpov it seems a little less so. But he could very well write a sequel to his first book. After all he has done a lot of analysing since. Of course, it's true that particularly among my generation there are many players who don't feel inclined to analyse their games for the public. Like Andersson and Ljubojevic, who don't think this is part of the job. They play and that's it. I've never seen any special comments by Short either. Of course, Speelman has written endgame books and some other nice books. And, of course, I shouldn't forget John Nunn, who has written a number of excellent books. I don't think there is any reason to be pessimistic. I believe that there are still enough books being published that are well worth reading.'

---

11 Arthur Mandler, 1889–1971, Czech chess composer.

Memorable Moments

The other day I was reading an article about the legendary baseball player Joe DiMaggio, when I came across the description of a familiar feeling. Having visited DiMaggio on the eve of his eightieth birthday, the journalist concluded, 'I don't think you interview Joe. I believe you have a conversation with him and consider yourself lucky.' Among my interviews the encounters with the great players of the recent past take up a special place. It is the kind of experience you regard as a particular privilege. There you are talking to grandmasters whose names have such a special ring. You know their careers, have played through many of their games, and there you are asking them questions to find out why chess occupied this all-important place in their lives. Gligoric amazes you when he confesses that every time he plays a game of chess he still sits down to it as if it was his first game. Portisch makes you feel sorry for him when he explains his conviction that he has always had to pay a heavy prize if he did not follow his principles and was always punished for his mistakes. Najdorf makes you fall silent when he recounts how chess made him overcome the personal nightmare of the second World War and brings back the smile on your face when he says that he still goes to the chess club every day for his daily diet of blitz games.

For good reasons several of the players selected here will find it too early to be dubbed living legends, so maybe we should speak of memorable moments. Memorable moments that sometimes came about very easily, sometimes required a lot of patience and perseverance. The interview with Viktor Kortchnoi, back in 1986, is the first talk we ever had. With his frank and straightforward approach he has always been a rewarding conversation partner and in the years that followed I regularly returned to him. This first talk was no exception. Generously taking his time he elaborated on the long list of topics I brought up. As a newcomer in the world of chess I felt honoured and tried to continue as long as he wanted to. As Kortchnoi did not give any clear signs that he wanted to leave either, it was finally his life companion Petra Leeuwerik who had to step in. 'Viktor, don't you think we should be going for dinner.' To which came the baffling answer that said it all, 'Please wait a little bit, I want the interview to be at least as long as the one with Ljubojevic in the previous issue.' Which proved to be no problem at all.

Others were less eager and drove it home to me that like chess, interviewing chess players can be a waiting game. The first time I approached Lajos Portisch for a talk was at the 1986 SWIFT. tournament in Brussels. With an apologetic laugh the Hungarian bass-bariton avoided my suggestion with a low-voiced, 'Well, maybe some time, but better not now', a reply I was to get in different but no less unambiguous forms for some years after, although it would be closer to the truth to say that at a certain point I gave up asking. In the meantime we had discovered a shared interest in classical music, more specifically opera and Lieder, and that was the subject we would talk about. Only when I thought it appropriate I might conclude an exchange of ideas and suggestions with the ceterum censeo that we should have an interview one day. Portisch would start, or laugh, or both, and say, 'Well, maybe some time, but better not now.'

My patience was awarded at the 1990 Hoogovens tournament. Having played an uncharacteristically short draw, Portisch was aimlessly wandering about the analysis room. We entered in a brief conversation on the game and then I added, 'I think we should do the interview now'. The Hungarian grandmaster drew breath to begin his, 'Well, maybe some time', but instead the answer he produced was a clear, 'Alright, let's find a place to talk.' We found it in the basement of the De Moriaan hotel and there Portisch talked and talked for two and a half hours, as if he had been saving up answers for four years.

Some of the interviews presented here have gained additional significance over time. Reading Gligoric's plea for a united Yugoslavia on the eve of one of the bloodiest tragedies in modern European history, reminds us that once there was a time when we knew there were conflicts sizzling under the surface in his home country, but still hoped that they would never erupt. The interview with Gligoric is also an interesting preamble to Fischer's return to chess. Still regretting the failure of his attempts, Gligoric relates how he even agreed to run for FIDE president in 1978, with the only desire to get Fischer back to play. He also says that he was the only person Fischer trusted when he came to Belgrade to discuss a match with him. After those vain attempts Gligoric gave up all hope that Fischer would ever return. Almost symbolically, Gligoric, as he later told me, sent this interview to Fischer, who let him know that he liked it. But we'll get to this later.

Viktor Kortchnoi

Tilburg, November 1986

'I have a very high opinion of the new Soviet leadership'

When in 1976 Viktor Kortchnoi defected from the Soviet Union, one of the first to send him a telegram was Robert Fischer who congratulated him on 'the correct move'. Ten years later when Karpov was catching up with Kasparov in their match in Moscow, Kortchnoi sent a telegram to Kasparov, signed with a neutral 'Petrovich', in which he warned him not to underestimate his opponent. Viktor Kortchnoi has always been full of respect for both Fischer and Kasparov, but much to his regret the most crucial moments of his chess career have been connected with the name of Karpov. After their match in Baguio his anger and indignation culminated in his book *Antichess* in which he openly accused Karpov of more than can be summarized here. In the following years Kortchnoi spared no efforts to repeat or reinforce these accusations. In view of this hostile atmosphere it came as no small surprise that when the antagonists met at the chessboard again in the grandmaster tournament in Vienna earlier this year, they exchanged some words. Maybe time heals all wounds for in Tilburg Kortchnoi and Karpov not only played bridge together but also spent more than an hour analysing their second game. Well, maybe it does.

After you won the Wijk aan Zee tournament in 1968 you said in an interview that despite your success you still thought that you had been at your best a few years earlier. Around 1965 you could have been a serious contender for the World Championship which was now definitely out of the question. Yet, in the seventies we witnessed a remarkable second flowering that brought you closer to the title than ever. What is your explanation for this?

'First of all it seems that I have had a bad basic school of chess. I do not want to accuse my first teacher too much, but you should begin by learning the alphabet of chess. I did not learn much when I was a young boy. So, after I had already become a master, a grandmaster, a champion of the Soviet Union, I realised that I had many white spots in my chess education. I was already a champion of the Soviet Union, and I had already won several strong tournaments, but I realised that this was just because of the tremendous energy I could put into my games, but my knowledge of the games of the best chess players of the past required serious improvement.

Then I started to work a lot, and I am still working a lot, and I am still learning something despite the fact that at my age it is more difficult to learn than when you are young. For example, I believe that I am still learning something from Kasparov. It is a good feature when you remain open to new influences and by this I explain why I improved over the last years.

'Also when I was still in the Soviet Union I experienced serious problems as I was not always able to travel and play chess normally. So when I defected I had the feeling that I had everything in my own hands. I used all these opportunities to work myself and to invite interesting people to work with. In the Soviet Union I could not play chess where I wanted to. That did not only concern me. Recently, for example, until the third match between Karpov and Kasparov, Tal had problems to travel and to play in the competitions that he wanted to. So it is not only me, but a lot of Soviet players who have these problems. Every time I wanted to play in a big tournament there were always these problems with documents, with people who tried to keep me from playing chess. This was another incentive for me to improve my play.'

When you came to the West you indeed started to play an awful lot. Where do you find the energy to compete in so many tournaments?
'Yes, this is a problem of ageing people. I have to recharge my sources of energy. Another problem of ageing people is to recharge your sources of ambition. For young players everything is important, but an old man, instead of playing, instead of trying to win, may want to read an interesting book or go to an interesting movie, because he no longer wants to be always in the position to prove that he is the best.'

After your defection it was often said that your wish for revenge was your main motive. Is this still your driving force?
'No, I don't think so. When someone leaves the Soviet Union, officially or runs away, it is always regarded as a political step. One has to grow up politically to undertake such a step. So, I made a political step, a step against the Soviet government. But let us consider how it happened. It happened because several people made my situation in the Soviet Union impossible. Actually I was pushed out of the Soviet Union by the hands of Petrosian and Karpov. But now, after ten years, Petrosian is no longer alive and Karpov is no longer World Champion, so it seems that everything is in place now. So if we could forget that it was a political step, I could come back to the Soviet Union and live peacefully. Especially because the Soviets, and more particularly the Soviet chess federation tries to establish good relations with me, as I am on good terms with the new world champion. So now it seems that I have no longer any stimulant to play and to strive for good results. I am enjoying my life in the West and playing tournaments wherever I want, which was what I wanted to achieve. But my personal enemies are down. This is a situation in which it is more difficult

than ever to find stimulants or new sources of energy to play as best as I can.'

Do you think that somewhere in the future it may be possible for you to go back to the Soviet Union to play a tournament for instance?
'No, I don't think so. This is still a political matter. I don't want to be accused of wishful thinking, but I have a very high opinion of the new leadership in the Soviet Union.'

A high opinion?
'A very high opinion, regarding everything, such as the personal qualities of the new leader (Mikhail Gorbachov – DJtG), and the way he is trying to improve the situation economically and

Viktor Kortchnoi: 'I was pushed out of the Soviet Union by the hands of Petrosian and Karpov.'

politically. Well, in every respect. How he is working on the image of the Soviet Union in the world. I appreciate this very much, just like his undertakings in the area of human rights. He allowed some people like Gulko to go to the West, even though this was a matter of principle. It was not just that Gulko was a refusnik like there are dozens in the Soviet Union. He was a case of principle, because by keeping him the Soviet Union wanted to stop the leakage of chess players to the West. Nevertheless they agreed to release him. On the other hand I have written several autobiographical books that were in a way political, especially the second one, *Antichess*. This book was written with fury, with wrath, with honesty, and it was strongly anti-Soviet. I felt, and still feel, that I had to write it this way. It was published in seven languages and from that time I am certainly an enemy of the Soviet state that will never forget or forgive. So despite these activities of the Soviet leadership I don't consider myself in the position to ever come to the Soviet Union, to play chess or whatever.'

How big is your own will to forgive in these matters? Would your autobiography be the same if you were to rewrite it now?
'This book was the result of the situation. My family was in the Soviet Union and I was fighting for them. I wanted the world to know the situation of my family. They are not in the Soviet Union anymore, so perhaps the book would be a little

bit different. But the book was dedicated to the match in Baguio and I still believe that Karpov did not play fair chess. When he is playing he tries to make use of the skills of the dozens of people around him. Not only chess players, but scientists, psychologists, magicians, doctors, and so on. This is wrong. Before Karpov introduced this nobody who was playing chess thought that he should be surrounded by a camp of supporters. People have to play alone, one against one.'

You yourself adopted the idea as well.
'Yes, I did, but the Soviet state has much more facilities than an individual can have. According to some sources Karpov in Merano was surrounded by seventy people, and it is difficult to imagine that someone could hire seventy people without the support of a big state.'

Of what help could they be? The usefulness of seconds is obvious, but what about all the others?
'Well, I can tell something. You see I have written a book on the match in Baguio, because it was a fighting match and because some foul play was discovered, so I had material to write a book. When I was crushed in the match in Merano, however, I could not understand how it happened and I had only suspicions, but I had never any solid evidence of what had happened.

'I know that the Soviets arrived in Italy with three containers. With these containers they were waiting for four hours at Milano airport before they could go through the customs without being searched. They managed to do so and they brought something, nobody knows what, to the villa where Karpov lived. They never allowed any foreign person to come to the villa. There was a group of Soviet tourists and a group of wives of the grandmasters who were supporting Karpov. They never allowed any Soviet woman to come to this place. And when the match was over, under the cover of the night, they put everything into trucks and disappeared. That is all that we know. I have now an inflammation of the eyelids, a so-called conjunctivitis, and the first symptoms of this illness I felt during and after the match. I believe it was that what was in those containers and many other technical things, which sometimes when foul play is allowed can enable a person to win a chess game or a chess match. That was one of the things that were never publicized. But time will come when it will be.

'Now I know that Kasparov was also in difficulties when playing Karpov, although they were playing in Moscow. I have heard many stories. That his seconds were drafted to the army, so that they had to avoid the draft. That they tried to send his mother away from Moscow during the match. I heard many different stories about psychology and parapsychology. The following story may be interesting to non-biased chess fans. The first part of the story is as follows. During the match in Baguio Dr. Zukhar, the so-called parapsychologist was always sitting still in the playing-hall trying to help Karpov, and sometimes trying to put me out of balance. After the match he got such tremendous publicity that it seemed that he had won the match and not Karpov. On this ground they had a row and Dr. Zukhar never worked with Karpov again. Then it turned out during the first match between Karpov and Kasparov in Moscow that Dr. Zukhar was a school friend of Kasparov's tutor Nikitin, and he invited him to the second part of the match to help him. Now it is hard to determine the effects of parapsychology. Parapsychology is a part of psychology which is still not grasped by the human mind, which is beyond our comprehension. Let's say, hypnosis is a very strange thing, but it is already accepted. I know that before each game Zukhar had been hypnotizing Karpov, but also during the games Karpov needed help, and he was sitting somewhere in the audience where Karpov could watch him.

'But let us return to the match Karpov-Kasparov where he was invited by Nikitin to help during the second part of the match and he similarly was successful because Kasparov managed to hold on to the edge of a gap and did not lose the match. That was the first part of the story. The second part I have heard from some sources. Whether they are reliable or not I don't know, but it goes as follows. In the Soviet Union chess is a political matter and very high officials are involved. During the match Zukhar was invited to the headquarters of the Soviet leadership and they said to him "Comrade, what are you doing? You are on the wrong side. Be careful, comrade." Dr. Zukhar did not stop his activities and according to my sources he was already in a lunatic asylum himself by the end of the match as a patient (sniggers sardonically).'

That's the rumour.
'Yes, that's the rumour, but not every gossip is wrong. It is like the proverb, there is no smoke without fire. I remember my own match with Karpov in Moscow. It was very strange. There were two Soviet citizens, and my group was surrounded, cut off from the world, and the people who were coming just to greet me or my wife were already under suspicion. They immediately got a bad political reputation. Being in Moscow, being a Soviet citizen, you felt yourself a foreigner while playing with Karpov, and I believe the same happened with Kasparov.'

Talking about psychologists, in your first match with Karpov it was you who started to come five or six minutes late to the games. In your autobiography you write that you did so at your psychologist's instigation.
'(Thinks for a while) I don't remember this exactly, but it is true that I had a psychologist who suggested to me several things like that. To be late, or to profit from the fact that I knew that Karpov is a very superstitious man. To force Karpov to change his shirt or his tie, or even his suit, you have to beat him, otherwise he is always wearing the same tie, shirt, suit, and this is not a joke. Well, in fact everyone who has a profession in which his life depends on a few seconds is more or less superstitious. Sportsmen, pilots and so on, but not to such a degree as Karpov.

'In that match Karpov was wearing one and the same tie, a tie with chess pieces from the United States. My psychologist suggested that I wear the same tie, as I had bought an identical one in the United States. I put on the same tie and I wonder how he felt at that moment (hilarity), because he could not leave the tie because he is superstitious. On the other hand there were two men with the same tie, and for several games we played like that, like twins. Well, O.K., this was suggested by my psychologist and from one point of view I would not say that I share all his views and the choice of his psychological weapons, but on the other hand, when you are surrounded by only enemies and you feel supported at least by your psychologist, you want to show that you also have friends.'

Did you choose this psychologist yourself?
'No, no, he came to me and offered his help.'

You spoke about the role that parapsychology sometimes plays in chess. It struck me that over the years you have shown considerable interest in several alternative methods or pseudo-sciences, such as astrology and biorhythmicity. What value do you attribute to these?
'Well, I'm not a specialist, I'm only a customer (laughs). I think that, let's say, the role of astrology has not yet been fully investigated and I believe that these methods are more important than people think.'

Did you become interested by personal experience?
'No, no, I had some fans in the Soviet Union, scientists, who came to me to talk about biorhythms, which is already accepted as it is based on astrology. A person is born at a certain time, so he has certain cycles. So humanity has already accepted some part of astrology.'

Some part.
'Well, O.K., it takes time.'

You say 'I'm only a customer'. Is that what you were in Baguio when these two guru's appeared on the scene. Were you only interested whether they could be of any use?
'Perhaps, in a way I am an adventurer who sometimes likes to try something new.'

What did you think of Keene's publishing Spassky's biorhythmic table in a newspaper? It must have been very unpleasant for Spassky.
'I didn't pay attention to it. He published it, I think it was an interesting journalistic step, as he published his table and mine.'

What is true of Karpov's story that you went to his doctor before your match in 1974 and then took Karpov's medical chart with you?
'(Looks puzzled) I can't remember that. (Thinks long) What I do remember is that once after a game had been drawn he had forgotten his thermos on the table and

we had taken it to analyse the liquid that he had in it. About his medical chart I cannot remember anything. I even don't believe that any doctor would have given me his medical chart, because he was always in a superior position. I don't think this ever happened. It is complete rubbish.'

As you said, the situation in the Soviet chess world has drastically changed. Petrosian is dead and Karpov is no longer World Champion. Is that also the reason why here in Tilburg you spoke to Karpov again after all these years of outright animosity, and even analysed with him for more than an hour in Russian, and in a rather friendly manner?
'No, this is more complicated. First the Soviet players already got the instruction two years ago to change their attitude towards their former countrymen. Originally they were instructed to stay away from these emigrants and to show them that Soviets don't deal with such degenerates. The new instructions, however, said, and of course, I can only speculate, that they should not show their fear. They are citizens of the great state and why should they be afraid of these people without motherland and so on. That is one thing. Now it is interesting to know how the boycott was lifted several years ago, and although I have not yet been able to verify my version, I feel that it happened this way.

'The boycott was installed by the Politburo, so only the Politburo could lift the boycott. In 1983 the Soviet chess federation and Campomanes were playing a very strange game, because they didn't trust each other. But actually they were acting in unison and together they made my match with Kasparov in the United States impossible. Campomanes was taken as a scapegoat and he was blamed for the match not taking place. Then Kasparov who has a very strong hand at the very top of the Soviet establishment whose name is Aliev, who was the second man after Andropov a few years ago, managed to see this man. This was very remarkable in itself as it is easier for a foreigner to see Gorbachov than for a Soviet citizen. Kasparov told him the whole story, and Aliev slammed his fist on the table and said: "I'll give you anything, all leverage that you need, and the match must be played." So the Soviet chess federation with all its officials and civil servants began to prepare this match and through the embassies all over the world they created the opinion that the match must be played. At the same time they had to find something to soften me, as I had legally won the match. And with the help of Kasparov and Aliev finally the boycott was lifted.'

There also was this rumour that you were paid a large sum of money.
'No, that is not true, but before and during the match with Kasparov the boycott was lifted, and they have even shown some games on Soviet television. An unbelievable thing. But still, now I have been away from the Soviet Union for ten years I look upon everything with different eyes and I no longer speak the same language as the other Soviet players. So, I'm not going to be friendly with them, like with other people. But something happened in Vienna where I played a

game with Karpov. The game was adjourned and we had to resume play a few hours later, of which I was not aware and I was, say, ten, fifteen minutes late. Being a Western citizen, well being not so cheeky as the Soviets, I have already this habit, as I am a normal person, and when I arrived I automatically apologized. But on him, who is a Soviet, this made a tremendous impression, this apology. From that time he felt that he also should make his step, and he made it here in Tilburg.'

Although you were involved in so many conflicts and quarrels you have always advocated a gentleman-like behaviour at the board. When Spassky started acting strange during your match you were very upset.
'Yes, I don't like strenuous situations during serious play, but I am cool and, well, that happened.'

Do you resemble Fischer in this respect, who could make enormous problems about anything but would always be a gentleman at the board?
'Fischer, yes he was a gentleman and never any chess player had objections to his behaviour, only organizers. I tried my best to give him the best publicity in the world by saying that he was, he is and will be the best chess player in the world.'

Do you still think so?
'Well, the situation is a little bit different now, because I highly respect Kasparov, not only as a chess player, but also as a very intelligent person, who is full of humour and who is outspoken. As far as chess creativity is concerned he is not worse than Fischer. As we are comparing the reigning World Champion to someone who is in voluntary exile we must prefer the one who is playing chess.'

When you were writing about sportsmanship in your autobiography you said that no one could accuse you of malice in this respect, except for Karpov, Petrosian and Fischer. The first two I can understand, but what about Fischer?
'I don't remember that, perhaps I was wrong when I was writing it. I normally got along well with Fischer and he was full of respect for me as a person. He was the first to send me a telegram when I was in Amsterdam at the police headquarters after I had defected, saying "Congratulations on the correct move".'

That was the last thing you heard of him?
'No, that was not the last time. I spoke to him in 1977. I was in Los Angeles giving simultaneous displays. I was making a simul tour of the United States and he was following me on the phone. He phoned me in Chicago and he phoned me in Denver, and so when I came to Los Angeles I went to see him and we talked. That was the last time, because it happened that I had a simultaneous display and a talk that same evening where I told that I had met Fischer. He was

very angry with me and he sent me a letter in which he accused me of spying on him. That was too much for me and at that moment I broke off all relations with him.'

Did you already get the impression that he would never return to chess anymore when you spoke to him?
'Yes, at that moment already. I got the impression that he was still very keen on chess and that he was still able to play very well, up to his Elo-rating, but at the same time I got the impression that he would never play again.'

We know your criticism of the Soviet system, but is there still some love left in your heart for Mother Russia?
'That is difficult to say for I was in a state of war with Mother Russia for many years. What kind of feelings can you experience when you are at war? When you are at war with Germany you may forget that there are famous philosophers, musicians, poets, and so on.'

Don't you sometimes think of these poets and musicians? You have often said that you were a lover of poetry and verse, I suppose that this was Russian poetry in the first place?
'Yes, of course, but I only occasionally read Russian nowadays. I am not interested anymore.'

Is this because you purposely want to cut off all ties with the Soviet Union?
'Well, it happened involuntarily. They deny the existence of this one person, and I deny the existence of this whole state.'

When you are listening to, let's say, a Shostakovich symphony, you are not listening to a product of the Soviet system, but to something Russian.
'Yes, I understand what you mean, but when people are talking like this I always remind them of a famous saying of Hegel that every people deserves its form of ruling. Well, I am a historian by profession and for hundreds of years the Russians have been dominated. By Tartars, by Normans, sometimes by Polish people or others, so they are accustomed to be slaves. That is quite essential. When you read Soviet prose, Dostoevsky or Turgeniev, you feel this. So you can't say, this huge state is so nice, but unfortunately they have been captured by the communist ideology and now nobody can say a word. Well, sometimes they have tried to say something, but in the thirties of this century they have again and again been taught to be silent. This is the Russian nature, to be humble and obedient.'

So, you don't have a Russian soul?
'Mm, there are exceptions of course, like this man Sakharov, who is a hundred percent Russian, but he is the conscience of the Russian nation.'

Of course there must have been many people who experienced difficulties like you did. Did you not feel any solidarity with them?

'I am not sure that they who are victims realize that they are victims. I have regularly spoken with dissidents, although I am not in that sphere, but I meet them sometimes, and we discussed the question what would happen if the Soviet people would be given their freedom. Some of them thought that nothing would happen. They are accustomed to be humble, they need instructions from above. For example, I have a few friends in the Soviet Union, and they asked me to send them my photograph. I correspond with them, and after they have been censored my letters get through to them. But I never managed to send them my photograph as the letters would always arrive without the photographs. A few months ago I met a Soviet grandmaster who was very friendly and trying to start a normal relationship with me. Then I asked him if he could do me a favour and take my photograph to an address I would give him. He looked at me with such strange begging eyes as if to say, "What do you ask of me?"

'This was several months ago. Now I have been watching the political developments and I know that the situation is changing. Gorbachov is doing his best and perhaps the time will come when he will start to deal with the censorship as well. But when I met this man, who is considered to be among the leading people, intellectually, of the chess elite in the Soviet Union, I realized that Gorbachov is ahead of the way of thinking of the Soviet population. He alone has to overcome the stagnation of the Soviet way of thinking (laughs). This grandmaster did not dare to take my picture. Was it a picture of a criminal? Well, I had already been on television in 1983. Now you say that I have to feel solidarity. I can only feel pity that they don't know their own situation.'

You referred to the fact that you are a historian. In your autobiography you write about the disappointing one-sidedness of your studies that were totally dominated by the Marxist-Leninist ideology. Do you still read books on history, in a broader sense that is, today?

'No, eh, (starts smiling) I now prefer to read detective stories based on polit-ical situations, which remotely remind me of the contemporary political situation. What I have learned, however, is the method. It is not only a historian's method, it is a communist method, the method of dialectical materialism which I apply on historical facts from the past and also on the present.'

You have always been very critical of the FIDE president Campomanes. He will now be president for another four years.

'As you can read in my book *Antichess* he has been my enemy since the match in Baguio. If we want to put back FIDE on democratic rails he must be removed. Otherwise it must be split.'

Do you mean that the leading chess nations and the developing countries should have their own federations?

'That is also a good idea, because the leading chess countries pay the lion's part of the contributions for the development of chess in the world, whereas the developing countries pretend to have the same understanding of what is going on, and they have the same vote, but they don't know what it is all about. Supported by their majority Campomanes can decide everything.'

You are also thinking of the Olympiad in Dubai and the tournament in Jerusalem?
'I'm also thinking of that. You know how this tournament developed. Somehow Israel had a deal with Campomanes that they would not protest against their exclusion from the Olympiad in Dubai. An independent organization then decided to organize a tournament in Jerusalem. But if the Israeli federation would not protest they should neither organize their own tournament, so they opposed the tournament and threatened not to recognize the tournament.

'Now, let's say that FIDE made a clumsy move by organizing the Olympiad and violating the major principle of an international organization by banning Israel, just for the sake of getting some money from the rich Arab organizers. In that case they should send an apology to Israel and greet and appreciate the tournament in Jerusalem as a substitute for those players who could not go to the Olympiad. But they opposed this tournament and in this way showed that it was not a clumsy move but a deliberate step. FIDE insisted on violating its major principle. This alone should be sufficient reason to dismiss the president of FIDE.'

For people who have known Campomanes for many years this does not come as a surprise. Also within FIDE people were very familiar with him as his career started many years ago. How could he ever become president?
'Yes, how could he come to power. This reminds me of a notorious part of the history of FIDE. In 1976 there was a chess Olympiad in Haifa and at the same time another Olympiad was organized in Tripoli, Libya. It has never been investigated how this second Olympiad came about, but as I am a historian by profession I think that it should be investigated. To organize an Olympiad is not so easy. Of course it is clear that there is a totalitarian state that always gives financial support to Libya, but such an organization demands more than money. About forty countries sent their team to Tripoli, some countries sent one team to Haifa and another to Tripoli. But who organized this Olympiad? Some say it were the Russians. No, the Russians did not participate. It should be someone who has the key to all the addresses, everything. Now we come to the point I would like to make, that someone, whose name I don't want to mention, of the FIDE-bureau at that time has managed to organize it, and I am absolutely sure that it was not Dr. Euwe or Ineke Bakker. So you may know who I mean (laughs). A sly politician with sufficient financial support, for instance from his former president, may reach a very high position in every international organization, whether it is respectable or not. That is why I still think that it should be investigated who organized the Olympiad in Tripoli.'

At a certain point in your career you started to work on your physical condition to improve your general fitness and your concentration during the game. What sports do you practise?
'Skiing, rowing, jogging, that's all.'

You quite regularly gave up smoking but never for long. What is it that makes you quit smoking and why do you start again?
'It seems that I don't have enough stimulation to stop smoking. I have heard that one who does not smoke plays better chess, so I have tried to stop. But after I had finished the tournament I would start smoking again.'

Let us consider your game. You hardly ever play 1.e4 anymore. Why don't you?
'The theory of the 1.e4 openings is very well developed and when you play 1.e4 you have to know all this theory, and sometimes when Black plays aggressively it takes much time to overcome his counter attack and so on. Karpov stopped playing 1.e4, or now only rarely plays it because he does not trust his energy anymore, and because he has grown tired of constantly keeping up with modern theory. When you play 1.d4 you are sometimes able to play the opening using only your common sense. Karpov won many games against me as White, but he won only one game when he played 1.d4, only because I badly wanted to beat him. In those games he had to rely on his common sense, and then he is not stronger than I am. So I would even say that in general, Kasparov excluded, it is a sign of ageing when one starts to play 1.d4 instead of 1.e4, or starts to play closed systems. But as far as I am concerned it is not a sign of ageing. Sometimes, once in every two years I play 1.e4 with good success, but I choose my opponents carefully, when I more or less know what will happen. These are not necessarily weak opponents. So when I am playing 1.e4 it is a sign that I am not old.'

You have a reputation of being quite materialistic as far as pawns are concerned. It is said that you like to grab a pawn and do your utmost to keep it.
'This is wrong. It is a very old idea that I told a journalist more than twenty years ago. After he had published it this story kept cropping up from time to time. You may ascribe my attitude then to my lack of chess education, the inability to feel the initiative and fight for it, but since then I have learned a lot.'

In Wijk aan Zee 1968 you played a beautiful game against Matanovic, that you considered to be one of your best strategic efforts ever. If you were to name your five favourite games, what games would you choose?
(Thinks very long) 'Eh, well, this is very difficult. Let's say Matanovic is included. OK, and then the seventh game with Polugaevsky in 1977 in Evian. Then my game with Spassky, from our match, also the seventh game, a middlegame with queens and rooks. That's three, yes? Well, there are so many games, I played about three thousand. Of course your opponent has to be strong, otherwise it cannot be a

masterpiece. I was thinking of my games with Karpov, but none of these games comes into consideration. Let me see, I won some thirteen games against Tal, but many were too easy. I remember one of my memorable games against Geller in the Soviet championship of 1960 which was very important at that moment and a good game. That's number fur. (Thinks long again) A very attractive game I played against Tal in 1962 in Yerevan at the Soviet championship.'

You will be less satisfied with your results here in Tilburg. After the first half of the tournament you still occupied shared second place, but in the second half you lost six games in a row, and finally ended in last place. Have you already found an explanation for this yourself?
'No, I don't have an explanation. It looks like in the second leg of the tournament I got possessed by some serious disease. That's what it looks like, because I was playing normally in the first leg of the tournament, and then something happened. It is beyond my comprehension and only time will tell if it really was a disease or the consequence of old age that suddenly fell upon me (laughs) or something else. So we had better wait and see.'

Could it be because you play so much? You hardly ever take time to recover from a tournament, but are travelling from one event to the other?
'Mm, in a way it is easier for Soviet chess players to maintain their ratings, because they normally play two or three tournaments a year, whereas I play in many more tournaments of different rank. In one tournament I play with extra class players and in another tournament I may play with weak players, or players of widely varying strength, which is more complicated.'

Why do you play so much? You don't have to do it for the money, do you?
'No, I don't do it for the money.'

You simply like to play?
'Yes, I like to play. When I was younger I played seventy games a year and that was not much for me, I wanted more. One or two years during my twenty years as a chess player in the Soviet Union I played 120 games, and at that time I thought that I had overdone it. Well, last year I played 170 tournament games and I think that that was normal (laughs).'

Other grandmasters sometimes complain that you ask a comparatively low starting fee. Of the players here in Tilburg you are the cheapest.
'Yes, that is true. I am not playing for the money, and I am independent financially. I believe that there are people who are born in very poor families, let's say famous millionaires like Rothschild. As they were born in poverty they have a complex for the rest of their lives. They want to make money not for the sake of money, but because they never ever want to be poor again. I was not born in a rich family, but I

never had this feeling that I was poor, so I never had this complex since I am financially more or less independent, I don't need to ask for more than I do.'

If you would not play so much and occasionally stay at home, would it make you nervous or would you become restless after some time?
'Well, a professional player needs practical play to revive his skill and perhaps this is one of the reasons why I have been playing worse in my last two tournaments. For during the last half year or even more, I have been involved in writing a book on complex rook endings, so that I have not been playing in tournaments as often as I was accustomed to.'

Vlastimil Hort

Amsterdam, August 1987

'Sometimes when I am sad I go out and buy a Rudé Pravo'

'A hallucination! I must have had a hallucination! How could I make such a silly mistake? I think I am getting old.' Vigorously and self-reproachingly shaking his head Vlastimil Hort shoots a final glance at the position in which he has just adjourned his game against Farago in the Amsterdam Ohra tournament. For hours he had been playing forcefully and had meticulously built up an advantage that seemed to make his win only a matter of time. Had it not been for this hallucination, this *Fingerfehler*, this mixing up of two moves that changed a winning position in a drawish endgame. Hort still cannot believe it and tries to conceal his frustration by laughing in disbelief. My suggestion to postpone our interview is, however, resolutely waved aside. 'No, no, let's do it', he says, smiling again, 'It will only be more philosophical.'

Since 1978, when he was asked to play for the Bundesliga team of SG Porz, Vlastimil Hort has been living in West Germany, where he has done a lot for the development of German chess and gained considerable popularity as a chess expert through numerous television appearances.

Although he went on representing Czechoslovakia in international events the relationship with his native country had been seriously strained and his desire to defect permanently had been growing steadily. Last year he finally took the plunge, and much to his relief acquired German citizenship. Now he can speak freely about his life in Czechoslovakia and the problems and harassments he had to endure. The story is often a bitter one but true to himself Hort tells it with little or no grudge or spite; he is in fact hopeful that the situation will change for the better, even though he has no great confidence in that actually happening. More than once Hort tells me that he is a born pessimist. As he had warned me, he was in a philosophical mood and candidly airs his feelings about other matters as well. Like his distrust in FIDE that dates back to 1970, or the ambitions of a 'middle-aged' chess player. But first he relates how he learned chess, a question that was left unanswered in his autobiographical *Begegnungen am Schachbrett* (Encounters at the Chess Board), an entertaining book on several aspects of his chess career that was published in 1984.

BAS BEEKHUIZEN

Vlastimil Hort: 'Fischer was playing there, so everything was fine and whatever happened to someone from a small nation did not matter.'

'It was all by chance. I learned chess at the age of six when I was in hospital. I had jaundice and had even been put in quarantine, because they could not decide whether I was some special case or whether my liver had been affected as well. At that time I was very small. In the hospital there was this doctor who was always there during the night and who also felt bored. Every night he saw me standing there behind the glass, where no one could actually visit me except for the hospital staff and one night he said to me, "I will show you a game". There in hospital this doctor taught me the moves and then at Christmas I got a present of a chess set from my grandmother. When I came out of hospital I was a chess player. I liked chess and tried to find my own way. In my chess life I have almost always worked alone. I had no trainer and was not pushed by the state or anything like that. In 1960, when I was sixteen years old, I played in the Czechoslovak championship for the first time. The championship was held in Presburg and I came second to fourth. This was more or less the beginning of my career. I made my grandmaster norm when I was 21 years old by winning a big tournament together with Keres in Marianské Lázne in 1965. This wasn't my first international success. In 1964 I had won, together with Portisch, a big tournament in Kecskemet in which the other participants were ten grandmasters of the older generation. Portisch and I came first, ahead of grandmasters like Barcza, Szabo, Padevsky, Simagin, Lengyel and Pietzsch from Eastern Germany. At that time this was quite something, but time is running, time is running.'

How was the situation in Czechoslovakia at that time. Did you get any support from the state?
'We did have some support from the state. I'm now talking about the fifties and sixties, not the seventies, because then everything changed very rapidly. This support entailed that if you played a tournament you got everything paid for by the

state. And if you had been working at another job you even got a refund. They call it a refund, so it means that you get the normal salary for that period. I think that today this is still the system in these countries, the way it works generally, because these countries differ considerably from one another. The Russians for instance get grants. In Czechoslovakia it wasn't that clear and it also differed from player to player. I did not get a refund in this sense. At first I was still studying and later I went into the army and then suddenly there was 1968 and the Russian invasion. At that moment, I think, people just got crazy. Many people had to decide how they were to live on. Many intellectuals left, others stayed and took to the bottle. Others started to collaborate in their attempt to get into bed with the system. Then, in 1968, I said to myself, Vlastimil, you'd better forget about all your ambitions of getting a civilian job. I was apolitical, my attitude was humanistic and I saw that if I was going to work as a journalist or in the field of economics, which I had been studying, I would constantly be at loggerheads with the system. I saw where it was going. From 1968 onwards Czechoslovakia has been going downhill in all respects. There was less and less freedom. From year to year people got more afraid of each other. Before 1968 I still had my doubts about whether I wanted a chess career or a civilian career, but then I directed my ambitions at chess. In the early seventies I was very ambitious. I was young and very tough and played some good chess.

'It was at that time that I had my first bad experience with FIDE. I am referring to this scandalous drawing of lots in Palma de Mallorca in 1970. It was done under Euwe, but Euwe was not guilty. The guilty party was Alberic O'Kelly, the chief arbiter. It was ridiculous. I still would like to explain what happened, because it was like a bad dream. At the beginning of the tournament it was decided that players from the same country would play each other immediately in the first half. So there were two Argentinians, Panno and Rubinetti, who immediately got corresponding numbers, and then Filip and I got numbers. Filip drew and he got number twelve and consequently I got number thirteen. Of course it is catastrophic to play after Filip in such a tournament because your opponent has always just had a free day. Either Filip consents to a short draw or he loses. Then Taimanov got up and proposed that players from the same country should only not play one another in the last three rounds or the last five. This was accepted but the draw proceeded as if nothing had happened. So I was trying to raise a protest and said, well then, let me now draw my number. This was the first time I recognized that FIDE was in fact a very political platform. If I had been, for example, an American, there certainly would have been a new drawing of lots. I really kicked up a ruckus there, and Euwe called me in the evening and said, "Well, young man, please try to forget this and play your games." Even today I am still indignant at this discrimination. I was so angry about this whole situation, all these people, this arrogance. Fischer was playing there, so everything was fine and whatever happened to someone from a small nation did not matter. The tournament started and I began with something like four losses and six draws. I really could not concentrate, I was so angry. In the end I still made fifty percent. In the second half I played quite well. When the tournament was over there was a formal protest by all the players. Fischer signed it too that something had gone wrong and that FIDE should take care of all this. But I was sick of this tournament. If something similar would happen to me today I would of course take the next plane home and go to my flat and enjoy life. I could not protest, because FIDE was considered an organization that favoured the system. FIDE is influenced by communism very much, so I could not attack FIDE. I even tried to write about it in a Czech newspaper but it was suppressed by censorship.'

When did you begin to think of leaving Czechoslovakia?
'After my first divorce, after 1975. I was waiting for my son. I knew that I was going to leave, but I was always hoping that I could somehow arrange for my son to come with me. You know, it is very difficult to keep this system at a distance. I always tried to stand aside, but you get involved very easily. I was very lucky when in 1978 Hilgert and Porz made me this proposition to come to Germany, because, you will not believe it, but I had no job in Czechoslovakia. I did not want a job, I just wanted to have a stamp on my identity card. In Czechoslovakia you have to "work" somewhere, otherwise you are a parasite, but nobody wanted to give me this stamp. There was no help from the chess federation. Maybe they could have done something, but Sajtar, the President of the federation has never done anything except for himself. What kind of attitude should I have towards FIDE if people like him have been in FIDE for thirty years already?

'To get a "job" you needed friends or had to collaborate, but that I didn't want. At that time the police had already started a file on me. They took me as a very unreliable element. So everybody was afraid of me, even though I wasn't politically active. I didn't sign Charta or anything like that. My second wife was always having problems with the police, too. I did not get anything from the state, and I was very lucky that they let me go to West Germany, although I had to pay terribly for it. You have to leave as fast as possible and you have to pay for it. During those years I was playing in Germany I paid to Czechoslovakia, without getting anything in return, one hundred thousand German marks. I gave it away for practically nothing. I was paying and still I always had problems at the border. Always this questioning. Spassky calls this the dance of the medicine-men. You see, they are always dancing around you and you never know the moment when the cage will drop. Suddenly I got the feeling that the situation was getting very hot. There was still no Gorbachov then. In the years under Chernenko and Andropov Czechoslovakia had been preparing for some sort of neo-Stalinism. When I left it was two minutes to twelve. The prisons were chock-full, many people were in preventive custody. They sometimes were held there for half a year, not knowing what the charges were.

'I played for Czechoslovakia in Luzern, in the Olympiad. At this time my wife had been convicted in Prague for something completely ridiculous, but as I said the police were watching us. I will never forget this. I played thirteen games on board one and put all my energy in these games. I had had to pay for my own expenses to come to Luzern, I made a plus score and Czechoslovakia came second. I don't think Czechoslovakia will ever be second again in the next fifty years, although I may be wrong and I wish they will. But for all these efforts I did not even receive a letter from the Federation. The other players received rewards and money, but I was not invited to the roll of honour. The other players were standing there and wondering where Hort was, but they didn't dare to ask. It was because of this atmosphere that I left. It was not enough that I kept my mouth shut, they demanded political commitment. So, I had to leave, but I was waiting for my son. I offered him this opportunity in our final talk at Cologne Airport. I said, "Either you come now, or never," and he went back to his mother, which I could understand. He was seventeen and a half and I thought that this was a critical age for him. Maybe he will be sorry, maybe he will not. I hope that the situation will improve in these countries but I am not sure. We are a very strange nation, Czechoslovakia. How many people have left the country, how many had to leave? This is very sad. Lendl lives in the USA, so does Navratilova. Some months ago one of our best singers stayed in the USA, Matuschka, who is 54 years old and very popular in Czechoslovakia. He had been experiencing trouble after he had made a joke about Chernobyl. He had said that Chernobyl had cost him his hobby, as he could no longer collect mushrooms anymore, and some comrade had complained about this. You may laugh, but it's no joke, but if I am sad sometimes, do you know what I do? I go out and buy the *Rudé Právo*, and when I read that I must laugh because it is so tragi-comical, so terrible that it improves my mood.

'Now I have got my German papers, but I would not say that I am German. I have many friends there and I appreciate what Germany has done for me but I feel more like a European. You know that at one time Czechoslovakia was part of the Austro-Hungarian monarchy. That was probably a better situation. If you were to ask people in Czechoslovakia today, many would probably like to get out of this system with all these Russian missiles and Russian troops and would immediately prefer to be together with Vienna again. But I will always be loyal to Germany, because they gave me the opportunity to feel what democracy is like. This year, after 43 years, I have cast my vote for the first time in my life. I voted for Genscher because I felt that if the Green Party was to be in Parliament, the liberals should also get more than five percent, and they even did much better.

'For me this really was a happening, because I remember that once in Czechoslovakia I forgot to "vote". This immediately brings you under suspicion. They think that you don't like the idea or that you want to damage the working class. So somebody visited me the next day. I had been drinking somewhere and still had a strong hangover. This person asked me, "Haven't you something to explain to us?" I said, "Well, excuse me, what do you mean", because I really had forgotten about it. And of course this got into my file as well.

'My father was a real idealist and till '68 he was a communist. I think my mother still has his certificate for the thousands of hours of voluntary labour he had given to a dam they were building. In the end he got this certificate and a very bad pension that he could hardly live on, even though he had been working his whole life. The tragic thing was that when in his later years he wanted to visit this dam, he wasn't allowed to, because it was under state control and only accessible to state officials. All his free time he had sacrificed. He went there every Saturday and Sunday and left us alone at home, and now he wasn't allowed to see the result of his idealism.'

You're forty-three now. Formerly this was considered almost the ideal age for a chess player. It seems as if you don't agree.
'I'm middle-aged now. Many years ago I had a talk with Donner about this midlife crisis and he said that now he was over forty, or forty-five, he did not fear anything anymore. I am still ambitious of course. I want to beat everyone I play, but when you reach this age you become more philosophical. Before you start working on a problem you have a lot of other things to think about. I am still ambitious, but it is my own small world. I no longer think of the World Championship and I will always think twice before I play FIDE events. I did not play in this cycle and I will see what happens next time. If I think that FIDE is doing a fair job I might take part. My ambition is to play good games and win some tournaments if possible. Life goes on, there is nothing wrong with that. I will also play when I am old, even if I will not be making my living out of it. I think it is a good thing that there are still a lot of players of my generation taking part in tournaments. It would be boring if only youngsters would play tournaments.'

You sometimes talk as if you were fifty or sixty, whereas you are still one of today's leading players. You are among the favourites in almost all the tournaments you play in.
'(Smiles) As you could see today, I had a hallucination in my game against Farago. New In Chess could introduce a new symbol "H" for Hort or hallucination. I used to be very practical in chess but I am not anymore. I always believed that chess should be creative. Today this is no longer the case. It has become more and more competitive and mechanical. People prepare variations up to the eighteenth move and they are always willing to play these eighteen moves in one minute. This is also important, of course, but there should be more variety in their play. I have seen many young players who can play the Dragon Variation very well. They have experience with this variation and have studied it and they believe that that is all. So I somehow feel sorry for them, because they will never get the feeling of all these other positions. And their development will necessarily stagnate. I don't like the new time-schedule. It is too quick for me. I have already blundered many games. In Biel I even lost my last round game against Lobron on time. I thought that I had still half a minute left, which shows you that even Swiss clocks aren't always punctual.

We will have to live with it but I think that it is not good for the generation over forty. It is also detrimental to the quality of the games.

'Another problem is the Elo system. If you play in a weak Swiss tournament this is very risky today. Let's say in Metz or in Bad Wörishofen. Even if you play well, you usually lose points. You can play well and finish second and realize that you just lost five points. But I think that the future of chess is bright. Look for instance at Biel this year, where more than one thousand players came. This is total chess.'

What may be the role of the Grandmasters Association in this future?
'I don't know. I want to wait before I come to a verdict. With the present status I will not join the Grandmasters Association. In my opinion it is impossible for an organization consisting of both players from the West and players from the East to really achieve something, because their interests are not the same. To me it seems that it would be better if the players here in the West founded some kind of trade union, a European union, and if they are so keen on it the players in the East could do the same. This might work out much better. I don't think the present formula is going to function. But it is not something that is on my mind. I do not want to think about it. I am not against it, I am simply not interested. I simply want to play my tournaments. I think there will always be chess enough in these three countries, Holland, Germany and Switzerland. I would say that number four in Europe at the moment is France. I mean as far as conditions for the players are concerned. I still remember playing in London, the Islington Chess Tournament, a tournament with a very long tradition. I could not believe what I saw. We were playing in a school in which the heating was not exactly what it should have been. This school really looked like a poorhouse, like a very bad railway station. It had not been cleaned. Because there weren't enough toilets we had to use a bathtub. Others preferred to go outside. We were sitting there like canned sardines. There were no flowers, no carpet, no drinks, everything had to be paid for. We even had to pay entry fees and I had to pay for my hotel. If I compare this with Germany where you are received by the mayor in the city hall. I think the situation is deteriorating in England. They have so many good players, but they don't play there, because the conditions are so terrible, with the exception of tournaments like Phillips and Drew. Whereas in West Germany all open tournaments have a certain level. You will play in a Kurhaus or something like that.'

It is generally known in chess circles that one of your hobbies is to go mushrooming. Do you still do this?
'Yes, I still do. In Czechoslovakia a lot of people do, because there are so many forests. It is a great way to relax. To go into the forest, jog a bit and collect mushrooms. I did so in Switzerland when I was playing in Biel and I will do so again in San Bernardino. That is why I like to play in San Bernardino, even if it will already be very late in the year.'

In your book Begegnungen am Schachbrett *you tell the story of Bobby Fischer who accompanied you on one of your trips in the forests around Vinkovci in 1968.With little hesitation Fischer only picked the most poisonous mushrooms. Do you never make mistakes yourself?*
'No, no, I never make mistakes. I only have hallucinations in chess games (laughs)'.

Some of these mushrooms have a hallucinatory effect.
'Yes, yes, but I didn't eat mushrooms today.'

Then suddenly we realize that it is half past eight and that Hort has to go down to the playing hall to continue his adjourned game against Farago. In the elevator I ask him about his plans. Will he propose a draw or will he still give it a try. A somewhat dispirited Hort answers that he knows this kind of endgame. The position is dead drawn and he will only play some three more moves. Later that evening Vlastimil Hort wins his game against Farago and one week later he wins the Ohra grandmaster group.

Boris Spassky

Belfort, July 1988

'I like to play with the hands'

Eleven years ago, after many an abortive attempt, Boris Spassky obtained a tempo-rary permit to leave the Soviet Union and to travel to France. Fed up with the harassments he had had to endure after his lost match against Robert Fischer, the ex-World Champion never returned to his native soil. With his formidable talent and this enormous experience Spassky can still be safely counted among the world's strongest grandmasters, but the joys of his tranquil and peaceful life in France have unmistakenly reduced his ambitions. 'If I had to describe my life here in the West I would say that it is extremely reflective'. During the World Cup tournament in Belfort Boris Spassky shared some of his reflections and talked with gusto and candour about Life after the Match. 'Maybe people are right when they call me a lazy bear, a Russian bear. But if somebody wants to fight, I will fight. And I can still be successful.'

What have been the effects of living in France on your personal life and on your life as a chess player?
'First of all I arrived in France as an ex-World Champion. After my match against Bobby Fischer I encountered many problems in the Soviet Union, so when I came to France I immediately felt very free. Unfortunately I was not rich anymore. After the match I had been quite a rich person in the Soviet Union. I had received nine-ty-three thousand dollars, which fortunately I managed to spend during my last four years in the Soviet Union. So, when I came to France I had to work somehow and I became a professional grandmaster, or rather a typically Western professional grandmaster. For me this was a crucial moment. I can tell you that I never tried to work very hard, because chess as a profession is not respected, either here or in the Soviet Union. In the Soviet Union chess is only used for propaganda purposes and in reality there are only three or four grandmasters who are paid really well. The rest has to fight very hard to attain a decent living standard.

'Perhaps the principal impression of my life in the West over the past eleven years is that it is very tranquil, very quiet. Nobody disturbs me. Because of my reputation after the match against Bobby Fischer I was sometimes invited to do simultaneous exhibitions and of course I am extremely grateful to my chess club in Solingen. It doesn't bring in a lot of money, but it is something, a basis, which gives me some sort of balance, an equilibrium in life. Of course, if this profession of chess player were paid better and respected more, I would work much harder. Maybe just for the money. Now I generally rely mostly on my talent. I don't make serious preparation before a game or study my opponent's games. I am very pragmatic in this respect, very practical. If I had stayed in the Soviet Union I would have had to work very hard, as the chess level is very high and the competition enormous, especially from the young generation. They have to prove themselves to be sent abroad to international tournaments.

'Yes. If I had to describe my life here in the West I would say that it is extremely reflective. My life has been very eventful. I have already been a rich person and very famous. Sometimes I have the impression that I have already been living for more than a hundred years. So many things have happened in my life, there have been so many changes and adventures, especially when I was living in the Soviet Union. Now, at fifty-one, I am very satisfied with my family life. I have my son who is a good boy to me, and I can pay some attention to him, which was impossible in my previous life in the Soviet Union when I was Champion of the World. So, I am quite satisfied. Now I have reached the stage between the middlegame and the endgame, if you compare it to a game of chess. But I don't have the feeling that I'm in the endgame already, I'm still in the middlegame.'

What concrete privileges did you lose after you had lost to Fischer?
'Well, I can tell you just in general. After the match the Soviet Sports Committee cancelled my right or rather the facility to have first choice with respect to international competitions. I was invited to many, many tournaments then, and I really needed to play then, from a psychological point of view. If you are beaten you need a revenge and I was eager to have this revenge and I also had the strength, but they blocked me for nine months. Eventually it made me ill. I sank into a depression which lasted maybe more than one year. As a result of this attitude towards me I started to fight against the Sports Committee. I started to fight against the political system. If a professional chess player is not sent abroad he can do nothing. I would have had to change my profession. I didn't become a dissident intentionally. Because I was a dissident, Kortchnoi wasn't. At that time Kortchnoi was a typical collaborator, an opportunist. The Sports Committee played a special game with him. (In a soothing tone) They forgave him something, some of his sins, some of his interviews. But my situation was very, very critical, as I got no tournaments.

How did you find a chance to come to France?
'I was extremely lucky. In Moscow I met my wife with whom I have been living for eleven years now, a very peaceful and good life. This is my third marriage. She was working at the *Mission Commerciale* of the *Ambassade de France à Moscou*. She is French. The way we got married was quite a story, a detective story. These were two years of fighting. I could write a novel about this, if someone was interested.'

Were there mainly bureaucratic problems?

'No, these were not bureaucratic problems. We were both followed by the secret police. I was followed by the KGB, she was followed by their secret police as well as by the KGB. I had already been divorced at that time and was living alone, but they didn't like to give us the permission to get married. Once in Moscow I was even robbed. I think it was in the newspapers somewhere. Eventually I got a visa which permitted me to travel *à la retour*, there and back, as many times as I wanted during one year. But when I came to France I realized that I had reached a very peaceful place. So it was better to stay there. As a chess player I was getting older, of course, and as I told you I am quite lazy. I don't like to change my style of living. If there is some interesting event, like a match against a young promising player, then this will motivate me and give me energy. But now even this tournament, although it is nice to play here, can hardly motivate me. I am very peaceable, but if someone wants to fight, I will fight. And I can still be successful. Maybe people are right when they call me a lazy bear, a Russian bear. Maybe this is correct somehow, because I am still a strong player. Unfortunately there is no challenge for me in France. We don't have any good players at the moment. There are a few promising young players, but they are nothing special.'

I understand that the French Chess Federation would gladly involve you in the training of these young talents.

'As long as I am still an active player myself I am not going to train other players, unless they can create some interesting financial conditions.'

Chess in France would certainly benefit from an experienced national trainer. You have often stressed the importance of your own trainers, Zak, Bondarevsky and Tolush, for the development of your talent.

'Oh, yes. I have very good recollections of all three of them. Zak is still alive. Maybe I will still have the chance to visit him in the Soviet Union. If I go there I would like to visit all my friends and especially the graves of those who have died. It is difficult to say how my trainers influenced me. I think Bondarevsky helped me a lot to become World Champion. At that time I was so strong that I couldn't imagine how strong I actually was. I was a rough diamond and Bondarevsky polished it. Bondarevsky was also a very interesting man, one of the cleverest persons I have ever met in my life. On the other hand he was also a terrible coward. I respected Tolush more. Tolush had an extremely rare quality. In Russia we call this *blagorodstwo*, something like "nobility".'

Wasn't it Tolush who incited you to play more aggressively?

'No, I had already become more aggressive of my own accord. So, I was looking for him. We found each other and then we started to work together. In 1953 in Bucharest he reached his peak. At that time he was only forty-one years old. In 1957 he almost became champion of the Soviet Union, but lost against Tal in the last round.'

There's this famous story about one of his games against Kotov.

'Yes, (broad smile) this story will go into my memoirs. Kotov wanted to ask Tolush for the point and so he visited him and said, "Sasha, I need this point". And Kazimirovich[12] said very simply, "OK Sasha[13], no problem, but... glory to you, money to me." After that, of course, they couldn't find a solution and there was no agreement. But Tolush was furious and said, "In that case you will be mated in the district of squares f7 and g7." So, they said goodbye and parted and during the game Kazimirovich sacrificed his knight on g7. There was applause in the hall and a nervous Kotov returned on the stage and asked, "For whom is this applause?" And Kazimirovich pointed his finger at him and said severely, "For you". So, after this game they became friends for life.'

You once said that you became a professional at the age of ten.

'Or maybe nine. What I meant was that at the age of nine or ten my life was already absolutely determined. I became a professional subconsciously, without actually knowing it.'

Your parents had been divorced by then. Was playing chess a way of creating your own world?

'I don't know. This is very private. You know that in the history of chess there have been several World Champions who spent their childhood without their father. For example Botvinnik, Bobby Fischer and I myself. Well, I still had my father, but in actual fact he was absent.'

Was this 'shared background' the reason for your sympathy for Fischer?

'My sympathy for Bobby Fischer stems from my childhood. In 1958 I met him for the first time when he came to Moscow together with his sister. What I liked in Bobby was that he was absolutely open and easily approachable. He liked to say openly what he was thinking. His approach to chess was also very honest and very pure. For the public, however, he wasn't a person you could easily get along with. The public needs some sort of social relation with a sportsman or an artist. So, on occasion Bobby was attacked by a lot of people, including chess players. Such as Botvinnik, who maligned him many times. His present situation is very tragic and he is living in really poor circumstances.'

Do you think Botvinnik attacked him because he saw him as a threat to the Soviet Chess School?

'I don't think the Soviet Chess School exists. I never met the Soviet Chess School, nor did I meet the Fascist Chess School. If you start from such premises this would mean that Bobby Fischer was a leading representative of the Soviet Chess School.

---

12 Tolush's patronymic.

13 As both of them were called Alexander.

This is nonsense, of course. It is just playing with words without understanding what they really mean. Chess is an international game and you could talk about national schools of chess, that I do believe, but not about ideological schools of chess. There exists a Jewish mentality in chess, a Russian mentality and a German mentality.'

Do you really believe this?
'Yes, of course, but nobody likes to talk about this. Newspapers like certain stereotypes, like Soviet Chess School. I can give you another example. The slogan of the French revolution was *Liberté, Egalité* and *Fraternité*. These ideas are completely contradictory. If

Boris Spassky: 'What I liked in Bobby was that he was absolutely open and easily approachable.'

there is *Liberté* there will not be any *Egalité*. But these are the stereotypes people like, and so there is a Soviet Chess School and a Fascist Chess School.'

Could you give an example of something in chess which is typically Russian?
'Take for instance two Russian grandmasters, Alekhine and Chigorin. I don't like to talk about modern examples. Both Alekhine and Chigorin have a lot of artistry in their styles, but sometimes they are not very fundamental. Now if you take on the other hand the best people of the Jewish Chess School, Steinitz, even Botvinnik, Nimzowitsch and Réti, you will see that they were very scientific. Their approach to the problems was extremely fundamental. Of course there is one notable exception, that is Tal. Which just proves the general rule.'

You said that you got a permit to travel from the Soviet Union to France and back. Do you still have this permit?
'No, not anymore. I still have my Soviet passport, but it has a special note to it. My permanent residence is abroad. If I want to visit the Soviet Union I will have to apply for a visa and specify the towns I intend to visit. I could also ask my relatives to send me an invitation. There is a special form for this which has to be sent to the consulate in Paris, after which it would be decided whether or not they would

give me permission to travel. But this would take five or six months. That is a long story, so I don't want to ask them. Apart from that one of my principles is, "Never ask gangsters for anything". I don't like dealing with gangsters. If they need something, they can ask me.'

Why would they ask you to come?
'I don't know. Maybe they want to have good relations with me, because I was Champion of the World. But they know I am an anti-Bolshevik, and this country is becoming more and more Bolshevik.'

Of late we've seen quite some changes in the Soviet Union. Don't you think that 'Perestroika' will bring about some fundamental changes?
'No, I don't. This is impossible as long as the mafia are ruling the country. Such changes can only occur if the body of the state is normal and based on democratic traditions. In the Soviet Union the basis is wrong, as the mafia took power by killing millions of people. This country was raped by Bolshevism. All countries which are taken by Bolshevism are in a state of civil war. The people try to maintain their culture, but Bolshevism wants to destroy culture. The worst thing is that they want to smash the soul of a nation. But let's talk chess. I don't want to talk about politics.'

Well then, what do you think of the future of chess and the developments that are taking place at the moment?
'Right now I am also very pessimistic about the prospects for the chess world (laughs). The general problem is to convince people that chess can be a professional sport. People have to be better informed about what it means to be a professional chess player. They should get a better impression of his daily activities and the problems he faces. In the future his work will be increasingly determined by the developments in the computer sciences. But despite these aids the World Champion will always be someone with a real talent for chess. At the moment we have this great talent, Kasparov, and still another great talent, Karpov, both of whom are far superior to the rest. I think that Kasparov is a very good thing for chess. Maybe he is better than Karpov, but I doubt whether he can exploit his talent as fully as Karpov did. As Champion of the World Karpov demonstrated a fantastic personality for ten years and won forty first prizes in the biggest tournaments. Of course Karpov was criticized, because he would travel like a king, with a bodyguard and things like that, but in the twenty-seven years that Lasker was champion he only took six first places in fifteen tournaments or so.
'Kasparov and Karpov have different natures. Karpov's strength is based on collecting small advantages. You know, in chess, too, he is a collector, like he is a stamp collector. This is a very fundamental approach. Kasparov's strongest side is his creativity. He needs the initiative, he needs some analysis. At this level this creativity takes much more energy than Karpov's approach based on his positional

talent. Karpov's talent is more natural, Kasparov's more artificial. You cannot stand such tension for ten years. Another two years and he will be finished as World Champion. Maybe three years. Of course I would not like to predict such things because it's an ungrateful business.'

One of the latest fads in chess is the introduction of the Active Chess cycle. What are your ideas about this Active Chess?
'(Beaming with pleasure) Oh, I love Active Chess. Yes, I am going to participate with great pleasure. If the time-control would be fifteen minutes I would even be happier. Yes, between fifteen and thirty minutes is alright for me. But I don't know why it is called Active Chess. If there is Active Chess this implies there is Passive Chess, too. I don't like this suggestion. But I already told you that chess needs money and organization. Maybe some sponsor will want to organize a thirty seconds tournament. I am not enthusiastic about the idea, but if some private business wants to do so... I only mean to say that the GMA should be more tolerant of such ideas as Active Chess or, who knows, a chess tournament on the moon.'

The GMA mainly objects to the special master and grandmaster titles, because they might cause confusion.
'Why couldn't one be Active Champion of the World? Who doesn't want this?

Kasparov for instance.
'Yes, I can understand that. But you can make a one-year cycle. (Laughs and quasi solemnly pronounces) Active Champion of the World 1988 or 1989. Why not? Or Expert of Rapid Chess? But jokes aside, where do you think that the old forty moves in two-and-a-half hours rule comes from? Why two-and-a-half hours? That was an idea of Mr Botvinnik, (starts mimicking Botvinnik and speaking slower), who was checking very carefully what would be the best time-control. Which time-control would guarantee the highest productivity. He played some training games underground in his dacha and invented this playing-tempo. And it was impossible to change this. But now the times have changed.'

You often suggested that you were writing a book on your games, but mostly you presented this in a jocular manner, a famous example being 'I am writing a book on my match against Fischer. At the moment I am working on the second game'.
'I am still writing this book. I would like to publish this book after my death, because it contains certain memoirs, certain ideas. There is no sense in writing such a book for the money, because it is very poorly paid. Nobody is going to pay you decently for it. If you want to write a good quality book you need time. I have many recollections from my chess career, I met many interesting people, but I wouldn't like to write a book like, for example, Kasparov did.[14] This is not a book, I could only read two or

---

14 *Child of Change.*

three pages of it, this is garbage. As Champion of the World I would pay at least one million dollars to get rid of such garbage. A shame! First of all, if you write a book as Champion of the World, you should write it personally, without any journalist.'

But your book, how do you go about it? Do you have a manuscript which gets bigger and bigger?
'No, I have a concept for my book and I have written a few chapters. Of course I will also include some analyses, but nothing serious. I don't like that. But I want to be very honest. If I didn't see something I would like to say, "Here I was blind, I didn't see this". I don't like this Botvinnik formula (in a solemn voice), "At this moment I had forgotten about something." No, he didn't forget it, he didn't see it! Haha, I had forgotten!'

You can't blame only Botvinnik for this.
'No, no, there are many others. Polu is always forgetting something, Karpov, too, even Kasparov. Alekhine was also forgetting a lot of things. But Fischer was more honest, Bobby was more honest, yes.'

I take it that your analyses won't be too long?
'No, I would like to point out the crucial moments. I would prefer to do a few games, but to do them well and honestly.'

As is generally known you are a keen tennis player. Do you think that your interest in tennis has an influence on your psychological approach to chess?
'Yes, absolutely. Like chess tennis is a game of balance, of equilibrium. Tennis gives you a very good balance of the body. It is fantastically refreshing for your mind if you can sweat once a day. You need a balance of mind and body. Paul Keres was a very good tennis player, but he didn't play very much, and so was Capablanca.'

Your tournament tactics, playing short draws and then suddenly energetically going for a win, reminds me of baseline tennis.
'It's a bit like baseline tennis, yes, that is correct. Once Smyslov revealed to me one of his tournament secrets. He said that first of all he didn't have adjourned games, because they cost too much energy. Secondly he said that he used to play not with the head, but with the hands.'

Trusting his intuition.
'Yes, because time-trouble doesn't allow for serious analysis during the game. If you have an idea, just play it. You must trust yourself. You know that in the game of chess there are two very important moments. The first moment is after the opening: plan. With this playing-tempo you can spend more than twenty minutes on your plan. Then the second moment: crisis. For this you have ten or fifteen minutes. But I like this idea. I love to play with the hands and draw, draw, draw (laughs heartily).'

Svetozar Gligoric

Antwerp, February 1989

'Everybody is for Yugoslavia'

In Yugoslavia Svetozar Gligoric is deferentially called 'The Legend', an epithet he earned himself during a unique career spanning five decades. In 1939 he created a sensation when he became Yugoslav amateur champion at the age of sixteen. With the threat of war already casting a gloomy shadow over Europe there was little time to enjoy his early successes. The outbreak of World War II brutally interrupted his chess career. Gligoric joined the Partisans and fought at the front. Twice he was decorated for bravery. Immediately after the war he returned to the game and also set out to restore organized chess life in Yugoslavia. For thirty years he was Yugoslavia's number one player and especially in the late fifties he belonged to the absolute world elite and was one of the very few to challenge the Soviet hegemony. Gligoric's tournament record is too long to be summarized. In 1947 he scored his first international success in Warsaw where he finished two points ahead of a field that included Smyslov, Boleslavsky and Pachman. In 1986(!) he tied for first in Sochi with Beliavsky and Vaganian, ahead of Razuvaev and Tal. All these years Gligoric has also been a prolific journalist and, more recently, an esteemed arbiter. A few days before this interview at the Portisch-Timman Candidates' match in Antwerp, Gligoric celebrated his 66th birthday. Yet, his lively and energetic manner do not betray his age. With candour and disarming openness he talked about his many-sided career, the War, Kasparov and, of course, Fischer.

Like many other great chess players you were raised by your mother. Should we deduce something from that or is it just an insignificant coincidence?
'Well, I must say that my mother didn't influence my chess career at all. She didn't play chess and she died early, when I was seventeen. At school I was a very good pupil and she was pleased by that, but when I began to play chess she didn't even know about it. Only after my photograph had appeared in the newspaper for the first time, because I had won the national amateur championship, did she realize that I was also a chess player. I was sixteen years old and was awarded the master title. Nowadays this would be nothing unusual but in those days this caused a big sensation. Of course she didn't prevent me from playing chess, because I was doing well at school and that was the only thing she worried about. We were very poor.

My father died when I was nine years old and as my mother had had only little education her salary was low. I do not recall my childhood with specific pleasure although I was healthy, young and optimistic at that time.

'My life, as so many other people's lives, was very much influenced by Hitler's war. That war interrupted my career for six years. When I started playing chess again in 1945 I had spent practically no time on chess for almost six years. Five months before the Germans attacked us my mother died. I was left with no resources, but was invited by three people who wanted to support me so that I could finish my school. One of them was the mother of grandmaster Janosevic, who was rich. The other was a very well-known Yugoslav journalist, Vasily Meden. Later he was executed by the Germans. Fortunately I accepted, just out of politeness, the offer of professor Miljanic. He had three sons and I was somehow his fourth son. I went to live with him and finished my last year in secondary school in Belgrade. When the war broke out and Belgrade was bombarded we left. First we were transported by train like cattle and from Sarajevo we continued on foot until we reached Montenegro, Doctor Miljanic' province of origin. In 1943 I joined the Partisans and for some time I was a guerilla. As I was an intellectual I was put in command of the semi-heavy weapons. I was even awarded two medals for war bravery and towards the end of the war I got the rank of captain.

'You see, we fought in a country without normal connections, without transportation. There was no regular supply of anything, no running water, nothing. For instance I once had to go on a small horse for three hours to get some water to drink and then another three hours back.'

How official was the partisan army as an army?
'It was made up of volunteers like me, but it was a regular army. Most of the soldiers came from the countryside, peasant sons who had had little education. We had ranks, we had weapons, we even had hospitals, everything. Of course we had no regular supply. We were hungry most of the time and we had nothing to wear. I had only one shirt which I wore for almost two years. Later the allies sent us things by parachute.'

In what way did this war experience influence you as a chess player?
'It changed me. I remember that before the war I was very optimistic and believed in my lucky star. I thought that whatever I played I would come out well, even if I made a mistake, because someone (laughs) was taking care of my intelligence and my ability to orientate myself in the game. But during the war I learned a lesson, that no one cares about no one. I mean, we care about each other, but when you lose your life it is just over. Everyone who survives is just lucky, so I'm nothing special. I'm just like the others. Maybe I was modest before the war, in a way, but after the war I was very modest. And it remained with me for the rest of my life. I remember my first trip to Sweden, in 1948 for the Interzonal in Saltsjöbaden.

Europe was ruined and we were travelling by train. When we came to Sweden and the train passed through the countryside and I saw these untouched houses, with flowers in the windows, beautifully painted and all in very live colours, I began to scream from joy. I couldn't... because I had been looking at ruins and dead people for so many years I could not believe that this still existed.'

Immediately after the war you also became active as a chess organizer. In what capacity could you do this?
'I was given the post of, let's say, secretary of chess in the Yugoslav central sports organization. We more or less copied the Soviet system. So we had a central sports organization and I was the head of the section for chess. That was how I organized the first tournament in Belgrade in 1945, and I also organized the first Yugoslav championship in Novi Sad that same year. We invited 24 players, because I wanted to have everyone with a title and because Yugoslavia was now a federal republic I invited representatives of all these republics. In the first two championships I finished second, which was a very high place for me as I had no practice. At that time Trifunovic was the best player, but that only lasted for two years. Then I took over. First I shared first place with him in 1947 and then I shared first place with Pirc in 1948. We had a so-called chess triumvirate for several years, but then I got the first board on our Olympiad team and kept it for about thirty years. With two small breaks. Pirc played on the first board at the Olympiad in Amsterdam in 1956 and also at the European team championship in Germany in 1965.

'During this first championship I got a call from the main newspaper in Belgrade, *Borba*. Borba, which means "struggle", was the newspaper of the Central Committee, very highly esteemed, and they asked me to work for them as a journalist. I was very honoured by that and accepted and this changed my career. I wrote about everything, I was a regular journalist and felt proud. I went to factories as a political worker, giving speeches and explaining to the people what was going on. It was also customary that at night you went to the printing house to supervise the printing and things like that. Later on the head of the whole enterprise decided that I had to get rid of all the other work except for the chess. So I had more time for chess. I got invitations to play in tournaments, which also improved my income, and travelled a lot. But I didn't work there for a very long time. In 1954 I realized that my colleagues did not like my position that much. I got the same salary but worked less than they did. Then I became a news-commentator for NIN, which is still the leading weekly in Yugoslavia. Something like *Time Magazine*. I remained with NIN until 1960 and worked very hard. And even today I do not understand that I had my best results in chess in that period. I was working like... Every Wednesday I would spend the whole night to finish my political commentary. NIN was a semi-independent magazine for intellectuals. We wrote about culture, about literature, about economics and politics, about all kinds of things. I also wrote about my trips in a, what shall I say, more literary style. In 1960 NIN had to move to the Politika house. I thought that the weekly would lose its independence by joining this bigger house. At that moment I had an offer from Radio Belgrade. Higher salary, less work. So I went to Radio Belgrade and there I worked for twenty years until I retired.'

What is your explanation for the fact that you had your peak as a chess player in those years when you were working very hard as a journalist?

'I have only one explanation. It is my theory that man, the majority of people, have their peak, their psychophysical peak between age thirty to thirty-seven, thirty-eight. That is when you are perfect. You have energy for everything. For instance when I went to Dallas in 1957 I had to write a political comment on the United States and to interview some politicians. Among them, on my way back, was Aneurin Bevan, the leader of the Labour party in England. At the same time I was playing in tournaments. Imagine that. I don't think that any grandmaster of my class has ever had such an experience. I was playing in tournaments and every Saturday night I had to prepare my commentary for the Sunday news hour, a special, long commentary, which would cost me a game. On Sundays I would lose my game. I got too little sleep.'

Which do you consider your best results in that period?

'Well, it began like this. I played in the Olympiad in Moscow in 1956 with a mediocre result. But I felt very strong. I had this strange feeling that I was giving only part of my strength. After the Olympiad I was invited to a big international tournament in Moscow. I was confident that I would do very well. I finished fourth, which was a very high place then. Botvinnik and Smyslov were first and second and Taimanov came third. Behind me were Keres and Bronstein and all the others, a very strong tournament. But I did less than I could because I missed wins in several games. Then we played against the Soviet Union in Leningrad in 1957. I played against eight Soviet grandmasters and made six points out of these games. That was wonderful. I scored more points than all the rest of the team together. I beat Petrosian, Kortchnoi, Furman, Kholmov and Tolush. I lost to Geller and made two draws. I remember that I shared a room with Trifunovic. He was complaining about the light, because you know they have these so-called white nights in Leningrad. And I said "Why are you complaining? We have our curtains and it is dark in the room. Why can't you sleep?" But he said "No, I can't sleep because I know that there is sunshine outside". (Laughs) In short, he was nervous. From Leningrad we went to Moscow and there they organized a clock simul for me against masters and candidate masters and I beat them easily, allowing only three draws. I was in great shape then. I went to Dallas and shared first prize with Reshevsky. And then I played in Munich in the Olympiad and had the best result on first board ahead of Botvinnik. Twelve points out of fifteen games. We had one more result like that, by Ljubojevic in Lucerne in 1982. I think he is my successor as far as his results and his position in the chess world are concerned. Of course his style is very different from mine.'

Were these results the highlights of your career?

'Well, there were many other good results. In Mar del Plata '53 I scored sixteen points out of nineteen and in 1958 I was half a point behind Tal in the Interzonal in Portoroz. I might have been first because I lost a completely winning game against Olafsson in his time-pressure. Three times I had a win and then I still had a draw, but I played fast because of his flag. But it didn't fall (laughs) and I lost. Another good result was the Sousse Interzonal. Interzonals then were not like the Interzonals today. It was only one tournament and the whole world elite was there. In Sousse Larsen was first and Fischer dropped out, but that is a story in itself. But I never think of my results, I forget about them. I had very good results later on too. I was seldom first in very strong tournaments, I was always second. Like Petrosian more or less. I had many second places. In 1970 in the Tournament of Peace behind Fischer, then in Vinkovci behind Larsen, then in 1975 behind Karpov in the Vidmar memorial.'

Svetozar Gligoric: 'The majority of people have their peak, their psychophysical peak between age thirty to thirty-seven, thirty-eight.'

Have you ever seriously aspired to the World Championship?

'(Hesitates) Well, some people in Yugoslavia wanted me to play for the title. I thought it was unrealistic, although maybe for a while... I remember the Candidates' Tournament in Zurich and Neuhausen in 1953, the big one which Smyslov won. I was somewhere in the middle of the rankings but in the last five rounds I wanted to go to the top. So I pressed hard and I lost three of these games and drew the other two. I remember I wanted to be dead at that moment. Not because of myself, I was healthy and never depended on my results in my life, but just because of the pressure from my fans at home. They wanted me to be the champion. After that I never thought seriously about it anymore. I realized that in Yugoslavia there are no chess schools, nor is there any financial support. All my life I had to support myself with my own work. I played so many simultaneous exhibitions to increase my income, hundreds and hundreds. It was awful. You got these terribly low fees and still had to be grateful. Nowadays they get more for one exhibition than I get as an arbiter for a whole match.'

Most grandmasters of your generation have already retired. In 1986 you proved that you can still have excellent results when you shared first prize in a strong tournament in Sochi. What is your explanation for this?
'I can explain that easily. It's a problem nowadays for older players, let's say Geller, Bronstein or me, to get invitations. So I play very little. When I play in a strong tournament it is always after a long pause and I am out of shape when I start to play again. I was lucky at that moment. I had played in Sarajevo and scored a bad result. I had also played in Plovdiv, in Bulgaria, and again scored a bad result. Not because I played so badly but because of health and sleeping problems. One of my problems is that I am very emotional and that I lose my sleep when something happens.'

It still affects you after all those years?
'Yes, very much. You know, when I play chess it is always as if I were sitting down at the board for the first time again. I always have the feeling that I'm not the person I am, but that I am just a novice trying to play chess. After Sarajevo and Plovdiv I got in shape. And when I came to Sochi I discovered that Sochi has a very hot, almost tropical climate. This hot climate suited me. I had no pains anymore and slept beautifully. And we still played forty moves in two and a half hours, which I am used to. After I had won the tournament another year passed by without me getting any invitations.'

I was somewhat surprised to see that you didn't get your grandmaster title until 1951 when you were 28 years old. By then you already had quite an impressive tournament record.
'Well, you see, everything came late in my life. The war postponed my marriage, everything. I married when I was 24, but I wanted to marry when I was 18. Well, (laughs) even earlier. I married the youngest sister of my school friend and I had known her ever since she was ten. I liked her very much, her nature and everything. Of course, when I came back in '45 she didn't want to marry me then, because she was only sixteen years old. We got married two years later. My chess titles came late too. The Yugoslav master title I got when I was sixteen, but then I had to wait till 1948 when I qualified for the Interzonal and automatically became an international master.

'But do you know how I got my grandmaster title? I had very good results in 1950 and 1951 and the FIDE President then was Folke Rogard. I was in FIDE as a representative of Yugoslavia and as a member of the qualification committee. Somehow I was quite popular with Dr. Rogard and without giving me any indication of what he was going to do he proposed me for the grandmaster title at the congress. Everyone applauded and I got the title by acclamation. This was the only time someone got the title without being proposed by his federation. My federation intended to propose me the following year, but I was modest. I thought I needed more results.'

There was something else which surprised me. Somewhere you wrote that until the mid-sixties you never did any serious or thorough opening preparation.
'That is true. I didn't like to work. I thought it was humiliating. Maybe I had something of Capablanca. Why should I prepare when I have ideas? Let me explain you how I worked on chess. As I said I was a lazy man in a way. I couldn't sit at the board for a very long time. I played fast and if I was analysing and the ideas wouldn't come in five minutes I would drop it. I would give up or say "there is nothing else to be found in this position". Which was wrong. All the new ideas I had in chess came in ten or fifteen minutes. For instance, one of my inventions was the Mar del Plata Variation. I was playing in Mar del Plata and my rival for first place was Najdorf. Three months before he had beaten me in Helsinki. I was tricked in that game and this was the first time I wanted to take some revenge. I had only recently begun playing the King's Indian and I had seen this new variation in the main line, which Bronstein played too. But they played it in a very artificial way. They put a rook on f6 or g6 leaving the knights on stupid positions at d7 and e7. This didn't look normal to me, so I tried Knight f6 and Knight g6 and this I liked better. I won a beautiful game. That was the first time the Mar del Plata line was applied. Then Najdorf copied my way of playing and won against Taimanov in Europe. So, many people thought it was Najdorf's idea, although it should bear my name. Also in the Sämisch Variation of the King's Indian, when White plays g4, everyone played knight somewhere and f5 and got a bad position. I realized that White is not developed on the kingside and Black should do something on the dark squares there. So I played h5 and that was new. No one had thought of this and I got this idea during the interzonal tournament in Portoroz in 1958 in five minutes in my hotel room.'

In recent years we have seen you as an arbiter at important matches or events quite regularly. When did you first act as an arbiter?
'The first time was in 1979, when Lubosh Kavalek invited me to be chief arbiter of the Tournament of Stars in Montreal, although I am not an arbiter and don't see myself as an arbiter. My next invitation was for the match Kortchnoi-Kasparov in Pasadena. But I declined because I had been invited to a tournament in Niksic and preferred playing myself. For well-known reasons this match was cancelled and put on the agenda again for London later on. Then I got a second invitation and this time I accepted. That was my first match. My second match was the World Championship match in Moscow. So both matches involved Kasparov. There were no problems until the very end. Then I was surprised by many things. I was also to be the referee of the second match and the Sports Committee begged me to come

to Moscow for the second match, but Kasparov made a statement for the Yugoslav press that he would not play if I were the arbiter. It was only during this visit to my country that he criticized me mildly. I could not stand this criticism, because it was unfounded.'

What did he criticize you for?
'He said that I was soft and that I was slightly on Karpov's side. This is stupid. I was playing a tournament in Slovenia, the Vidmar memorial. Shortly after the first round this interview was published in a Yugoslav newspaper. I read it, I was shocked. I lost my sleep again for the whole tournament. Then I began to write an open letter to him and published it. Maybe he was shocked by my answer. He replied to me after several days, but this reply wasn't written by him. It was written by Adorjan. He criticized me for not standing up against Campomanes' decision to break the match. And I said, "Why should I stand against that decision when it was identical with your proposal of February the third?" I will write an article on that. I have been waiting for years till they were finished with their matches. I didn't want to influence them. But now I want to write the truth as I see it. I have plenty to say about it. That was his proposal. To stop the match, no more games, and begin a new one with 0-0. Campomanes made his decision to stop the match all by himself. He didn't tell anyone what he would do at the press conference. I didn't know what he was going to do. Afterwards he said that he didn't know what he was going to do himself either. I think that he was considering whether there should or should not be a revenge match for Karpov, but he didn't mention this. So it was just Kasparov's proposal which he read out.'

Then how could he criticize you?
'(Laughs) Well, if you didn't join his campaign, that quite unnecessary campaign, you were guilty in his point of view. In that way it is impossible to do anything objectively. I think that the people to blame for this whole idea of stopping the match were the players themselves. It was them. They played for draws and Kasparov initiated this situation. He is mainly to blame, let's say 55 percent, and next is Karpov, 45 percent. They created this situation which gave rise to the organizers' wish to stop the match. I wrote to him that he is a strong player and that the world expects him to win at the chess board. He was burdened with his rivalry towards Karpov. He thought that Karpov was favoured in the country where he lived and he thought that he should have as much or more attention as a young and promising player. But you cannot rely on your emotions when there are objective decisions to be taken. If this match had been played somewhere else it would have been stopped much earlier. For financial reasons, for lack of financial support. I will write this down one day. I cannot explain this in an interview. I didn't understand how it could come to this. But now I understand, after all of his writings and statements.'

You mean his personal drives?
'Yes, I didn't understand them. Especially his attitude towards me. We never talked in Moscow.'

Don't you give him any credit for the reasons why he acted as he did?
'Well, you see (hesitates), I do not give him the credit, although he may be right that some of the people in the Soviet Chess Federation were Karpov's fans. But that was all. I think that he had his fans too. You cannot attack people for wanting someone to win.'

But how would you react when someone tells you, 'We already have a World Champion, we don't need you'. This must have been pretty tough.
'Yes, that's true. But why should he pay attention to that at all? I do not know the inner relationships in the Soviet Union, except for what I've seen. He had a whole floor in the hotel, just like Karpov and he was treated in the same manner. His team was probably bigger than Karpov's. Or at least he had a better team at that moment. So he had nothing to complain about as far as the match was concerned. He played for draws all the time, he even offered a draw in the 47th game which he won. Maybe he wanted to tire Karpov out to get his chance. But what kind of champion would he have been if he had won that match with six to five after seven or eight months of play? He only got his title deservedly when he won the next match. As a matter of fact it was a deal, Campomanes' decision was a deal. The only unclear question was the question of the revenge match. Because of that revenge match the whole thing went on, I think. The whole thing went on because Kasparov wanted to kill that right for the second match in Moscow. And Karpov wanted to have it, because he had it before he played the first match, which he didn't lose. On the contrary. That's where the dispute was. It was the revenge match. That was the whole point. But he covered it with all kinds of moral questions. And that wasn't the truth. That sounded more like a political campaign than a chess campaign.'

Wasn't it terrible that you had to remain in Moscow for all these months?
'No, it wasn't terrible at all. People were very attentive to me. But the outside world didn't understand what was going on in Moscow. Ever since this series of draws began the match was dying off. Television stopped paying special attention to the match and the newspapers limited themselves to two lines. And we had no hall. There was always this discussion where we would have to move to. So we continued to stay there with all these technical time-outs. I wasn't paid for this. I spent six weeks longer than I should, free of charge, without my private life, without my usual work. I remained there just for the sake of them, not to leave them. I was honoured that they had invited me to be the referee, both of them. So I thought I should be faithful to them and stay till the bitter end. In my heart I wished to go

back, of course. I had asked the organizers to give me an apartment with a piano. This had been my only wish, and this piano was a great comfort. I started studying the piano when I was sixty. I'm self-taught at the piano and I learned the theory of music all by myself. Like I learned English, Spanish, Italian, Russian. I am not a great player, but I can entertain myself and I am improving all the time.'

Does it still give you pleasure to be an arbiter now that in Saint John at the Candidates' matches there were some problems with Kortchnoi too?
'Yes, that's true, we had a problem and I tried my best. What happened was Kortchnoi's fault. He was to blame for the situation.'

He was vigorously pacing up and down the stage disturbing Hjartarson...
'Yes, everyone saw that and my two deputies were much stricter than I was. I respect Kortchnoi as my colleague. My first thought was, "He doesn't do it on purpose", so I told him that he was disturbing his opponent. He took heed of that but only partly. So I had to write him another letter and again it was very polite. But when he lost the match...'

He sent you a letter accusing you...
'You know about that letter? I said that I wanted to publish that letter, but Kortchnoi didn't like the idea.'

It was a bit too strong, wasn't it?
'Yes, he wrote a letter which was very unfair and I replied to him privately. That's how it ended (laughs). I didn't mind a public discussion. Like I am ready for a public discussion on the marathon match all the time.'

Some ten years ago there was a rumour that you were going to play a match against Fischer.
'That was true. That was in 1978. I was very friendly with Bobby. I liked him very much and I respected him deeply, not only as a player but also as a person. He was misunderstood by the world and it was very bad that FIDE didn't give him his system of play. He was the first World Champion who could not play according to the system he proposed. Everyone in the past played the way he wanted to defend his title. What he proposed was quite normal to me. Maybe ten wins was a bit much, but it was the Steinitz system. What he argued and what killed the whole thing was that in case of a nine-nine result the next win would be a matter of chance. So this should not be allowed and in that case the money should be shared and the title should remain with the champion. That was all. That was very fair. Fischer didn't ask for a revenge match at all. And he was accused of wanting too much, too many advantages and so on. That was unjustified. FIDE killed his match with Karpov, in fact the whole chess world did. There are many federations that are guilty of this. They helped remove Fischer from the scene for ever.

'Our friendship began when he was fifteen and visited Belgrade after his first and only visit to the Soviet Union together with his sister. I was one of his hosts there and he probably realized that he could trust me. For instance in 1972, when I was in Reykjavik as a radio correspondent, I went to a reception at the American embassy. Everyone was pushing towards Fischer, so I stayed in a corner not to disturb him. When he realized that he came over to me and invited me to play tennis after midnight. Twice I accepted, twice I refused, because I had a journalistic job to do. When he dropped out of chess we remained in contact, and when I came to Lone Pine he would always invite me to visit him in Los Angeles. We began to write to each other and I began to try to persuade him to play chess again. That's how it went. The idea that he would play me in that match wasn't mine at all. I'm twenty years older and secondly it would seem as if I were looking for money or something. He gladly accepted the idea, because he wanted to play someone he trusted. He unexpectedly came to Belgrade for six days. It was shortly before the Olympiad and the congress. I was already a candidate for the presidency of FIDE. It was the only time I accepted, because I had been asked several times before that, and it also happened several times after that. In 1978 I accepted because I had some hope that I could persuade Fischer to play. As president of FIDE I wanted to perform miracles to bring him back. That was my main ambition. But when I flew to Buenos Aires after these six days I had lost the wish to be president, because I no longer believed that he would play. I didn't say this openly, and I still fought for Fischer, but I wasn't sure anymore that he would play even if I were president.'

What had given you that impression?
'There were many psychological mistakes, also by the Yugoslavs, although they were very well-intentioned. But he is very sensitive. And some other things happened in Europe. He was on a private visit in Berlin, with a chess player and organizer, who afterwards published an interview with him with photos which had been taken for his family album. Fischer saw this interview on the airplane and was disgusted. The match wasn't cancelled immediately, but he changed his conditions and they were impossible to meet. When he was in Belgrade he gave a statement for Yugoslav television. All out of his own free will, because he was very mindful to me. I promised him that the cameramen would not take any shot of him before he gave the sign. But the moment he entered the hall they started pushing forward. He was very tense and I thought that he might say nothing at all, but instead he gave a very kind, polite and wise statement for the Yugoslav public. After this was over the only personal contact he had in Belgrade was with me. He came to our house a few times and we talked about all kinds of things, but I realized that it would be tough to get him to play. Even if I were president of FIDE. What I wanted was to turn back the clock of history, which is maybe impossible. I wanted to create a situation similar to the one we had in 1974 and 1975. I wanted to have his match system accepted for a match with Karpov. I wanted that match very much.'

In 1977 a booklet was published in which Fischer was portrayed with a beard and long hair. What did he look like when he visited Belgrade in 1978?
'He had a beard when he arrived in Belgrade but he shaved it rightaway.'

A real beard?
'He had a real beard at Belgrade airport when I met him there. He was treated like the chief of a state. I drove up to the plane with a police car, a big Mercedes, and all. I was there alone, but he didn't want to get out of the plane without me. There was no passport control and he was immediately driven to the secret villa where he lived. I was the only one who knew about this villa and I also slept there a few times, because he was alone.'

Did you also play chess with him?
'Yes, at his request.'

Which impression did you get?
'He was strong. We played with a clock. It was his wish, I never play chess that way. I only play chess in serious tournaments. I did so when I was young, but not anymore. But he was strong.'

There is one final question I wanted to ask you, seeing you have been a political commentator for so many years and have fought in the war for a united Yugoslavia. What do you think of the current problems in Yugoslavia?
'Well, what do I think. I think that we should bring about a change of the economic rules as fast as possible. Both regarding enterprise and private initiative. As we also have national and ethnic problems at the moment too much time and energy is spent on these, and too little, or too late, on what should be the first issue, economics. That's my opinion.'

You think that national unity is the first priority?
'The idea of a united Yugoslavia is very old. It dates from the 19th century and it is a very strong feeling among people, no matter what you may read or see on television. That is not the real situation. The real situation is that Yugoslavia as a whole should exist, because the small republics, the separate republics, would soon lose their independence. This is the lesson of history. It's no use. My nationality is Serbian, but I am Yugoslav in the first place and only secondly Serbian. This feeling also exists among many musicians and well-known writers in our country. Everybody is for Yugoslavia.'

Lajos Portisch

Wijk aan Zee, January 1990

'I always had to pay a heavy price when I didn't follow my principles'

It is hard to imagine that there was once a time when Lajos Portisch was not around in the international chess arena. For more than three decades he has been Hungary's uncontested number one player. Before he lost interest in the Hungarian championship Portisch won the national title nine times, while he defended the Hungarian colours at sixteen Olympiads, the absolute highlight being Buenos Aires '78, when he led the team that broke the perennial Soviet hegemony. Eight times he qualified for the Candidates' matches, twice reaching the semifinals. In countless international events he took first prize. A paragon of dedication and discipline, Portisch is the only player in the world whose Elo has never fallen under 2600 since the ratings were introduced in the early seventies. Yet, this sphinx-like man is the kind of celebrity every chess fan knows, but no one really knows anything about. Shunning publicity as much as possible he never revealed what makes him tick and it was only after repeated requests that he allowed himself to be persuaded into granting an extensive interview. 'I don't like to give interviews, so you must realize that this is an exception'. That did not sound very encouraging, but his warning was accompanied by a loud laugh and for two and a half hours he talked freely about the changed chess world, Fischer, Sax, Kadar, weightlifting, music and much more. So that was why we had been looking forward to this talk for so long.

What strikes you in particular as having changed in the chess world since you started on your international career?
'When I played my first international tournament there were hardly any good magazines or books available. The first good international periodical we had was Euwe's *Losbladige*, which appeared every month. It is still being published in Germany as *Schach Archiv*, and I still get it. Now there are so many chess magazines that there's no question of reading them all, unless you have people who do the work for you, like the Russians. Another thing I simply hate are these chess diskettes and computers. I think I have such experience in chess that I can do without them. It's not important if I don't know the latest analyses, because my chess intuition is such that I can always choose the right method of play. Of course, I don't want to reveal any chess

103

secrets, but I'm not so familiar with these modern lines, like the Dragon. But I have my own theory, which I know very well.

'I have always liked analysing a lot. I was so productive. A lot of variations and novelties that were adopted by other players were actually mine. Take for instance this Nimzo-Indian Variation which they call the Hübner Variation. I'm always angry about that, because I already played that line in the fifties, from 1952 till the Bled tournament in 1960. But it was forgotten because it wasn't considered very good. Then suddenly a few years later Hübner started to play it and also Fischer and now they call it the Hübner Variation. I have all respect for Mr Hübner, but they forgot that it was actually my idea. But I was not such a well-known player at that time.'

Is it true that you worked or still work eight hours a day? Or is this the Portisch legend?
'This is the legend, of course. The truth is that I'm still capable of working as many hours as I want, but the point is that I don't want to. If there's something that interests me I'm still able to work eight or even ten hours a day, but nowadays I work two or three hours a day on average. Of course, I've always been working hard in chess. I had to do a lot of things on my own. I didn't get much help in Hungary and I didn't have as many good seconds as the Russians. Well, Fischer once asked me, "Lajos, is it true that you work eight hours a day?" And I said, "Why are you asking? People also think that you work eight hours a day." Then Bobby said, "Oh yes, but they think that I am crazy." '

In Hungary you succeeded a generation of players like Szabo, Lengyel and Barcza. It wasn't till the seventies that a new generation of strong grandmasters appeared with Ribli, Sax and Adorjan. Was it bad luck for you to be the country's only strong grandmaster for such a long period?
'My bad luck was that I was born in a small village far from Budapest. There was no chess life, although there was a nice old man who taught me the moves. The elements of chess I learned from him, but I had to learn a lot of things from books in those years. When I got to Budapest I was already a master player. Within two or three years time I won the Hungarian championship. Then the problem was that there weren't so many international tournaments and it was very difficult to get good invitations. I was just lacking experience. The other problem was that I started a little late. When I was twelve my brother and I got a chess set for Christmas, but it took at least a year before I realized that I had some talent for chess. Maybe that's why I'm still playing, because the sooner you start the quicker you lose your interest or ambitions.'

Did it help you that you could train together with your brother[15]?
'That was only in the very first years, because I became stronger much more quickly than he did. So we stopped analysing together. But I almost always work alone.

---

15 Ferenc Portisch, who became an IM in 1975.

Sometimes I meet friends and we check some variations. Or when I was preparing for my match against Timman, I worked with my second a little. But the ideas come from me and I'm still very creative. In every game of that match I introduced a new move that was playable.'

How much confidence do you have in seconds ever since your Candidates' match against Hübner in 1980, when three seconds proved unable to analyse a winning position properly?
'This is a fundamental problem, of course. There was a time when this whole problem of seconds irri-tated me. I think chess is an individual game and there shouldn't be any help from a third party. Not only when the

Lajos Portisch: 'I always thought that Fischer was a great player and it's a disgrace what the chess world has done to him.'

game is in progress, but in general. Especially the Russians have all the advantages of this, which is why they are still fighting to have adjournments in tournaments. For Botvinnik it was one of his principles to adjourn in a good position and then analyse it at home. I think that for reasons of principle it is unfair to have seconds. What happened in this game against Hübner was my own fault. I had three seconds and the position was simply won. I just left them to work out how, because I was already thinking ahead to the next game. My fault was that I didn't check it. I just sat down for fifteen minutes and they showed me everything they had analysed. I was very tired and said to myself, "You have three seconds, why should you worry?" This was just the proof of my theory that maybe it is better to have no seconds at all. In a tournament I can afford to have no second, but in a match where your opponent has two or three seconds you have little choice.'

I've always been impressed by your disciplined attitude towards chess. Is this something you have learned through the years or is it part of your character?
'Maybe it's just my character. In many other things I'm disciplined as well. Maybe those who live a bit more like bohemians have an easier life, but I always had to pay a heavy price when I didn't follow my principles. There are many rules which

you should follow, but the older you get the more difficult it is. For example, in my very first years in the international arena I said to myself, "You'd better be on your own. You'd better not talk much with anyone else, it might bother you". This is because of my lunch with Fischer and Benkö during the Interzonal in Stockholm. I don't blame them, but I made a stupid mistake. The three of us had lunch together before the last round, in which I was to play Aaron from India. During the meal they were joking and said things like, "Lajos, you'd better be careful. This guy is very dangerous. You may very well lose this game."

'Psychologically this shocked me a bit and then I really lost the game. Benkö is still unhappy when I mention this (laughs). Of course, it wasn't their fault. But people like to play with words and sometimes they don't realize how heavily these words affect you psychologically.'

How did you get along with Fischer?
'I think we always had good relations. I still remember our last game at the Siegen Olympiad in 1970. It was on a Sunday and we both showed up for the game in black suits. Because it was Sunday and out of respect for each other. Unfortunately many things have changed. I always paid a lot of attention to stories like the one I read in Alekhine's book. When he was about to lose the match against Euwe he showed up in evening dress. It was probably very difficult for him to have to resign the world title, but he didn't show that. I'm always saying that many chess players do not realize that they should show some respect for their opponents. I also understand that there are a lot of chess players who feel more comfortable in leisure clothes or don't want to wear ties (laughs). I still remember Larsen during the Interzonal in Palma de Mallorca. We were staying in the same hotel and in Spain at that time you couldn't show up for dinner without a tie. So when he was about to enter the restaurant without a tie the head-waiter didn't let him in and offered him a tie. Larsen was very upset, but he accepted the tie saying, "The last time I wore a tie was at my wedding".

'Another thing that disturbs me is that there are chess players who discuss their games and simply want to get advice from others, while they are playing. I'm not saying that all the people who are chatting while the games are still in progress are talking about their games. They may speak about the weather or music or girls, whatever, but still it's a bit irritating. Unfortunately I don't know any arbiters who take steps against this, although I think this is in the rules of chess. I never saw Fischer speaking with anyone while he was playing. He was absolutely fair in these matters. People think this is not so important, but it is. At the beginning of this century you were not even supposed to analyse adjourned positions and the players went for dinner together. There was this code, but then everything changed. Unfortunately this gentleman-like behaviour among chess players is out of fashion. It's my principle that you should respect your opponent as much as you respect yourself. When your opponent is suffering to find the best move and you are laughing and chatting with somebody else, this is not done. But you asked about Fischer. I always thought that he was a great player and it's a disgrace what the chess world has done to him. It was obviously FIDE's fault. Something like that should not be done to the World Champion.'

Was this one of the reasons why you wanted to be involved in the GMA?
'Kasparov asked me to be a member of the GMA and I thought that was a good idea. One of the reasons was that I had a lot of bad experiences with FIDE through these many years. The whole chess world was so badly organized. I can give you an example. When FIDE was about to take a decision on this famous Fischer-Karpov match, I was on a simultaneous tour of England and the English Channel Islands. On one of these islands, I don't want to say exactly which one, because I don't want to insult people, the president of the federation was a tomato farmer. A very nice gentleman, but a very weak chess player. He played in a simul against me and on the reception following this simul he came to me and asked me, "Lajos, what do you think. At the FIDE Congress I have to vote either for Karpov or for Fischer. Whom shall I vote for?" And I said, "Look, it doesn't matter what I am saying to you. I am sure that Mr Edmondson, the president of the American Chess Federation and also Mr Baturinsky from the Soviet Federation will soon pay you a visit and try to persuade you."
   'And people like him, although he was a nice man, and many more such delegates from countries all over the world decided on very important chess issues. So I thought that the GMA would be a good opposition, but unfortunately I'm not very satisfied with what's going on right now. Right after the Skelleftea tournament I resigned as a board member in Brussels. I don't want to go into any particulars, but in general I don't like what's happening.'

One of the reasons why you wore this black suit against Fischer was that it was Sunday. Has it ever been a problem for you to be a Catholic in a socialist country?
'Actually never, because they never dared to say anything about it. When they realized I was a religious person I was already a well-known chess player. For example, the morning after we had won the Chess Olympiad in Buenos Aires in '78, me and two other players ran into the chief of the Hungarian delegation in the hall of the hotel. Well, he was a nice man, but a strong communist. And he said, "Where are you going?" And I said, "To church to give thanks that we won the Olympiad". And his answer was, "Yes, well done, well done. Go, go." (Laughs) It was a bit funny and we started to laugh, well, smile at least, that a communist leader should say something like that.'

Did they never ask you to join the Communist Party when you had become a famous chess player?
'Actually they never asked me. They probably realized that I would say no. Of course, I never wanted to be a member. I never was a member of any party in my whole

life. Now there are so many parties in Hungary that maybe it's high time to start with one of them. But I don't care very much about politics. Of course, they wanted me to be a member of the presidium of the Hungarian Chess Federation, but I never wanted that. I've always thought that there would be a conflict if a leading player took advantage of his membership of a governing body. I didn't want to be blamed for that. That's why I was so surprised when I had to read that stupid interview with Sax in the latest Interpolis tournament book.[16] This interview is full of nonsense. I don't remember ever having done anything against another Hungarian player. My only answer to this interview is that now Timman is making a serious mistake by including Sax in his camp.'

Were you aware that there was so much envy among your colleagues?
'Of course, there is much envy. That's the problem, we are only humans. The younger grandmasters still cannot... how shall I put this without insulting them too much... they have to understand that I'm still there. Twenty years ago they may already have thought that it was time for the takeover, but it still hasn't happened. This interview irritated me very much, because of all the lies and nonsense. For example, he says that the president of the Hungarian Chess Federation visited me in my villa every weekend. My answer is that unfortunately I don't have a villa (laughs). Anyway, you must realize that nowadays with this rating system, organizers are thinking in categories. They invite you if your rating is high. It's as simple as that. So that has nothing to do with my relations with organizers. I never stopped organizers from inviting other Hungarian players, although they have asked me many times what would happen if they would. My answer was always, "That's your problem, not mine. Please do what you want." Maybe they expected that I wouldn't play in that case, but that's absolute rubbish, of course. That's why I'm so surprised by this stupid interview. I really don't understand.'

Were you in the position to achieve the things that Sax is accusing you of?
'Of course not. As Hungary's best player for many years I have obviously often been asked my opinion, but I have to tell you that unfortunately my view was seldom accepted. For example, in this Adorjan case. Perhaps you remember that in 1980 and 1982 he was left out of the Olympiad team and especially in 1982 there was a boycott against him by three Hungarian grandmasters. I thought this was unfair towards a colleague and I told the president and the vice-president of the Federation that I hated that kind of thing and thought that Adorjan deserved a place on the team because of his strength. But he was left out of the team anyway. I have always been opposed to boycotts, be they personal or political. I remember very well that

---

16 In this article Sax accused Portisch of having frustrated his generation's development and opportunities for many years. According to Sax, Portisch carefully protected his own privileges and opposed international invitations for other players. Together with Szerenyi, the federation's president, he allegedly determined the course of Hungarian chess in his own interests only.

in 1960, when I played in the Zonal Tournament for the first time, there were some problems with the East German grandmaster Pietzsch, because the Spanish organizers refused to put the East German flag on his table. And then Mr Pachman, who at the time was a communist fighter for Czechoslovakia, said we should not play. But I said "No, this is my first Zonal Tournament. You can do what you want, but I'm going to play." The consequence of this Adorjan boycott was that during this entire event in Lucerne I carefully avoided any conversation with these three players. That was the reason why after the last Olympiad[17] I decided that I will not play on the Hungarian team anymore. In the meantime I have already been asked several times by the new Hungarian federation to change my mind, but I'm afraid I can't (with a muffled laugh).'

Maybe your colleagues also envied you for the fact that you were a good friend of the mightiest man in the country, the late Mr Kadar ?
'Well, I wouldn't say that I was a good friend of his, but he liked chess very much and obviously knew me as Hungary's best player. But I didn't get any special help from him. Except for once, when I wrote him a letter. This was before the second Piatigorsky Cup. The Hungarian Sports Committee refused to let me play in a tournament in America, saying, "You'd better not go there, because the Americans are bombing Viet Nam." That was how they actually put it. So, I wrote a letter to Mr Kadar explaining that this was such an important chess event and that I would lose a lot if I couldn't go there. He accepted my points and took steps so that I got permission to play there. But we couldn't have been friends. Firstly there was a big difference in age and secondly he had other interests and I never had any political interests. I think that he was an honest man, although there has been a lot of criticism. I'm not a politician and it is up to others to judge his political mistakes and his political heritage. As I knew him as a man, I think he was an honest person.'

What role do you think the Polgars will play in the future of Hungarian chess?
'The Polgars go their own way and probably they are right in that respect. The father realizes that you will always face difficulties when you do something original. I'm not convinced by their theory, but that doesn't matter. It's not my problem. Still, we have to admit that they are doing something original. It's an interesting challenge. Of course, I'm impressed that the girls are so talented, but I cannot believe that a woman can be overall champion in chess. This is just against nature, both physically and mentally, and you cannot ignore nature. But we have to give them some credit. Maybe I'm too traditional. Not so long ago people didn't believe that mankind could reach the moon, but maybe it's even more difficult for a woman chess player to win the male title. Of course, this is not their fault.'

---

17 Where Portisch scored 8½/11 on first board, the second best result after Kasparov.

When I asked Judit about the help she got from Hungarian grandmasters her mother answered, 'Portisch said he couldn't help us because he was too much on his own.'

'I said that I was so busy with my own problems in chess that I simply cannot help anybody else. Maybe I am too individualistic. I don't care so much about other persons' problems. I'm too difficult for myself (laughs). You understand what I mean. It's very difficult for me to handle myself and I do not want to force my ideas on anyone else. And this is what I certainly would do if I coached somebody. For example, if I worked with the Polgars I would certainly insist immediately that they fight for the female title and we would immediately have a conflict. Why should we, when we have normal relations? I don't say that we are friends, but we have been in the same club for many years. Actually there is a young Hungarian talent whom I occasionally give some advice. Once a month or once every two months. But this is just because his parents are friends of us. I don't think I could coach someone regularly. I have other interests and life is too short. I have already sacrificed too much for chess.'

Talking about other interests, at the drawing of lots in Skelleftea you were the only player who could lift this gold bar with one hand. Somebody said this was because of the weightlifting you had done.

'Yes, that was one of my favourite sports, but when we moved to a new apartment I had to give it up. My wife simply forbade it. She said it had ruined our previous apartment, because I always fell to the floor with these weights. But these were only exercises with small weights. I wanted to get acquainted with the technique and I wanted to know how strong I was. I didn't work with heavy weights, the maximum was fifty kilo's. But the point is that it doesn't matter so much how big the weight is, but how many times you can push or lift it.'

What other sports do you like?

'Well, I've played tennis, but I'm a very weak tennis player, because I never had a talent for the ball. And, of course, I always liked soccer, but I wasn't a good soccer player either. When I was at school I was always the goalkeeper. But I'm a good swimmer. When I'm at home I regularly go to the swimming pool and they let me swim in the same lane where (Tamas) Darnyi, the Olympic swimming champion, normally trains. He is Hungary's best swimmer. Actually he won the Olympic games with the same glasses I gave to him in the pool. He saw my glasses and said, "What nice glasses", and I said, "Well, please, it's a present. I hope you'll win."

'But again these sports we are talking about, except for tennis, they show the loneliness. You swim for one hour and you are in the water alone, just like in chess. It looks like (thinks), I would say like *Einsamkeit* from the Winterreise[18]. Sometimes being on your own is sad, but it also gives you confidence.'

---

18 *Einsamkeit* is the saddest song from Schubert's most famous song cycle.

You generally make a serious impression. Are you never afraid that you put people off?
'Well, I don't know. Chess is a very serious game and with my behaviour and principles I put some ideas into chess in the hope that someone will discover them and perhaps sooner or later follow them. Even if it's so difficult. Well, you never know. Once, for instance, I was very surprised when Sosonko blamed me that I had been disturbing him during the game. This was in the last round of Reggio Emilia, which was played very early in the morning. I know it's terrible to play very early in the morning, but as it turned out I played very well that morning and won a beautiful game. Of course, he was very unhappy and at the end of the game he said to me, "You're not supposed to push the button of the clock with a piece in your hand." I replied, "I don't know. Why?" and I said, "But you are not supposed to continuously look for dust particles on the chess board." But this was the only conflict I ever had when my opponent lost a game.'

I remember Sosonko once told me a story about a game against you. He had a very good position and when he got up to walk around and started talking to someone you shushed him. He was scared stiff, returned to the board and lost the game.
'(Starts laughing loudly) No, I can't remember that, but maybe I did. Maybe I felt that I had to warn him to stop talking. I haven't done this often, I would rather shoot a glance and make clear that I found that this wasn't fair. This is in the rules. Like it is also forbidden to leave the playing room during the game. For instance, in Reggio last December I had forgotten my chocolate in my room and I went to the arbiter and asked her, "I want to go to my room, can someone come with me?" And this guy who accompanied me didn't understand why I asked that.'

Of late, music has become more and more important to you. Have you always been an ardent music lover?
'Even before I started playing chess I was already playing the violin, from when I was five or six years old. My parents actually wanted me to become a violinist. But it is more difficult to achieve results in music than it is in chess. You don't feel the taste of victory so quickly. When you are a young girl or boy and play chess, pretty soon you are able to beat an adult, but when you are a small musician you have to work and train every day and I hated that very much. When I began playing chess I slowly lost my interest in the violin. I thought it was much easier to achieve success in chess than in music. Nevertheless music has always remained something special and beautiful for me. I still have this old violin, but I very seldom pick it up anymore. My fingers no longer move like they should because I lost the technique. And I was always singing, even when I was still young. Every time I came home from Budapest, after I had moved there, my mother would say, "The neighbours can hear that you are back." I always knew that I had an acceptable voice and I dreamed that I might have been a good opera singer. At that time, when I was eighteen or nineteen, I was mostly singing opera songs. I never liked this so-called light music, except for really good musicians like Elvis Presley, Bing Crosby or

Frank Sinatra. I always preferred serious music, although even today I will occasionally sing Hungarian folk songs. Which is very nice, especially when you are sitting at a table with a glass of wine and have a nice gipsy band behind you. Then, in 1985, came the time when I thought it was my last chance to start my serious music education again. And ever since I have been working with my teacher. She's a professor at the Hungarian Academy of Music and when I'm at home I go to her at least once, but mostly twice a week.'

When we talked about music a couple of years ago you were still very much interested in opera. This interest has obviously shifted to songs. Your recent recital on Hungarian radio was entirely made up of songs.
'My teacher is a Lieder singer, so... And also now I think that these songs fit my voice better than the arias. I still like opera, but for me learning a whole opera doesn't make much sense. Where can I sing an opera? Although there is one role from a Hungarian opera, well, not exactly an opera, but something in between opera and operetta, that I know. Last year I was given the honours of the town where I was born. At the reception I talked about the dreams you have as a chess player and a singer and I said, "I will probably never become World Champion in chess anymore, but I can still hope that I can arrange something with the opera company in Zalaegerszeg and sing that role." '

Your colleagues cannot fail to notice that you continue your singing exercises during tournaments. Does this help your chess?
'It certainly helps my mood. In chess it's very difficult to get rid of your problems when you lose a game or miss chances. In those cases music is a very good outlet.'

What did you do at such moments when you weren't singing yet?
'(Laughs) This is a good question. Probably I was suffering more. I didn't have any compensation then. This is the problem. All chess players suffer and those who take it more seriously suffer more.'

Have you always been able to find a balance between the joy you derive from chess and the sorrow it obviously gives you?
'It is difficult to find this balance. After all chess is not only my profession. It's also part of my life. And you only have a very short life. I don't know what I could have reached in music. Of course, I know that I wouldn't have become a world top star like I am in chess, but who knows what's better. Everybody has this problem. We all have different talents and it's probably a matter of luck which of these talents we use for our whole life. When you are in secondary school you are asked this foolish question, "What are you going to be, my dear pupil?" Of course, you don't know, because you're sixteen or seventeen years old. I remember by first day at university. I arrived at the Karl Marx Polytechnic seven days late, because I had been playing in the Hungarian semifinal and qualified for the Hungarian championship for the

first time. I dropped into a two hours' lecture on political economy or something, anyway something foolish and while I was sitting there the four years that lay ahead of me appeared to me and I said to myself, "Oh my God, this is not the kind of thing I want to study for four years." I immediately went to the dean and said, "Either you give me a one-year break or I leave the university." I was lucky, because he didn't grant me the break. This was thirty years ago and I was heavily criticized for taking chess as a profession. I was only a master and chess wasn't so well paid as it is now, when young players can play everywhere in the world. Then it was very difficult to get out of Hungary. Fortunately my parents didn't say anything. They were a bit sorry when I gave up music and started to play chess, but they didn't try to persuade me to do something else. I was playing for a club and I took a small job, something administrative. But still a full-time job, I had to sit there for eight hours a day. I didn't have any privileges in the very first years, but this changed when I became champion of Hungary. That's why I don't understand Sax, because they were in a much better position than I was at the time. Szabo always says that my generation was much luckier than his, because his best chess years were during the War. My answer to that is that in the fifties, especially from 1950 till '56 it was a terrible time in Hungary, both economically and politically.'

How did you experience the Russian invasion in 1956?
'Maybe chess is the reason that I'm still alive. At that time I was fortunately very busy with Capablanca's games, so I didn't have any political commitment and didn't get into any fighting. I was only eighteen years old, but a lot of youngsters were fighting. It's sad to say that Capablanca's games were more interesting to me than the Hungarian Revolution, but this is how it was.'

How was this among your friends?
'Well, maybe I was lucky that I had just moved up to Budapest and didn't have so many friends yet. I was living in a very small room and my landlady supplied me with some food. It was very difficult to get food. Most of the fighting took place in Budapest, but not in the district where I was living. But one day I was almost shot. I was walking down a street when suddenly there was a rattle on the pavement behind me. Then I realized there was a tank standing a couple of hundred yards away from me with its gun pointing at me. So this rattle had obviously been bullets from a machine gun. Now either they had shot at random, or it was a warning or they just missed me. I remember I was cool-headed and realizing the danger I didn't run, but calmly walked on. Because had I run I might not have been able to speak now. You never know. Anything could have happened. Just like in Romania now.'

Do you also have this detached attitude towards the recent political landslide in Hungary?
'No, of course not. I follow the political developments and the economic problems. There is real freedom now and I'm glad these changes are taking place. And these

problems affect us all. First of all the problem of inflation. You have to be interested, because what are you going to do with your money? There are a lot of economic problems and I don't know how we can solve them, but we will see.'

What are your plans and ambitions as a chess player for the coming ten years?
'(Another resounding laugh) Thank you. The coming ten years? I just want to play good acceptable chess. I don't want to cause too many problems to myself. I'll probably have to be a little bit less aggressive, which is my nature actually. I'm not such a solid person, I'm too aggressive. Sometimes it's very difficult to direct this aggression in chess. Probably I have to learn to be satisfied with small things, like an occasional small quick draw (laughs). When I was young quick draws used to affect my confidence very much. That's why sometimes at critical moments I had to suffer foolish defeats, because I was trying to win the game at any cost. Even against weak opponents, when I couldn't forget the fact that they were weak players. On the other hand I always tried to play against every opponent as if he were a champion. I always had to take everyone very seriously.'

Miguel Najdorf

Manila, June 1992

'Do you want to hear a beautiful story?'

At 82 Miguel Najdorf exudes a vitality, drive and energy that would make many a young man envious. 'I am the oldest active grandmaster in the world', the maestro beams without false modesty. Active he may certainly be called, given his participation in last year's Argentine championship. And totally devoted, too, to a game that has been with him for all his long and eventful life. A successful business man who still spends long working days at his office, Najdorf will only rarely skip his daily diet of free games at a Buenos Aires chess club. Even though my own part in the conversation was limited, having an interview with the legendary raconteur was the fulfilment of a long-cherished wish.

Talking to Miguel Najdorf is a unique experience. Going by stories from players who had known him for many years, I was fully aware that I had to expect a change in the usual questions-answers, answers-questions routine. That feeling was correct, but contrary to what I had feared, I was not treated to a gushing monologue either. During the two graciously granted sessions, the first in the lobby of the Manila Holiday Inn and the second in his room overlooking Roxas Boulevard and Manila Bay, the grand old man remained true to his well-developed technique of using questions as stepping stones for his stories or opinions. Sometimes he would give a straightforward answer to a question, but mostly one or two words or a name sufficed to remind him of a nice 'history' which urgently needed telling. Inevitably the structure of the interview suffered from this procedure, but who would nitpick about structure when there are 'beautiful stories' on offer?

It is Najdorf's fourth visit to the Philippines. Twice he was here as a player. In 1978 he reported on the Karpov-Kortchnoi match from Baguio. For 35 years he has been writing for *Clarin*, the most chess-friendly newspaper in the world, which sent him all over the globe to cover World Championship matches and Olympiads. This time, too, he writes daily reports, not a mean feat in combination with his duties as captain of the Argentine men's team. However, the first and foremost capacity that he is recognised in when he enters the playing area is that of 'Najdorf', the living legend who warmly greets old friends and treats them to one of his stories.

Miguel Najdorf: 'Now chess is a sports industry aimed at making Elo.'

Miguel Najdorf, who was born in Poland as Mieczyslaw ('Moshe') Najdorf 82 years ago can talk from experience when the subject is Olympiads. Three times (1935, 1937 and 1939) he played for Poland. Eleven times he represented Argentina, the country where he sought asylum when World War II broke out. Both in Dubrovnik in 1950 and in Helsinki in 1952 he achieved the best score on Board 1. While he reminisces about the Olympiads he played in, his thoughts inevitably wander back to the Olympiad that marked a tragic turn in his life, the 1939 Olympiad in Buenos Aires.

'I went to Buenos Aires just like you came here. Then the War broke out and I suffered a very big tragedy. I never saw my family again. I lost all my family. My wife, my daughter, all my four brothers, my father, my mother. Three hundred people in all. All killed by Hitler. So, in 1939 I stayed in Buenos Aires. I started to work in an insurance company to make some money, a company which I later bought. And I played chess. One of the things I did was play forty games blindfolded. Do you know why I played these blindfold games? I had a very special reason. Not only a chess reason, but also a private reason. Somebody told me that it was impossible and it took me 24 hours, but I believed that if this was a sports record, that perhaps someone from my family might hear about it. If they were in the concentration camps this news might somehow reach them. They would know that I am alive and that I am playing chess. So maybe they could hope to come to Buenos Aires too after the War and start a new life. I believe that they received this notice, but I never saw them back.

'When the War began in 1939 many chess players from the Olympiad stayed behind and didn't go back home. As a result chess life got a boost. You may remember Stahlberg from Sweden, who stayed till 1948, the German, Eliskases, who is still in Argentina. Chess in Argentina benefited a lot from this. After soccer, chess is the second most popular sport in the country. Everybody plays chess. That is the reason why every newspaper has a big chess section.'

At this point one of the Argentine players comes into the lobby. He has just finished an adjourned game and lost. Najdorf is unpleasantly surprised and sternly tells him in Spanish 'We will look at it tonight.' Then turning back to me he continues as if he had been interrupted: 'Chess is an art. But nowadays chess is no longer the same as it used to be when we didn't have Elo's. I think that Elo is very bad for chess. Now chess is a sports industry aimed at making Elo. Chess is no longer an art, no longer clean. In my time, many years ago, chess used to be more friendly. Of course, the computer changed all this. Chess used to be only art. Keres, my good friend, once asked me "Hast du mit dem eigenen Köpfchen gespielt?" (Did you play with your own little head?) Today they have no "eigenen Köpfchen".

'I believe that Kasparov really is a genius. But he is an industry. Four people are working for him every day. Analysing everything. You see, Kasparov doesn't play the Kasparov Variation. There is no Kasparov Variation. There is a Petrosian Variation, a Najdorf Variation, a Maroczy Variation. Everybody played something himself. New ideas. Kasparov is a wonderful chess player, the greatest player in the world. Now he has to play against Short or Timman, which will be very difficult for him, although I think... You know Timman. Sometimes he plays very well. He is a chess genius. But he is not as Kasparov who always plays well. Sometimes Timman is a genius and sometimes he is like a patzer.'

Are you proud that there is a Najdorf Variation?
'I played my variation. You see, when I was a young man and began to play chess I had a chess book that told me that in a certain position Bishop c4 was not a good move. But I could not understand why. And even though the book said that Bishop c4 was a bad move, I played it. I remember a game I played against Timman in Reykjavik. I knew that he would play the Leningrad Variation and I was looking in my room where I could improve my play. Not by taking the *Encyclopedia*, but by looking myself. I must play my own idea. If you want to be a chess champion you first of all have to be a composer. Like Bach or Mozart. They play Mozart music, Beethoven music, Tchaikovsky music. Do you understand? Good or bad is not the point. You may like it, another one may not like it. But they play their music. The same goes for chess. Fischer played Fischer music. Petrosian played Petrosian music.'

Who do you think was the Mozart of chess?
'The Mozart of chess was at one moment Bobby Fischer. Many years ago the Mozart of chess was Capablanca. Now Kasparov is right that they didn't play in the times of the big competitions. Chess is very popular these days. Everyone who begins to play has a computer and books and plays his first twenty moves because Botvinnik and Karpov played them in Wijk aan Zee or Hastings. They know all the moves. I believe that if Bobby Fischer would now play against Kasparov, Kasparov would,

of course, win very easily. But give Fischer five years time and make him five years younger and I don't know who would win.

'Do you want to hear a beautiful history about what it is to be old? I play a lot of blitz games at my club, that's my specialty. Not so long ago I had big difficulties when my opponents played the line with Knight e2 against the Benoni. I had many problems with the black pieces after Knight e2. So, one Sunday, because I'm very busy at the other days, I started leafing through some books looking for an antidote against Knight e2. I go from one book to the other and then I find the following game. The Olympiad in Havana, Argentina against Yugoslavia, first board, Ivkov: White, Najdorf: Black. Ivkov plays Knight e2 against the Benoni and I won a wonderful game (bursts out laughing)! Yes, now I knew how to play against this line.'

You are one of the rare examples of a chess player who is also a successful business man. Do you think that in general chess players are bad business men?
'I am still working. I believe that chess is very important. After my family, that is my wife, my two daughters who are both physicians, and my grandchildren, my love is chess, chess, chess. I must play chess every day. That is the reason why I feel so strong. I will never give up chess. Every day I go to my office at nine o'clock in the morning. I used to go at six, but nowadays I go at nine. At six in the afternoon I go from the office to my chess club and play till eight. Two hours. This is my relaxation. I play my games and I feel wonderful. Like after a Mozart or Beethoven concert.'

Is working hard the best way to reach a high age?
'Working hard. If you want to be an old man, your work and your chess will make you younger every time. Sometimes people wonder when I will give up. I'm only beginning (laughs loudly).'

But are chess players bad business men?
'Chess is a good business for maybe twenty people. Tell me who makes good money in chess? Kasparov, Karpov, Timman, who else? Short, but not so much. Kortchnoi, but he is not a rich man. They make some money. Chess is not a good profession. I prefer to have my business and to play besides. You see, many people claim that they are so busy and that they are so occupied that they have no time to play chess. Let me tell you, a man who is that occupied does not have time for chess, for his business, for his social life, not for anything. If this man had nothing to do he would have no time either (laughs triumphantly).'

What makes a good chess player?
'Chess is a combination of ten games. I'll tell you which. Attack, defence, endgames, openings, few pieces, more pieces. A combination of ten games. Who is the champion of the world? The man who excels at all these ten games? Look at Tal. A wonderful chess player in the attack, but not in defence. Not in the ending. Look at

Petrosian. A genius of defence. Not of attack. Look at Smyslov. One of the best chess players in the world in the endgame. There are ten games together and nobody is the champion of the ten games together.'

Which were the games you were best at?
'I believe that I was very good at the initiative. I never studied chess. I have a very good intuition. I didn't play with my head. I played with my nose. You understand what I mean? I have a beautiful history about Dr. Alekhine. I played together with him in a tournament in England and he played a wonderful game against Böök from Finland. In a Queen's Gambit Accepted, Alekhine, who was White, sacrificed a rook. Alekhine was very nervous and while Böök was thinking he asked me in Russian, "Miguel, I sacrificed a rook. What do you think?" I was a young man of seventeen or eighteen years old. I couldn't say I was a patzer. But I looked and saw nothing. So, I told him, "Very interesting". But in fact I had not seen anything. Fourteen or fifteen moves later he won a beautiful game. After he had won the game I went to my hotel saying to myself, "He must be a genius. Such a rook sacrifice. I saw nothing and he saw so many moves! How can this be? I don't think that chess is for me. Maybe I should play domino and not chess (laughs heartily)." This was, I believe, in 1938. In 1939 at the Olympiad in Buenos Aires he said, "Miguel, let's go for a drink". I told him that I was a poor man and that I had no money, but he said, "I pay". So we went to a nightclub and every time he would take not a glass of whisky, but a bottle of whisky. Of course, I only took one glass. So, I said, "Doctor, I want to ask you something. Do you remember this game you played against Böök where you sacrificed a rook and asked me my opinion? And I told you 'Wonderful'? Well, you know, actually I didn't see anything. So, may I ask you, why did you sacrifice?" He smiled and said, "The same goes for me. I didn't see anything either." "Then why", I exclaimed, "Did you sacrifice?" And he told me, "I have a big nose." You understand? A big intuition. The same applies to Capablanca. A big nose (laughs his high laugh, leans over and much to my amazement pinches my nose)!'

Which of today's players have a big nose?
'Today they don't have big noses. They have big computers. Sometimes of course they have. Kasparov, he plays everything well. Karpov is a really wonderful chess player. The number of tournaments he won. But, you see, his nerves are not that good.'

Larsen once told me how well informed you were about the latest news in chess. One day when he came to have lunch at your place and wanted to show you a spectacular game he had just received from Europe you took him to your study where the crucial position was already on the board.
'Yes, I receive about fifty different magazines, but I don't have the time to read them all. And I write a bit. Now I want to write a book about my life. I don't have much time, because I work a lot, but maybe I will finish this book. I have many stories.

You know, I played Alekhine, Capablanca, Spielmann, Bogoljubow, Nimzowitsch, Botvinnik, all the champions, Tal, Smyslov, Spassky. And I won and lost. I won against Botvinnik and I lost. I won against Smyslov and I lost. I won against Petrosian and I lost. Against Kasparov I played only one game in Bugojno and I lost.'

How was Nimzowitsch ? How was he at the board?
'Nimzowitsch was terrible. A small gangster. Also at the board. Not fair. Rubinstein was a big gentleman. You know my history about Groningen 1946? I played against Vidmar. I had a bad position and he said to me, "Young man, are you playing for a win?" I was worse, so I answered, "Thank you very much. I agree to a draw." To which he replied, "No, I didn't offer you a draw. I only asked whether you played for a win. I don't play for a win, but I play to beat you. But I wanted to know whether you play for a win (roars with laughter)." So, we played some twenty more moves and then the game was drawn.'

How big was your ambition to become World Champion?
'When I was young I wanted to be World Champion, of course. But when I was 32 or 35 I realized that chess was a big pleasure for me, but that it was not my career. Not the way I wanted to make money. But chess helped me very much, because nothing is easy in life and chess taught me to fight. You are like you play chess. If I don't know you and I have talked to you for two hours I will tell you who you are. Temperamental or not, and so on. The same with chess. People play chess like they are. If you want to do business with somebody you can first play a game of chess with him and you will know whether he is a gentleman or not. Also when I suffered this tragedy chess helped me a lot. You see, in chess you may lose today, but you may win tomorrow. How many games did Timman lose? But he is still fighting. And he still has chances to become champion of the world. This is very important. To fight all your life. It never stops. Chess is very good for your education. I have five grandchildren and I have a professor who teaches them chess. You know, many young people react terribly when they lose. But chess teaches you that today you are a loser, but tomorrow you will be a winner. Even when you are a student. A young boy fails an exam and goes, "I don't like this subject" or "The professor is bad", etcetera. Chess teaches you to fight.'

Nowadays there is a tendency among young players not to smoke. Did you pay any special attention to the physical aspects of chess?
'No, not particularly. But I think that now it is very important. It is important not to smoke when you are a young player. Also very important, I will tell you a beautiful story, is your sex life. Sex before the game is very bad for chess players. I can tell you this story. I was playing in Saltsjöbaden and my wife came to Sweden as well. But after a few days I told her to go home. She didn't understand and said to me, "But I love you. I came here because I want to be together." So I told her, "Do you

know why I want you to go home? Why? Because I love you too much (smiles)." Loving is not bad, but loving too much...'

You just mentioned that Alekhine spoke to you in Russian. Today English is the lingua franca in the chess world. What languages did you speak with the great masters of the past?
'You know I was born in Poland, so my mother language was Polish. At school I was taught German. So I speak both German and Polish very well. Then I speak, because I'm a Jew, Yiddish, some Hebrew. I travelled to so many countries that I never really studied languages. I speak a little bit of English, a little bit of French. I can make myself understood in eight languages. A couple of chess players speak a wonderful number of languages. One of them is Ljubojevic. O'Kelly was wonderful. Larsen. But normally speaking we are talking in chess language and for that purpose one thousand words is enough. Because d4-d5 is the same in every language. Our language is d4-d5.'

Have you often been back to Poland?
'Yes, I went back, but now I have some problems in talking Polish. I arrived in Argentina in 1939 and now it is 1992. That's 53 years in Argentina and 29 years in Poland. I went back several times to Poland. In 1945 when the war was over I returned for the first time, because when I left I had a daughter of three years old and maybe someone had taken care of her. I was looking for all my family, but I didn't see them back. This was the reason why after Groningen 1946 I travelled on to Prague and played in Warsaw. After that visit I have been in Poland four or five times. To see my old friends. But they are very old now or have died. Do you know that the Pope is a good chess player? He wrote a book on chess problems. Yes, this is true. I know him personally. Even now, when he has time, he still looks at chess problems. I received a letter from him. I put one of his problems in my newspaper and sent my column to him. And he replied and thanked me.'

You knew Alekhine well...
'Of course. A man like Kasparov. He loved chess very much. I know a history about him. In 1939 in Buenos Aires he comes to my room and says, "Miguel, I invite you to dinner." So, we went and then he said "I want to see some chess." There happened to be a tournament, category five or six, very far from the centre. One hour by car. Alekhine had heard about it and persuaded me to take a taxi with him and go there. I had told him, "Doctor, it's not interesting", but he insisted to go there. So we came there and he was looking around and writing down things and then he told me, "Miguel, they are all patzers!" I said, "That's what I told you, but you wouldn't believe me (laughs loudly)." He loved chess.'

Do you think that Alekhine wrote the anti-semitic articles in the Pariser Zeitung?
'(Without hesitation) I believe so. You want to know a beautiful history? In Mar del Plata they always organized a beautiful grandmaster tournament in which all the

great players took part. I am a lucky man, because I won about ten tournaments out of twelve. I beat Stein. I won my first game against Euwe in this tournament and came first with a three and a half points difference. These were my best years, from 1940 to 1950. So, when we were playing in this tournament in 1946, the president of the Argentine Federation, Paulino Monasterio, comes to the club and says, "Please, stop the clocks. I have some bad news for you. The champion of the world, Alexander Alekhine, has died in Lisbon. I would like you to be silent in his honour for one minute." Everyone stood up, except for Miguel Najdorf. Why? Because I had learned about these articles. That he was a Nazi. So he was one of the people who killed my family. He was a very good chess player, but I cannot stand it when someone says "Heil Hitler". What would you have done in my place? I will never forget that. A couple of months later I was taking a ride in a taxi in Buenos Aires. The taxi-driver said to me, "Aren't you Mr. Najdorf?" "Yes". "I don't like you. You are a bad man." I asked him why. "I am not a chess player, but I read the newspaper and I read the story about Alekhine and that everybody stood up except for you. How could you do that? He was the champion of the world and a genius?" So I told him, "Do you know my history?" "No." "I lost three hundred persons. My father, my mother, my daughter, my wife, everybody. And he was a collaborator, a big Nazi. He was one of the people who killed my family. So what would you have done in my place?" The taxi-driver didn't say a word. When we arrived at my office and I wanted to pay he told me, "I don't charge you. I apologize. Please give me your signature. I didn't know your history."

'I believe that Alekhine wrote these articles. I will tell you why. Alekhine was not a Nazi. He was an opportunist. A terrible man. He loved money very much and for money he would be Jew, Catholic or Protestant. Just depending on how much. He had no morals. One of the greatest chess players of all time. When he came to Germany they just told him to write these articles and he did.

'I can tell you a story. At the Karpov-Kortchnoi match in Baguio I was the correspondent for *Clarin*, my newspaper. When I was in Baguio someone called me from Tehran, from Iran. From Manila I was going through Bangkok to Paris. This man told me that he was the director of the Iranian television and that it would be his pleasure if I stayed in Tehran for a couple of days. Not to play chess, but to give some lectures on the match. They offered me a certain amount and I accepted. They took me to the television studios. This director was not a chess player and it was a few weeks before the Shah was expelled by Khomeini's followers. You remember that Khomeini prohibited to play chess. I found myself in a political situation when this director asked me to say some favourable words about the Shah and all the things he had done for the country. I told him that I was Argentine and that I had no views on their political life. And that secondly I was a chess player and my only language was d4-d5. I could say that he was very nice, I could say that the girls were beautiful, I could say anything. If you ask me about chess I can answer any question. But not about politics. They kept begging me, but I refused until I finally came up with this. I said, "I want to tell you something. The one who will most remember the Shah is not the Iranian people, but me." "You? Why?" "Because in many languages, German, Polish, Russian, chess is 'schach', the name of the king of Persia. Every day I play ten games and keep repeating 'Schach, schach, schach.' So I will think more about your king than you will." He explained me that that was not political enough, but I explained that I could do nothing more.'

Before he came here to play in the Olympiad for Bosnia Predrag Nikolic stayed at your place because it was unsafe to return to his hometown Sarajevo which was under siege. Did his fate remind you strongly of your own situation in 1939?

'His situation is very similar to mine in 1939. His family is in Sarajevo. But bad as the situation is, Sarajevo now cannot be compared to the times of Hitler of course. Nikolic is a wonderful man. That is another thing. In chess you have many good players. But not so many gentlemen, senors. If you ask me who are or were the biggest gentlemen in the world, I can tell you. I knew Spielmann, I knew Bogoljubow, I knew Capablanca, I knew Nimzowitsch, I knew Alekhine. Somebody once asked me who was the biggest gentleman in chess? You know who? Max Euwe. Tartakower. Keres was one. Akiba Rubinstein, Nikolic, Jan Timman. Not Kasparov. Not Karpov.'

What makes up a real gentleman in chess?

'You can be a strong player and not be honest. Kasparov is not a gentleman. He is not sympathetic. He's a god. You cannot be a god. The Israeli Government asked Einstein to be their president. And Einstein told them, "I am too big an idiot to be President (roars with laughter)." You understand? I am too big an idiot to be your president. Einstein. Albert Einstein. In former days there were more gentlemen who played chess. That's why in Buenos Aires my first aim is not to organize a strong tournament, but a tournament for gentlemen. I would never invite Kamsky[19]. I don't like problems. I would not invite Kortchnoi. Nobody wants to play Kortchnoi, because he thinks "If I want to play I must want to kill my partner." In private Kortchnoi is not a bad man, very sympathetic. But during the game it is terrible. He wants to kill you. Every year now, in April, when I have my birthday, I organize a big tournament, which costs me about one hundred and twenty thousand dollars. I believe this is the first time in chess history that a chess grandmaster is at the same time a Maecenas. Normally chess players don't spend money. They take money. It costs me one hundred and twenty to one hundred and fifty thousand dollars each year. My aim is twofold. Of course I want a strong tournament, but at the same time all these players should be gentlemen. In the old days the girls cost me money. Now it's chess (laughs).'

---

19 Kamsky shared first prize with Shirov in the tournament Najdorf organized the following year.

Bent Larsen

Brussels, April 1987
Prague, August 1990
Cannes, February 1993

'To win is the main thing'

You talk about his great victories and he will tell you that Havana '67 was special because for the first time in his life he went to thirteen different night clubs in seventeen rounds. You bring up the subject of faster time-controls and he will come up with a Romanian experiment in 1964 where they tried 45 moves in two and a half. You drop the name Enevoldsen, five-times Danish champion in the 1940s, and instantly he will ask you: 'Did you know that after Folkestone 1933 Enevoldsen walked home? Via Antwerp?' Apart from listening a lot, talking to Bent Larsen is going for a never-ending journey through the realm of chess. A journey that may easily be interrupted for an exposé on young Danish cinematographers or some statistics on earth quakes. Small wonder that this interview was not done in some lost hour between rounds. Actually it started in 1987, was continued in 1990 and finished, or rather, was taken up again in 1993.

This is not only an interview but also a story about an interview. A story that began almost six years ago at the second SWIFT. tournament in Brussels, the first ever event where the bitter rivals Kasparov, Karpov and Kortchnoi played together. New In Chess produced the daily bulletins and had also been commissioned to record this historic occasion in a tournament book. Having just taken my first eager steps into chess journalism I was looking forward to doing some work at this marvellous gathering of chess stars. I couldn't believe my luck when unforeseen circumstances forced Wim Andriessen to throw me right into the deep end by asking me to write the round reports and the interviews for the book.

High on my list of celebrity interviewees was Bent Larsen. Ever since his emigration to Argentina in 1982 the great Danish fighter had become an ever rarer guest at European tournaments. Obviously this was a splendid opportunity to meet the first Western player of the postwar era to put the wind up the Soviets, who established his name amongst the very best when he won the Amsterdam Interzonal in 1964, the first of three Interzonals he was to win. Boldly he took the lead and did not waver when he faced five consecutive Soviets in the final rounds. Larsen.

Who won so many tournaments in his magic years 1967 and 1968. He came first in five international tournaments on the trot, including Havana and the Sousse Interzonal, a feat he followed up by winning three Opens. Who played in Hastings three times in thirty-one years, but who conquered when he came. In 1956(!) he shared first place with Gligoric. In 1973 he claimed unshared first. A couple of months before Brussels he had been back to Hastings for a third time and, guess what, in the 1987 edition he had shared first with Chandler and Lputian !

My only worry was that I had not unearthed many interviews with Larsen during my background research in the chess department of the Royal Library in The Hague. Did he have a thing with interviews

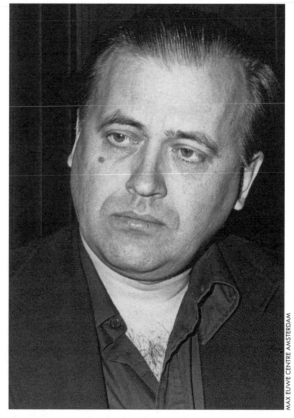

Bent Larsen: 'After losing the match against Fischer in 1971, I win Hastings and I win Teeside. Immediately.'

or was he just reluctant to give them? Any such fears were quickly dispelled at the opening ceremony. His answer to my request was one that will not be forgotten. 'Yes, of course. No problem. Call me any time between ten in the evening and three in the morning.'

A splendid interview seemed in the offing, an expectation which blossomed into certainty when Larsen proved to be in great shape and got off to a roaring start in Brussels. After five rounds he was on plus three and shared second place with Ljubojevic, half a point behind Kasparov, who was picking off the opposition like sparrows. At this point, he told me later, he was convinced that he was going to win the tournament.

And what was the ambitious reporter doing instead of calling Larsen somewhere between ten in the evening and three in the morning now the time was ripe? Well, he was enjoying the fascinating tournament to the full and putting off till the final week what should have been done today. This proved to be a costly mistake. With the wisdom of hindsight one could say that the seventeen-move collapse Larsen suffered against Kortchnoi in Round 6 was the first sign of the imminent gall-bladder attack that was to affect the remainder of his games.

When I finally got round to giving Larsen a late-night call, I knew that he wasn't in the best of forms. But I still was mightily nervous when at half past eleven I took a seat opposite to the man I had been so eager to talk to. Pale and motionless Larsen listened to my often clumsy questions, while the bleak light in the room did little to dispel my unease. Listening back to the two hours of tape years later I find it difficult to understand why I was so bitterly disappointed afterwards. True, Larsen is not at his best, but the tone and manner in which he answers my haphazard list of questions bespoke goodwill and great patience. My dissatisfaction was to lead to two more sessions in Prague and Cannes, which I will come to below. Let's first sample the juicy bits from the Brussel Tapes.

(Some weeks after the tournament Larsen sent two analyses from the SWIFT. tournament to the New In Chess office, with a note containing a comment on his physical state which is funny enough to enter chess history. 'I am better now. But I am afraid to explain illnesses in English since the time Najdorf's haemorrhage became hemorrhoids in *Schaakbulletin*.')

When you look at the recent developments in chess, the information boom, the professionalization, which are the things that you don't like?
'I don't like ratings for instance. Nothing is wrong with the rating system, but the way people read it is very wrong. It's an interesting way of summing up the results of the last few years. If you're into that. But apart from that... It's one of the new gods. People think they have no religions anymore, but they have lots of religions. For a lot of people it's the Elo-rating. In the statistics it should appear not far below the great religions. No, I'm serious. In these statistics there are sects which have probably fewer followers than Elo. As for the question of information, there are things in it that are terrible. If a normal player studies all the games in the *Informant* or in the New In Chess Yearbooks, that is much more than enough. People get more information than they can digest. And they get a lot of information that they don't even understand. There is not much to do about that. Even one hundred years ago or more they analysed a lot of variations of the Evans Gambit and everyone copied what Anderssen or Zukertort had played. It's not so new. But it's a little strange when young chess students get all this information without really understanding it. In some fashionable openings they know a lot of moves and they play against young players of the same kind. Therefore it looks as if they play like grandmasters in the Najdorf Variation of the Sicilian. But apart from these twenty moves they don't play very well (laughs).

'I normally get out of the books as quickly as possible; if possible on move two. Recently I played 1.e4 e6 2.b3. Now we're out of the books. On move five I intended to play h4 and then we would have definitely been out of the books. It's the following position, 1.e4 e6 2.b3 d5 3.♗b2 ♘f6 4.e5 and now he played

Knight d7, but if he had played Knight g8 I would have played 5.h4. The general idea is to see at once if Black can get square f5. My next move is h5 and if Black plays h5, I play Bishop e2 threatening his pawn, and if he has to play g6 he is already weakened. An excellent idea. A few days later I saw a Chilean master by the name of Campos actually play this. So, there is somebody who understands me.'

How should a young player go about it if he wants to improve his chess?
'He should study master games with master notes. Of course, the lack of language in the books I mentioned is also a sad thing. But I cannot change it.'

One of the great grandmasters you were brought up on was Nimzowitsch.
'Yeah. There was a strong Nimzowitsch tradition in Denmark. The best players when I was young had known him personally and he wrote very much. There is a Danish book about Nimzowitsch by B. Nilsson. I got that book when I was thirteen or something and liked it very much. Much better than *My System*. It's not trying to be a manual. Just a collection of good games with interesting notes by Nimzo-witsch and some others. It's called *Nimzowitsch, Denmark's Chess Teacher*. I completely read it to shreds.'

From the stories I know Nimzowitsch was quite a character. How was he looked upon as a person in Denmark?
'He was, of course, a strange person. He became quite accepted, including his nervousness and so on. He had a lot of humour. But he was very nervous, probably because of some events during the Revolution and during his escape from Russia. He never talked about this much. His nerves also got better in Denmark and he became accepted because he was good at giving lectures with something funny in it. The tragic thing was that he only lived in Denmark for twelve years before he died at 48 years of age.'

Did he also learn the language?
'He learned the language very well. I have somewhere a postcard he wrote after he had been in Denmark for one year. There are no misspellings. He was good at languages. Maybe he learned some Swedish first, because he was two years in Sweden first. That would have been a good introduction to Danish. He mixed his Danish with some Latin and German, but later this became part of Danish chess terminology.'

You're not too bad at languages either. I understand that you speak some Russian.
'I speak some Russian. I may have been able to write a word or two in Russian, but not anymore. I learned Russian in the Army Language school when I couldn't avoid military service anymore. Because I had good high-school marks I got into the Army Language school and that means Russian.'

But you didn't have to work as a spy or something?
'No, not as a spy. These intelligence services work very badly. First they take you in and then they start studying you and find out that you've travelled in Eastern Europe. So I could not be authorized for top secret work and then they didn't know what to do with me.'

Did you study a lot of Russian chess literature?
'Yes, for a long time I studied *Shakhmatny Bulletin*. But there's not much text in it. Now I use it less. And also books, of course, but not so much as people would imagine.'

In 1970 you stunned the Dutch television watchers by answering a few questions by the writer Godfried Bomans in his own language.
'Well, I had been reading Euwe's *Losbladige* from 1952 till 1970 or something like that. It's not such a difficult language. It's simplified German. Or German is complicated Dutch. You have to speak your languages when you're from a small country. Spanish was so to speak my latest acquisition. I never studied it. I went to live in Spain in 1974. For several reasons. For the climate, for tax reasons. Las Palmas is very nice. I'm not overly fond of extreme heat, but the Canary Islands being there in the middle of all that water, you don't get more warmth than you can take. In Buenos Aires the air is also very humid. That is not such a pleasant climate.'

Over the years you've met many grandmasters. Do you share Timman's idea that in general grandmasters get on well?
'Yes, they get on very well. It's different if you're a boxer or a footballer. You may be in the same hotel for one night. But during a chess tournament you're together and often eat together for something like three weeks. It would be tragic if they didn't get along. Of course, there are some cases of players being enemies. Most of these cases are of players from the same country.'

Whose company do or did you prefer?
'Well, at one time, many years ago, Donner was very interesting company.'

Many grandmasters invariably mention Keres.
'Yes, but Keres is not interesting. Not interesting at all. He was a polished gentleman and never made anybody angry. About his personal history he would say very little, he generally stayed away from these themes. Some Estonian refugees in Canada may have known more about this. Many Baltic refugees in Canada told me such things. Secretly they were hoping that on his next trip to Canada he would stay. People admired his quiet and balanced way, but in general I find that is not so interesting. People are more interesting when they're not so smooth. I prefer conflicting views. Not too much, just a little. When I was young I found it very interesting at times to talk to Botvinnik. With most of the other Soviets it was impossible to talk about

politics, because they had not thought about it and just told you what *Pravda* had said about the last Party Congress. With Botvinnik you could have very correct discussions. At one time he was a convinced Stalinist. He wrote a booklet about chess and Marxism with the thesis that Marxism is the only sound basis for really good chess. Around 1970 he moved away from many viewpoints he had had before.'

What about the other Soviet players?
'Well, Bronstein was very interesting. A very nervous type, but with many interesting ideas. Many things. He believed in telepathy and all these things. I didn't. He told me examples from chess. For instance, you look at a position together and then you say exactly what the other was going to say. I don't think that is strange, because you are both strong grandmasters. You know many of the same things. Why shouldn't you think the same thing?'

How did you experience Fischer ?
'Fischer I had quite normal relations with. And I was his second when he was sixteen. Normally when you could get Fischer to the table and the board there were not so many problems. There were not so many problems with Fischer and the other players. The problems he had were with organizers, journalists and photographers. Of course, he also created problems with some players when his rules totally dominated the others. When the organizers wanted to do anything for Mr. Fischer. Afraid that Mr. Fischer would leave the tournament, you know (grins). That is annoying.'

How did you come to be asked as his second?
'His mother wrote to me. I never met her so I never got much of an impression. The trouble was that they had to take a European second to save travel costs and that Fischer had said that it could only be Larsen or Donner. Because she had done something terrible. She had employed O'Kelly and when Bobby found out he was very angry. If it had to be a European it had to be Larsen or Donner (laughs). He had met me at the Interzonal and the two of us at this tournament in Zürich. We got along very well.'

Did you try to give Fischer any advice?
'Yes, but he wouldn't take it. He knew everything. Still, I was probably not useless. Also what happened was that between I think Rounds 6 and 9 he lost three games in four rounds. Then he knew he wasn't going to win the tournament and from that moment onwards he didn't want to analyse much anymore. That made my job much easier.'

Earlier on you mentioned Nimzowitsch. Were there other great examples, guides that inspired you?
'I don't know, but I know two people who made me switch from the King's Gambit to the Catalan. Tartakower and Barcza. Tartakower wrote about the Barcza system in

the Danish magazine. I had been playing the King's Gambit and then I started to play this completely different opening and with that I became a grandmaster. This is one of the many examples that some openings you have to play when you're young. Then they give good results. Later they don't give such good results and they lose their surprise value.'

That doesn't sound much like a search for objectivity.
'It's very nice to want absolute truth, but you won't find it. Tournament chess has to do with beating your opponent. It has nothing to do with finding the truth in the Najdorf Variation or anything. It's just beating your opponent. Winning a pawn or whatever. To win is the main thing.'

So the German title of your games collection is not 'Ich spiele auf Sieg' for nothing.
'Several titles were suggested. Kühnle, the publisher, wanted a good title and I don't know if this was his or my suggestion.'

You always liked to fight till the bitter end?
'Yes, terribly. It gives you a lot of long games. That's not good. Maybe for this reason the new time-control is better for me. Now games get longer because people are no longer afraid of adjournments. Many games that now last sixty moves would not have lasted 16 moves in the old schedule. People drew games at move 16 because they were afraid to adjourn at move forty.'

Did you have any examples in mind when you were writing your own book?
'I don't think I did. A book I liked at that time was Keres' *Ausgewählte Partien*, but I was not trying to copy it or find the same style. It is strange how fifty or more years ago many games collections had very short notes. For instance, the typical Capablanca comment is, "Here the improvement Knight g5 has been suggested, but I have analysed this and I can assure you that it loses as well." Without giving any variations! Typically Capablanca. He is not a player I have much sympathy for. He was lazy, a playboy, and didn't give much to chess. He didn't study much, only played well.'

If you were to draw up your list of the greatest players of all time you would seriously take into account their merits for the game?
'Yes, and that would mean that people like Steinitz and Nimzowitsch would come much higher than Capablanca. Alekhine would come much higher, too. When they ask about the greatest player I don't know what that means. How can you ask such a question? Then I answer Philidor, because he was fifty or seventy years ahead of his time, while the others were only five years ahead of theirs. Of course, time moves faster these days, but still as an answer Philidor is as good as any. Was Morphy the greatest player of all time? He played only 35 master games. That's a bit silly. The question is unfair.'

You mentioned the opening switch that helped you get the grandmaster title. The first grandmaster you beat was Osip Bernstein at the 1954 Olympiad on the day that he celebrated his 72nd birthday. Did you meet many of the great players that now seem to belong to a far and distant past?
'I met Bohatirchuk, for instance.'

Who?
'Bohatirchuk, the Soviet co-champion of 1927. He was a Ukrainian who escaped to Canada after World War II. I met him there. That was someone from the past. He was very sad that he had lost a book by Botvinnik with a dedication that played on the fact that he had beaten Botvinnik three times. One of the games was in '35. Or Edward Lasker. Him I've known quite well. Champion of Berlin 1910, of London 1913, of New York 1921, I think. I met him several times. He was in Montreal in 1979, when he was 94. He gave an interview to a very charming girl. Afterwards he said, "I don't like to give interviews to people who don't know who Steinitz was." (laughs) Whom he had known. I don't remember how, because I do not see how it could be. It must have been somewhere in Europe when he was a boy of twelve or thirteen.'

You said that the main thing that mattered in chess was winning. Did it disturb you when you won the Sousse Interzonal after Fischer had left the tournament after a seven out of eight start?
'What was annoying was that everything had become reduced to the question, "Does Fischer play or not?". For instance the day he returned for the second time and played with Reshevsky, that day the rest of the players could hardly play. When he finally got out of the tournament, which was to be expected sooner or later, it came as a relief. Now we could play. There were terrible things. Reshevsky was very busy negotiating that if Fischer withdrew, his points would not be counted. I don't know whether as an orthodox Jew he was allowed to conduct negotiations on a Saturday, but that's what he did. Gligoric and I retired from the whole thing a bit. It was very disturbing to have a player leaving the tournament all the time. They had made a special program for Reshevsky with all these free days because he was a Jew. I asked Bobby at the opening ceremony, "What is this? You also want these free days? But you don't respect them?" And he said, "I don't want to talk about it now." That was his mistake. He started talking two weeks later, when it was too late to change it. Then he made some very bad suggestions. He claimed that he couldn't play five days in a row and suggested a change that implied that somebody else would have to do that. It was very difficult to understand him in these things. At that time he was already involved in this Armstrong's Church of God. But he also had some Jewish ideas. It was a bit difficult to find out how he was religiously. There was also something strange with this Armstrong Church. Bobby lived far away from their centre in New York. Their centre was in Pasadena. But he was more strict than the others just to make sure he wouldn't do anything wrong. For instance, on Saturdays he ate in his hotel room. That wasn't necessary, but he wasn't quite sure.'

~ ~ ~

Three years went by. Occasionally I would come across the Brussels Tapes that were sitting patiently on a shelf among an increasing number of new tapes, and wonder whether I should write an article based on the material I had. I always came to the same conclusion: There was enough in it to write such an article, but in the case of Bent Larsen more material to illustrate his many-sided personality was called for.

The occasion I had been hoping for cropped up in the summer of 1990, when Bessel Kok had another of his bright ideas to combine business and pleasure. In Prague he organized a small chess tournament to pay a tribute to Czechoslovakia's new-found democracy. Bent Larsen did not play in the tournament but flew to the city of the Velvet Revolution to attend a GMA Board meeting. This time I came better prepared and was more successful in getting across what my questions were meant to mean. Yet, the ultimate result was once again not to my complete satisfaction. Due to a crammed program of meetings, dinners and an official reception by president Havel, Larsen found only one hour to respond to my questions. He was also slightly out of sorts with a nasty case of jet-lag. This time it was a very lively conversation I had with him in the nightclub of the Intercontinental Hotel that convinced me that the Prague Tapes were not going to round off my Bent Larsen project either. Which does not mean that they did not contain interesting material.

You've been around on the international chess scene for more than three decades. Do you endorse the much heard complaint that the grandmaster title has devaluated?
'Yes, the grandmaster title has been devaluated, but I admit that with many more tournaments, with more players trying to become grandmasters, it is only natural that there are more grandmasters. But, yes, it has been devaluated.'

How do the grandmasters of, say, the fifties and the sixties compare with today's leading grandmasters?
'The best grandmasters of the fifties were very, very strong. But you can say that much more about the grandmasters of the sixties. They were so strong that for instance the Russians had a generation problem, which is reflected in some other countries too. This generation was so strong that the younger generation could not push through. A lot of young masters who should have become strong grandmasters or world champions gave up. There is something I am very proud of. Do you know the last book Keres wrote? It was published in Estonia, a readership of less than three million people and, despite the paper rationing, in 15000 copies. He wrote it together with Nei and the title was 4x25. The book contains 25 games from Spassky, Fischer, Kortchnoi and me. I was most pleased when I got this book. Those were tough guys. Those four and some others. They ruined the chess careers of a lot of softish people. (With a broad grin) I am sorry about that, but I am not. They ruined them in a way different from how Botvinnik ruled Soviet chess for a long time. His role was to be number one.

'Imagine the number of tournaments the four of us won. Quite depressing. Fischer didn't win too many, but Kortchnoi did and so did I, and Spassky won a few too. Later Tal, when he shot up and became World Champion also impressed so terribly. A lot of people were scared of Tal. I am proud to believe that a lot of people were scared of Kortchnoi and me, too. I'm sure they were. Look at the bad positions we won. That was not because they had bad technique. It's because they were scared (laughs sarcastically). So, how do they compare? It's not easy and not fair to compare them. There are more strong players now. The top is not better, but it's broader.'

Is it true that for you a tournament was or is practically a failure if you don't win it?
'There was a time when I thought that you should only congratulate me if I won. I could be satisfied tying for first, but I didn't do it many times. Look at Petrosian, he was different. Petrosian hardly won a tournament in his life. He won a couple of tournaments, but the normal thing for Petrosian was to tie for first. People come to you and congratulate you on a second or third prize (smiles). I know they mean well, and I don't insult them, but maybe I'll laugh a little bit and maybe I'll tell them.'

At the peak of your tournament career there was this dispute with Fischer about first board in the USSR vs The Rest of the World Match in Belgrade in 1970.
'There was not much of a dispute between Fischer and me. Euwe had been, let's say, a swine. He had given Fischer first board based on some thinking along the lines "Well, there will be no problem with Larsen". I told the Yugoslavs that I would not play and they invited me as a journalist. That was nice. I didn't expect the match to be very interesting, but it became more interesting than I had expected. I knew there were some talks going on, but I didn't want to influence them and quietly went for a walk. When I came back there were all these people, like an army, and the man who is in front of them, a Yugoslav organizer, is smiling. Because Fischer had said, "Yes, let Larsen play first board. What's the problem?" Fischer has said later that he liked it. He hadn't played for one and a half years and was a little rusty. Fischer's words, yeah, yeah.'

It has often been suggested that you never fully recovered from the 6-0 Candidates' loss against Fischer.
'No, I don't see that. After losing the match in 1971, I win Hastings and I win Teeside. Immediately.'

Did you ever analyse or evaluate clinically what happened during and after your match against Fischer?
'Yes, I did. I was very badly treated. Fischer played his first match against Taimanov just north of the border, financed more than half by the USCF. I now expected to be forced to play just south of the border financed by the USCF. Denmark is a small country and I didn't have any support from my federation, so I finally agreed to play in the United States. I hated to play in Tijuana or something like that or Mexico City. There were no other bids. So I agree. Otherwise they might have done like they did with Taimanov,

when they had the match in Vancouver but with fifty per cent of the budget being paid by the USCF. So, the USCF is running the show and that is very unpleasant.

'If you asked me about mistakes in this match I could say that I might have called the Meteorological Institute in Denmark and they would probably have helped me. I could have asked them, "How is the weather in Colorado just now?" And then I would not have gone. They had the hottest summer in that place in 35 years. And very, very dry. This is not for me. I cannot sleep. It is absolutely impossible. After Round 2 I asked to see the doctor. The bad thing is that the doctor is part of the organization. He just thought that I am someone who always runs around with a high blood pressure and doesn't believe that I am not. He would be ready to have me not play on this day but over the weekend they really hoped to have some spectators. They had very few spectators, of course. I met two young chess players from Denver in the supermarket and they didn't know that the match was going on there. The United States is like that. That is why such organizers are desperate. He may postpone this game, but it is obvious that he is not going to postpone Saturday or Sunday's game. I have to just put down my foot and leave or I have to play on. I didn't put down my foot.

'This was a very unpleasant situation and, of course, I had no help from the Danish chess federation. It was very much a question of dry air and a little lack of oxygen. Fischer could take these things better. These things are not the same for everybody. because Fischer was able to play tennis, maybe an hour, just before the game. It doesn't sound like the best preparation for a game, but the idea is simply to get more oxygen in. He could do that and I couldn't. These are not equal conditions.

'After Game 2 I knew the match was lost. I should have won Game 2. Ask Piket's father. He's the one who pointed that out really. There was some really bad analysis going around the world, but Piket's father pointed out exactly how I should have won. After Game 2 I considered the match lost. Also that is not normal. Game 3 was played on climatically the worst of these days and I lost a pawn in the opening. All very sad, but, well, nothing to do about it.'

~ ~ ~

In Brussels I had not dared to tell Larsen that I intended to shelve the tapes he had filled so generously. In Prague I immediately told him that we needed one more session. If that was what I wanted, he retorted without a trace of indignation, then so be it. Again we had to wait close to three years. The 1993 *Festival des Jeux* in Cannes offered several good reasons for a visit to the Côte d'Azur. Easily the best reason for me, however, was Larsen's presence on occasion of a GMA Board meeting. Three eventful years lay behind us. The Soviet Union no longer existed, Yugoslavia was being ripped apart by a gruesome war and Bobby Fischer had returned to chess. On the evening of the Board meeting we met in the *Palais de Festival*, the epicentre of the annual film festival, to continue our talk. Again Larsen effortlessly filled a one-hour tape. And I made up my mind. Was the Cannes Tape the tape that completed my interview? No, of course it was not. However, to this conclusion I had already come when I was thinking the matter over on the plane to Nice. The idea of a rounded-off interview with any player is an illusion. With a fascinating and versatile personality like Bent Larsen even more so. After three meetings the time had come to at least try to write the interview that I had been daydreaming about in Brussels six years ago.

What chess thoughts came to mind when you saw the Soviet Union disintegrate?
'I remembered the second time I was in Moscow. That was in 1959. At that time they were talking in the chess federation how wonderful it would be for the federation to be free. If they could do their own business, they could make money. They could pay everybody, trainers and so on. But alas they were under government control. I understand that now they have their freedom it scared them a little bit (laughs). But it doesn't totally change the country. There is so much chess in all the parts of the former Soviet Union that it will not suddenly disappear. Maybe a lot of chess trainers are out of work now, but the fact that they play a lot of chess and have a lot of strong players will not change. The funny part is that for the top players it is now economically much better than before. It is now in the open that for the Soviet Union these are very rich people. Down to medium grandmasters they are some sort of upper class now. I think that chess in the former Soviet Union is still prestigious for the reasons why it was prestigious before and also because of the money.'

You must have been shocked more by the events in Yugoslavia.
'What happens there is terrible. Most chess masters with some experience have been to Yugoslavia many times. I was there for the first time in 1955. That is a long time back. What happens there is tragic and terrible. Not much you can say about it.'

How strongly did you experience these national divisions when you were there?
'Not very strong. Sometimes you had some of these jokes. Like the first time I saw Pirc and Trifunovic, people told me that Trifunovic says that Pirc is the secret police and Pirc says that Trifunovic is the secret police. That was very funny. Of course, they didn't like each other very much. Pirc is from Slovenia and Trifunovic is a Serb. And he was a state employee already before World War II. He had an education in law and later he was in the service of the Interior Ministery. But that doesn't automatically make him a spy or a secret agent. Apart from such jokes I have never seen many things that resembled ethnic conflicts. It is a terrible tragedy. I know history and know that terrible things happened in World War II. But I thought that was so long ago. I don't like to see that forty or fifty years is not enough.'

Were you stunned to learn that Fischer was making his comeback there?
'I did not believe it when I heard it, but I said at once, "Well, if he really wants to play then it sounds logical that it's there." It didn't disappoint me on Fischer's part

or anything. I thought it was wrong to have the match there. When you talk about a United Nations boycott, chess players should not try to stay aloof, trying to make themselves something special.'

Were you delighted by the idea in itself?
'It's nice. It's the closest you can get to the old question what happens if two hundred years ago you freeze Philidor or maybe sixty years ago you freeze Alekhine and later you take him out of the icebox and see what happens. This is the closest you can get to this old fantasy. Of course, we didn't see a Fischer model '72, but there is no doubt that he improved during the match. We really still don't know how strong he is now. When you're five points ahead, neither you nor your opponent plays at your or his best. He obviously improved during the match, although it wasn't a good match towards the end. But it was quite obvious during the first part of the match that he was studying and improving and probably getting used to it again.

'Game 1 was very good, but it was very easy. Some of the other games also showed confidence. For instance, Game 7 with the b4-pawn sacrifice. Not a clear pawn sacrifice, but it is nice, a good idea. When you get the idea you either do it or you don't do it. But if he does it, it shows that he is beginning to enjoy it and to believe in himself.'

What did you think of his general behaviour? Had it grown worse or was it just the same?
'Some of the things he said at the press conference were rather terrible. The journalists should protect him against that and should never publish this. Some of what he said was rather childish. I mean, when you're asked whether you are an anti-Semite and then start all over again that the Arabs are also a semitic people. That is a little childish. We know that from very early in school. If he doesn't like the question he should just say that he doesn't want to answer it. Some of these things were very bad. Most of it was horrible reading. It was not only because of him but also because of some of the questions.'

Many people believe that Mr. Vasiljevic's money is rather suspect. Is this something the chess world has not seen before?
'At that level and of that size it is pretty new. I don't know if Vasiljevic's money was in any way suspect. There have sometimes been plans by some people of whom you didn't understand where they got their money from. Normally these plans don't happen. It's basically new that it is so much.'

Have you ever been involved in or approached for something shady?
'I have once done something I don't like to do, which was to play a tournament that made propaganda for nicotine. I even played two such tournaments. The second one was at least in a tobacco-growing district in the Philippines. The question of smoking or not smoking is not a very hot question in the Philippines. There are a

couple of tournaments that I have said no to for political reasons. But I have never published these political reasons. For instance I boycotted Greece for some time after the colonels took over.

'I admire a South African lawyer who called me and with whom I had only a very short conversation. The whole conversation may have lasted less than three minutes. He put the question about the tournament he was planning very correctly and I told him that I was not interested in getting an invitation. And he thanked me very much.

'When you make a point because a government has a certain colour, there is the question how long such a boycott should last. Sooner or later you may say that that is obviously the government that they have and that they maybe even like. You cannot go on saying for many many years that a military dictatorship is horrible and that they should kick them out, if they don't. Then sooner or later you must accept that as that country's government.'

Where do you see yourself in the political spectrum?
'You cannot compare your own political ideas or a party from one country with a party from another country. But in the political spectrum I am a bourgeois when they talk about money. And a little further more left when they talk about almost anything else. It is very nice to have ideas, but it is very often the money that decides whether you can have them or not (laughs). If I had been a politician in Denmark, and the opportunity has existed several times, I would have been in a non-socialist party, which is exactly in the centre.'

Do you have the idea that you have changed a lot over the years?
'Not a lot. But if I try to think of my political views when I was seventeen, that is when I finished high school, then it is remarkable how I never believed in street demonstrations. There I might have changed my opinion during the last five years. It's just incredible to see what happened just because one hundred thousand nice citizens decided to have a little walk or stand in some big square. And how effec-tive these demonstrations were. The people of Leipzig and Dresden took to the streets and that I thought very surprising, because I thought they had no leaders. In Czechoslovakia they had leaders. In East Germany the people who could have been leaders had been allowed to leave many years ago. That has changed my idea about the effectiveness of such demonstrations. And there are some other things. When I was seventeen, you must realize, that was so close to the War, I was more conserv-ative than I am now. Most people go in the other direction. I am not a leftist, but I sympathize with them on more things than I did when I was seventeen.'

Have your views on chess and the role of the game in your life changed greatly since you first started to play chess?
'My views on chess when I was seventeen, that is very easy. I started engineering. Chess was obviously something you couldn't live on in Denmark. Denmark is

an amateur country. They got their first professional football league in 1978. In Holland you got it in 1959, I believe. People in Denmark are anti-professional in some ways. For some good or bad reasons.'

Has chess been an inescapable vocation in life for you or would you prefer to see it as a job in the first place?
'It was obviously what made it possible for me not to have another job. I could have imagined to have another job, though. Now it's not so realistic, but I could have imagined very well going into politics twenty years ago. That would have been very logical. I decided not to do it several times. It was tempting even, because my father's most important thing in life was politics. I decided not to fulfil my father's ambitions in that respect.

'I also decided several times not to become FIDE-president. I was asked several times and a couple of times it was probably serious. But I had decided long ago that the answer was a quick no.'

Six years ago you were immensely active as a chess journalist. You wrote a daily column, two weekly columns and one biweekly. How busy are you these days?
'I am still writing for *Extrabladet* every day. I lost the provincial newspaper chain. This provincial newspaper chain broke up and the remaining newspapers thought me too expensive. And I lost *Expressen*, the largest Swedish newspaper. That's much worse.'

Next week you will be in Denmark to play an exhibition match of four games against Deep Blue, IBM's successor to Deep Thought. In the history of computer chess you have the dubious honour of being the first grandmaster to lose a serious game against a computer. Was this something that annoyed you?
'It annoyed me that I had to play against the thing. It annoys me when people send me a special invitation, pay my travel costs and don't tell me the rules. This was in an open in Long Beach. I was not playing badly, I tied for second in the tournament. But it was a crazy tournament. We play two games a day and this was in the morning. I come downstairs and one of the arbiters grins at me and says "No, no, you don't go in there." And takes me down under the hall, the worst place. Where all the air comes in from the air-conditioning. I was very annoyed. I was even more annoyed when I was told that I could have put my name on a list if I had not wanted to play the computer. Which I would have done if I had known about it.'

Are you playing Deep Blue just for the money?
'Yes. It is also in accordance with what I said many years ago. That we should not have computers in the tournaments. If they want me to play a computer I will do it in a laboratory or a circus. This is part of a thing where IBM wants to show a lot of novelties. This Deep Blue is ten thousand times quicker than Deep Thought.'

Did you have any special preparation for this?
'Well, not much. I was sent some material that didn't contain many surprises. The program is brand-new and nobody knows it yet. I have looked at a number of openings, but I don't even know if the machine plays e4 or d4. It's funny to face an opponent of grandmaster strength and you have never seen a game by him or her or it[20].

You're writing less for newspapers now and playing a little less in tournaments than you would like to. Does this leave you enough time to finally write a sequel to your book?
'Maybe, maybe. This project is very often talked about. But it's not so easy to write a book. You write the first half of it with great energy and enthusiasm and the last half of it is horrible. I think I should write that book in about three years. And I even don't know what kind of book it should be. If it should be a games collection or if it should be like my memoirs.'

Both ideas would be welcomed by many people.
'Thank you. Thank you, very much.'

---

20 Which did not prove too much of a handicap. Larsen won the first game and drew the remaining three.

Vassily Smyslov

Vienna, June 1993

'Intuition is much more important than knowledge'

'Don't forget I come from the family of champions.' Soft-spoken, with an almost apologetic smile, Vassily Smyslov uttered the words I kept hearing when I listened back to the tapes of our two-hour conversation at Joop van Oosterom's Ladies vs. Veterans Walzer tournament in Vienna. Forget? How? Smyslov, winner by a two-point margin of the legendary Zurich 1953 Candidates' Tournament. Smyslov, who did not lose heart when a tie with Botvinnik in 1954 did not suffice for the highest title, but bounced back to smash his fellow-Candidates again in Amsterdam 1956 and beat his arch-rival 12½-9½ to become World Champion in 1957. Smyslov, whose second flowering stunned the chess community, when he reached the final of the Candidates' matches a quarter of a century later. Vassily Smyslov who, at 72, still has a burning desire to restore the harmony in his chess life and exploit the gift that God invested in him.

It is a pleasant coincidence that I finally get a chance to talk to you at a chess tournament in Vienna, a city famous for its musical heritage. Did you ever think of your chess style in comparison with the style of one of your favourite composers?
'Both in chess and in music I have always tried to find harmony. The most logical and intuitional way to come to the right solution. It is no coincidence that the title of my book is *In Search of Harmony*.'

You once said that the composers you like all have this classical clarity. Which is part of the harmony you are talking about, I assume?
'All the famous classical composers had a high level of melody. For instance, Bach, and of course Mozart. Or, from the Russian composers, Tchaikovsky. Or Chopin. Even for Verdi and the old Italian composers melody was the main aim of their music.'

Is there or has there ever been a Mozart of chess?
'(Hesitates) I didn't think of this before. We might compare Mozart, because he showed his talent for music at a very young age, to Capablanca. Capablanca was also

very young when he showed his touch of genius in chess. Both demonstrated great clarity and intuition. I think that intuition is the unconscious feeling for harmony.'

What does harmony consist of?
'In chess you find harmony when you can come to an intuitional judgement of a position without analysing it. Intuitional understanding. The same you see in other pursuits. It is a matter of feeling. However, the times are different now. Nowadays people are living faster. They think differently from the days of Mozart and later Capablanca. The modern composers don't like the classical approaches and they look for new ways. Chess players, too, like to change. They have computers and more information and no longer think as intuitionally as they did before. Intuition has become less important than knowledge. But nevertheless, of course, intuition remains important. In my view it is much more important than knowledge. Also today you can find players with a high intuitional gift. Like, for instance, Kasparov and Karpov. They are modern players, but their games are very clear. They have a very high level of intuition. A level that you only find among world champions.'

Your sense of harmony is not only restricted to chess. You also try to find harmony in your life. To be one with nature and things like that.
'In our lives finding harmony is more complicated than in chess. In principle the foundation of my life view is the connection between earth and cosmos. My cornerstone is religion. In the face of all the hardships and adversities in my life religion leads me to this feeling of harmony.'

Have you been religious ever since you were a boy?
'My father was religious, but the feeling grows more profound when you get older. When your age begins to approach eternity (laughs).'

What kind of religious feeling do you have? Is it based on instinct or is it a matter of vocation?
'Mostly it expresses itself in my awareness of the good moments in my life and the negative moments. It's not a matter of prescience. It is not even completely clear to myself, but one way or another I have a feeling that something is wrong at a certain moment. Or whether things are in order.'

Does this have something to do with biorhythm?
'Perhaps. Partly this may be so. Perhaps some mistakes in my life may have been connected with my biorhythm. All this is very subtle. But apart from my own life there is life in a broader sense. In general I can feel whether life is better or worse. You cannot link that to biorhythm, as biorhythm belongs to one person. I don't believe that everything that happens is only connected with life on earth. Everything is under control from some different sphere.'

GERARD DE GRAAF

Vassily Smyslov: 'Caruso was very diplomatic and in order not to disappoint me he said, "Not bad."'

Could you give some examples connected to chess?

'I could point out many instances. Now for instance, there is general chaos and turbulence in the world. And the same goes for the chess world, where we have two matches for the world championship.'

All this didn't come as a bolt from the blue to me either. Yet, I do not claim to have such feelings as you describe.

'No, it is something else. I am not a clairvoyant or a soothsayer. It is not some intuitional feeling in advance. My feeling is to do with the moments when harmony is destroyed. When things tend to get unbalanced and there is room for mistakes. Either you have harmony or this harmony is unbalanced.

'For instance, I wrote a book on my best games from 1935 to 1991, a collection of 321 games. From the point of harmony and intuition only one tenth of the games satisfied me. From the best period of my chess career I could select more examples of harmony. That is typical of my style, as my style is very strongly connected with the harmony of the situation. I try to have this approach in everything I do. But life is more complicated than chess. There are more possibilities to make mistakes. I most clearly feel it when something is wrong, when the situation is unbalanced. Then the feeling is more pungent.'

Obviously music and chess both played big roles in your life. Were they very much different roles?
'That is very difficult to tell. You see, I turned professional at a very young age. To be a professional singer at the same time I would have needed a lot more time. To take lessons, to practice. My father introduced me to chess and music at around the same time. When I was about seven. We would play chess and I would accompany my father, who was also a singer, on the piano. Just like me he was not a singer by profession. He was an engineer who very deeply loved chess and music.'

What was your reaction when, on auditioning for the Bolshoi Opera, you were turned down? Was it a shattering blow or merely a disappointing experience?

'No, it wasn't such a big blow. One year later I was to play in the Candidates' tournament in Switzerland. The fact that I never became a professional singer left me a lot of spare time to think about and to work on the quality of my singing and the quality of my voice, in which I was most interested. I started to take private lessons with a professor in Leningrad in 1948. I worked hard on my singing and even took part in several musical programmes. At that time I was not so satisfied with my style of singing. Now, I think I am better.

'I don't know whether this is a correct thing to tell, whether this doesn't sound impolite, because my teacher died at the age of 92. After that I had no other teacher and worked alone. But what happened is that I had a rather mysterious experience. The great Caruso also loved chess and in one of my dreams the Italian tenor, whom I admire more than any other singer, appeared to me and gave me some advice on how to change the style of my singing. After that I changed my style of singing completely and now I am more satisfied.'

When was this?

'This was in 1975. I worked for approximately fifteen years to find out what he meant. It was like a *perestroika* to me (laughs). Very difficult, because any *perestroika* is not so simple.'

What did Caruso tell you?

'I asked, as each amateur asks a great maestro, "How do I sing?" Caruso was very diplomatic and in order not to disappoint me he said, "Not bad." (Laughs) "But", he added, "You must learn to sing from your chest." I woke up and even felt something in my chest. To achieve the change that Caruso proposed I had to change everything and that took a lot of work. It was an absolutely different style from what I had learned. A completely different breathing technique. Now I try and sing like this, in the tradition of the Italian school. Under any circumstance, even without warming up and regardless of my age, I can sing whenever I want.'

Did you have more such dreams?

'Yes, but this was my only musical dream. Caruso was my idol. When I was a boy I was deeply impressed by the quality of his singing.'

Did any chess grandmasters from the past speak to you in your dreams?

'Yes, of course. For instance I dreamed about my friend Levenfish after he had died. With whom I wrote a book on rook endings. He appeared in my dream and said hello to me. I asked him how he was and he said, "I'm OK." And there were a lot of other chess players whom I had known who were asking for help.'

What kind of help?
'They were all dead and apparently not everyone feels well there. They asked for spiritual help.'

Were there any legends from the past whom you had never met that spoke to you in your dreams? Anything comparable to your Caruso dream?
'No, there weren't. When I was a boy and I devoured every chess book from my father's library I got the impression that I already knew everything I read. That all this was only too familiar to me. When I read these books I didn't come across anything new. However, in my singing I never attained the level I was dreaming about. That's why Caruso came to give me advice. In chess this was not needed. (Starts laughing loudly) Perhaps I may need some help now.'

You probably heard about Kortchnoi playing a game against Maroczy through a medium. Do you believe in such things?
'Yes, I do.'

Would you like to try something similar yourself?
'I don't like to disturb people if they are not coming by themselves (laughs).'

You mentioned the role of harmony in your life. Is this striving for harmony the main reason why as a player advanced in years you could still play high-level chess?
'Three years ago at the Interzonal in Manila, Nekrasov, Yudasin's coach who is interested in palmistry, read my hand. He told me that according to a long line on my hand I should have had a long reign as World Champion. But I was champion for only one year. According to him my strength as a champion therefore has been stretched over a prolonged period of time. I also asked him what should be the name of my book. And he answered: *Life, Creativity and Harmony*. These are the three points that should be stressed in this book.'

You always make such a balanced impression. Did you ever grow impatient to become World Champion when in the early fifties it was increasingly clear that you were the best player in the world?
'I was not sure that I would be World Champion. I only knew that I had to do my work and perform my duties. I think that people who become World Champions have been born World Champions. The same goes for other cultural pursuits, like music for instance. These are predestined courses of fate. The second factor that counts is how diligent and faithful you are towards your duties.

So there is predestination combined with the fulfilment of duties. Before your match against Ribli you stated that never before in your life you prepared so thoroughly. Was this true?
'Yes, I worked a lot then.'

Shouldn't you have prepared equally hard for your matches against Botvinnik ?

'Well, perhaps. But this is something in chess that fluctuates. It's a matter of ups and downs of your spirit. Creativity is the most important factor in chess. This creativity depends on spiritual energy, inspiration. The strength of your spirit is a gift from God.'

How strong was this rivalry with Botvinnik? Did you manage to play against the board when you were sitting opposite him?

'I thought about how I was to play against Botvinnik, not only as a chess player, but also keeping in mind his psychological structure, his personality. I tried to find the right approach that would benefit me. I must say that Botvinnik was very strong in strategical positions that could be analysed in a scientific manner. Perhaps I didn't see this right at that time, but I thought that the best way to fight against Botvinnik was, for instance, to play the King's Indian as Black. Where you don't have a fixed or determined situation anywhere on the board. No clarity anywhere. This method, I thought, might offer me the best chances. Maybe I was wrong, but we saw matches with a high number of decided games. And each game contained a lot of creativity.'

How strong a grip did this rivalry with Botvinnik have on you? Did it occasionally drift away from the chess and turn into something highly personal?

'Not permanently, but sometimes it also was a personal conflict. However, there came a moment when I understood that my play improved whenever I had positive feelings towards my opponent. When I approached him with respect instead of thinking about personal conflicts, my results became better. Also against Mikhail Moisevich. I respected him as World Champion and my head worked better. This attitude benefited my mind which became more open for intuition. When my feelings were negative my intuition was clearly less and my results accordingly.'

When did you discover that in fact you could not stand these conflicts?

'Subconsciously I had already understood this earlier. Later I became consciously aware of this, after fate had given me the opportunity to make a second attempt. Fate gave me a new chance to meet the strongest chess player in the world. Then I understood.'

I remember a passage from Botvinnik's autobiography in which he describes an incident before the 1952 Olympiad in Helsinki. There was a vote on the Soviet team and he, the World Champion lacking recent successes, was voted out by his colleagues. The next morning Botvinnik goes to the bathroom of the 'Voronovo' rest home where the players were staying, runs into you and straight out asks you about your involvement. According to his version your reaction is supposed to have been a hesitant 'I didn't know that it would all come out.' *That doesn't sound like a man who is very happy to be involved in this sort of business.*

'Yes, I remember. As a matter of fact this incident may throw some light on my personal opinion of Botvinnik. I read this book and must say that Botvinnik describes this situation as he experienced it himself. In fact I can tell you that all through my life I have tried to stay out of such matters. Such intrigues. I can explain what really happened. I was most surprised that Botvinnik, who was World Champion and who held the highest position in our chess hierarchy, did not know about this and asked him, "Why, you didn't know? You didn't know that such measures were going to be taken against you? How can that be? You are the World Champion. You are a top person in our chess life. You should know everything. And you didn't know that all this had been prepared? You, as a member of the communist party?"

'Botvinnik erroneously deduced that this answer meant that I had been involved in this matter. There had been a team meeting that Botvinnik also attended. When I was asked my opinion about Botvinnik's participation in Finland I said that it was not up to me to decide. That Botvinnik had to decide by himself whether he wanted to play or not. It was not my job to decide. He was the World Champion. Then fate was very favourable to me. At the Olympiad in Helsinki I showed the best result of the Russian team. Therefore I can say that I was right and not Botvinnik (laughs slightly triumphantly).'

And now people say that Botvinnik and you have dachas close to one another and that you go for walks together. Is that true?

'Not exactly. Our dachas are not that close. They are twenty kilometres apart. What can I say? If you know Mikhail Moisevich you may know that his character is such that if he holds an opinion he will stick to it for the rest of his life. For that reason I will not argue with him about what happened exactly in this case. As it is impossible to change his mind anyway. But we have good relations. Practically each day we talk on the phone. And he likes to talk to my wife. Sometimes when I am out of the country or out of Moscow and Botvinnik wants to take a decision in some matter he calls my wife and asks her opinion and then uses her opinion to decide this question.'

Who were your closest friends in Soviet chess?

'A lot of coaches whom I respected a lot. And many outstanding chess players. And players with whom I wrote books, for instance Levenfish whom I mentioned before. To everybody who helped me in my life I am very grateful. A life that was not so simple.'

Why not so simple?

'You may understand this yourself. If you are World Champion or if you are on your way to become one, a lot of people are not too happy about this (laughs exuberantly). I understood later, when I became older, that to become World Champion is a crime.'

Could you forget these things when you got older?
'Yes, for sure. I give the opportunity to make mistakes to everybody. I made mistakes myself, so I could forgive those of others.'

As you kept being unusually successful when you grew older, the length of your career is an unavoidable subject for discussion. Perhaps I may confront you with two statements by well-known colleagues of yours. The first one is by Gligoric, who told me a couple of years ago that every time he sits down to play a game he feels as if he is again playing his first game. He still plays with the same enthusiasm. Is this something you recognize?
'That is very good, but it is not so simple to keep that appetite. I wrote in my book that a player is ready to fight on the board if there is a creative fire burning within him. Then he can fight.'

The other player I wanted to quote is Viktor Kortchnoi. After he had lost his Candidates' match to Timman in Brussels, he mentioned that in the foreseeable future he might give up chess altogether. When in a reaction I mentioned your name and the age at which you were still playing high-level chess, he responded that this was different, because as a Soviet citizen you had had no other option if you wanted to make hard currency and travel abroad. Is this the reason why you kept playing?
'That is a very outspoken statement. Nevertheless I don't think that that was the most important factor. Sometimes when your results are below par the feeling may occur to you that it is no longer necessary to keep playing chess. As for that I think that some of the mistakes in my chess were caused by the mistakes I made in my life. This had nothing to do with my age. I can explain what I mean. I was talking about harmony. Well, over the last few years I have been working on my book and not working on my practical chess. You might see this as a mistake and point out the consequences, my lesser results on the board. I worked on my book and had no time to follow chess theory. I got *Chess Informants* but would not look at them. For my practice this was a mistake. But such things happen. My theoretical knowledge right now is insufficient to fight successfully against modern chess players. I might prepare as I did against Ribli and still have good results. I could be more successful, but I spent a lot of time on my book and did not have enough time to check all the new findings in theory. I lost track a bit with modern theory. Generally speaking it was not a mistake to write this book, but for my active chess career it was.'

Have you ever considered writing an autobiography like Botvinnik did, giving your points of view?
'No, never. Many things in life you should write down in a diary, because your memory does not suffice to remember the details. And apart from that, we don't like to remember everything (laughs).'

What were your reactions when the perestroika started?
'This is a period on earth directed from above. As was predicted by the greatest prophet from all history, Nostradamus. He had foreseen this and gave exact forecasts. Therefore it is clear for me that life on earth is passing through certain periods and this period is a test of the human spirit. The heads of government do their duties according to their views and understanding. According to their understanding of our time. But everything goes according to the laws of life that have long since been established.'

You believe in the predictions of Nostradamus?
'Yes, absolutely.'

For someone striving for harmony, living in a totalitarian state like the Soviet Union must have been very difficult. Maybe extra difficult.
'That is right, but the issue that counted for me was chess. And chess is so abstract that no one will tell you to move your knight when you feel you have to move your pawn. Chess was a good way to escape, while at the same time it offered the opportunity to show one's artistic possibilities. If you had to show your talents in other fields you would be subjected to restrictions from a totalitarian regime. Fate gave me chess and music which were both quite independent activities. That was a felicitous combination.'

Several times you have stressed that chess is an art. At the World Cup tournament in Belfort I spoke to you briefly to ask your opinion on Active Chess, which with your intuitional approach seemed highly suited to your chess. You said, however, that you were actively opposed to Active Chess. It took chess back to where it came from, the coffeehouse. Do you still worry about the future of traditional chess?
'I am myself now playing Active Chess, but I would not include any of these games in my games selection. You can only play these tournaments and that's it. These days chess as an art has lost something. Chess has become more competitive.'

The quicker time schedules seemed ideal for your style.
'Yes, I am very relaxed when I play. I find it quite easy to play Active Chess. You just follow your intuition. But I don't take it too seriously. It's nothing like classical chess. Although I must add that the change from the old time-limit of forty moves in two and a half hours to forty in two has been to the detriment of classical chess. This reduction has certainly limited the possibilities.'

In 1935, when you were fourteen years old you saw Lasker and Capablanca in Moscow. This made a very deep impression on you. What was it exactly that made this impression? Their personalities or their chess?
'To begin with, for me these were legendary names. Secondly I observed how Capablanca played and even more attentively how Lasker played. They were playing in the same hall, the Museum of Art. Capablanca was playing very relaxed and

easily, whereas Lasker was thinking all the time and never got up from his chair. You could see that each move had been deeply pondered. He thought deeply about each move. Capablanca was a chess genius. His play was very intuitional, which filled me with admiration. Lasker surprised me with his hunger for struggle. I was particularly impressed by the game he played against Chekhover. Lasker played a very complicated Vienna Variation of the Queen's Gambit and spent a lot of time. In the endgame he was in time-trouble but still he took the right decisions very quickly. I watched the games of these two chess geniuses very closely. They left a deep impression.'

Which is the strongest asset in your own chess style? Your natural feeling or the will to struggle?
'You know, I think the most important part is intuition, but you couldn't play very well solely depending on intuition without a feeling for struggle. Again some kind of harmony is needed. Life forces us to struggle at the board.'

Suppose you were fourteen years old now and you went to a strong grandmaster tournament. Which players might make a similar impression on you as Capablanca and Lasker did?
'Difficult to tell. Of course, World Champion Kasparov is a brilliant chess player, that's for sure. And also former World Champion Karpov is an extra-class player. (After a slight pause, with a twinkle in his eyes) Don't forget that I am from the family of champions (laughs).'

So you're only watching your relatives?
'Yes (laughs). Who else? Fischer. Naturally Fischer deserves respect. And Spassky. Irrespective of the fact that he doesn't always have the wish to struggle. But if he can mobilize himself...'

Did Fischer lose some of your credit recently?
'There are two sides to this. Fischer's comeback may mean that he wants to play chess again. If he wants to come back to chess this is a good step. If he doesn't want to come back this is his personal decision. Everyone has his free will, and can make whichever decision he wants. It's his personal business.'

You said that religion is an important factor in your life. Do you belong to a specific church?
'I belong to the Orthodox Russian Church, which has much in common with Christian churches. Close to this hotel there is an Orthodox church, but if it had been a Catholic church I might have gone there as well. I respect all kinds of religions and may just as well go to a Catholic church. I don't hold narrow views in this. My cornerstone is all that is written in the Bible.'

Were you baptised?
'Yes, I was, in the Russian Orthodox Church.'

Has this ever been a problem for you in the Soviet Union?
'Of course it was less of a problem in 1921 when I was baptised, than somewhat later in, let's say '31 or '35. In 1921 it was no problem. Nothing much was happening. No problem.'

Was it something in those later years that one had better not talk about?
'Let's say that I didn't propagate it (laughs).'

Did they ever urge you to join the Communist Party after you had become World Champion?
'A few times I was asked to join, but my religious convictions did not allow me to do so. Of course I could not tell them this, but I tried to stay away from the subject.'

With a person like you, who takes a highly philosophical attitude towards life it is difficult to predict what might make him happy. Was winning the World Championship the victory that made you happiest?
'Yes, it made me very happy, but I had only one year to be happy (laughs). The World Championship made me happy, yes. That had been my aim. This was what God had invested in me. In 1928, when I was seven years old, my uncle, a chess player, but not a very strong one, gave me the odds of rook and played a match with me. I won that match and he gave me a book for a present, *Alekhine's Best Games*, and he wrote in this book: "For the future World Champion, the winner of our match. From your uncle." '

People often say that after achieving an aim you have this empty feeling. Did you experience anything like that?
'I only had one year for that. (Smiles) I didn't have enough time to feel empty.'

Is there anything you would like to add to the matters we touched upon?
'(Starts to talk as if he had been waiting for this invitation) I already explained my philosophical point of view which is the central part of my life. This feeling takes a lot of my attention. All questions concerning the lives of other people, all questions related to any society, any country, I observe from my personal point of view and my personal feelings. The situation in the world has deteriorated, there is unrest. This forces people to consider the fact that they should look to heaven above more. Any individual, I am one hundred per cent sure, has a cosmic predestination. Life is given to man to decide how he relates to religion. Whether he is interested or not. This is the crucial point in a man's existence, whether he reaches at a belief in God or whether he rejects it. This is the essential point in life.

'For me chess and music offer the possibilities to develop my artistic side, which does not leave my spirit cold (with a satisfied smile). But I look at the situation in the world from a religious point of view. Mankind is divided in two categories. One believing in God, the other side striving against Him. This is the main conflict.'

You think that everyone should believe in God?
'O, yes, without any doubt. But it is impossible to achieve this. Because of man's free choice.'

You would rather convince them by force?
'How could I force them if God Himself cannot do this (laughs loudly).'

And why doesn't God force them?
'Because each person has an innate freedom of spirit. And the possibilities to make their own mistakes.'

Did God ever talk to you in your dreams?
'I am afraid that he mostly punished me. Because I am not free from weaknesses either.'

What were these punishments?
'Some bad luck in my professional work. Also problems connected with my voice. Other problems. All these I experienced as strong control from God.'

You mean that when you made a mistake you saw this as some sort of punishment?
'No, not like that. I am thinking more widely. Not just about one move.'

A bad tournament result might be a punishment?
'Yes. Such things can happen when you have not looked after your mission in the way you should. As is the case with me now. I have to be much more strict in my preparation for tournaments. Prepare, rest at the right moments, etcetera. No chess player allows himself to play chess the way I do now. Without any preparation. I am probably the only one in the world now. (Starts moving pieces on the board) I am prepared to make any opening move. Because it doesn't make a difference anyway as I didn't prepare. It doesn't matter. Any move. Sometimes during the games I could not muster the kind of concentration that is needed for each move. Sometimes I suffered from blackouts. Maybe I am defending my eyes which are so weak now. My eyesight has deteriorated lately due to glaucoma.'

In a way your strong religious feelings are a remarkable phenomenon. I always had the idea that only very few chess players were religious because they think they are their own gods on the chess board.
'I don't know. Wasn't Fischer religious? I don't know of anyone else. Yes, Portisch. I don't know. They have no understanding. All matters concerning religion are very subtle. If you want to be in contact with God you have to have this wish yourself. If you don't try it's impossible (laughs). It's as simple as that.'

Karpov-Kasparov

I vividly recall the gusto with which I read about the extensively documented quarrels between Alekhine and Capablanca about their world championship match and the rematch that was never to be, in Edward Winter's monumental Capablanca book. The details were not always equally riveting or fascinating, but the tenacity with which these World Champions stuck to their guns made even the dullest document compulsive reading. Yet, even the protracted feud between Alekhine and Capablanca dwarfs to a petty squabble compared to the relentless rivalry that has been raging for over ten years now between Anatoly Karpov and Garry Kasparov.

Talking about Karpov is talking about Kasparov and vice versa. But also talking to Karpov is talking about Kasparov and vice versa. Whether they like it or not, the best two players of the moment are condemned to be stuck with each other like Siamese twins. When he talked about the knowledge of the public at large of chess Kasparov stated in one of our interviews, 'Maybe they have heard about Kasparov, Fischer, maybe Karpov,' only to add the telling afterthought, 'They probably mix up Kasparov and Karpov.'

Hardly anybody will contest the common view that Kasparov is still the greatest player around, possibly the greatest player of all time. Yet his PCA world title has not generated the same acclaim. Is this only because Kasparov chose to play the World Championship match outside FIDE? I don't think so. To my mind Kasparov's PCA world title is under suspicion for the simple reason that his opponent was not Karpov.

Describing Karpov and Kasparov as I have come to know them over the years would require more space than I have here. Instead, by way of an introduction, I might describe some observations I made during the many hours that I watched them analyse with their opponents. In such sessions Kasparov is a miniature of the Kasparov the entire chess world knows: the thirteenth World Champion, whose stormy ascension to the throne earned him a popularity that came close to and at times even surpassed that of Fischer's. But it is a popularity which he just as easily loses huge chunks of as he tries to realize his chess political dreams with an immense drive that often suffers from the unpredictability of his inspirations. In the post-mortem Kasparov's face is an open book. Utterly miserable after the rare loss, full of self-reproach after a missed chance, and happy as a child when he has played another brilliancy. In the latter case his opponent has to sit passively by while the beautiful defeat he has just suffered is spun out, knowing full well that Kasparov does not care too much about his sentiments. This happened last year in Linares, for instance, after his devastating win with black over Karpov. Getting happier about his attack by the minute he spread his arms and, virtually ignoring Karpov at the other side of the table, crowed, 'The entire board is black!'

The comfort Kasparov grants his victims constitutes of showing wonderfully impressive tactical possibilities that he saw during his calculations as only Kasparov can impress. Having just returned from the Madrid tournament this May I went to see Kasparov in Amsterdam for an interview for the Dutch evening newspaper NRC Handelsblad. As he flicked through the bulletins from Madrid I had brought with me and came to the final round, I pointed out that Judit Polgar had been rather lucky. In a winning position her opponent accepted a draw offer because he had only a few seconds left on the clock. Kasparov studied the gamescore without diagrams for five seconds, looked up with a smile and said, 'Yeah, king f1 and it's over.'

Kasparov's uninhibited and egocentric behaviour seems in marked contrast with Karpov's more restrained attitude. Yet, although Karpov tries to be diplomatic about it, there can be no misunderstanding that he has the same self-centred will to win at all costs as his rival. The main difference is that Karpov hardly ever tries to prove objective truths. Karpov's sole wish is to show his opponent that in any given position that might have occurred in the game he would have played better. I witnessed a fine example of this at this year's Las Palmas tournament. After a fairly regular draw with Ivan Morovic, Karpov, who had played the white pieces, sat down to show that he had missed some practical chances. Among the endless variations and regroupings there were certainly enough moments where Karpov could claim an edge, but the overall impression with the onlookers was that Morovic had never been in real trouble. Having analysed the more cautious approaches for more than an hour Karpov decided to have a go at some wilder attacking schemes. At first he was quite successful in tricking the unprepared Morovic, but gradually suitable defences for Black were found. At one point Morovic even defended so well that he got a raging counterattack. Quietly he evaluated, 'Now I'm much better.' Karpov contemplated the position for a split second, moved a few pieces and challenged him saying, 'I'm not so sure. I play this and this and it's not so easy for you.' With a resigned expression Morovic mumbled, 'Ah, I see. I'm never better.' He had finally understood.

Anatoly Karpov

Tilburg, September 1988

The Collector

Boris Spassky once characterised Anatoly Karpov's strategical approach as follows: 'Karpov's strength is based on collecting small advantages. In chess too he is a collector, like he is a stamp collector'. Well, it seems to be an undisputed fact that Karpov is generally looked upon as today's representative nonpareil of the Steinitz-Lasker theory of accumulation, but what about these stamps? Everybody is always talking about Karpov and his stamps, but what do we really know? Does he have an interesting collection? Are they chess stamps only? What else does he collect? And several more questions that we no longer could keep to ourselves. Anatoly Karpov answered them all.

'I started collecting stamps at an early age, although at that stage you couldn't really call it collecting. I got my first stamp, a Russian stamp, when I was ten years old. I wasn't very much impressed by it. At first collecting stamps was just one of several hobbies. I did it just for fun, just like I collected, for instance, all sorts of badges. In the Soviet Union collecting badges is a very popular pursuit, and at that time it was even more popular. But then I started coming across more intriguing stamps. Stamps with paintings or historical scenes. I was very much interested in the history of our state and acquired some interesting stamps from the Soviet Union, and especially Russia. One day I got this set commemorating the tercentennial of the Romanov family from 1913. These were very tall stamps with portraits of the czars and pictures of their palaces. From that time I started paying more attention to stamps.

'My first idea, of course, was to collect chess stamps. Later on I also decided to collect Olympic stamps. Of course such a decision alone is not enough. If you start collecting seriously and take up a subject as wide as the one I chose, you need a lot of money. That's why I didn't begin to collect seriously until I became a grandmaster in the early seventies and started to take prizes in tournaments. When I had become independent this way, not only as far as I myself was concerned, but also to the extent that I could help my parents, I started to collect more or less seriously. Now I have a very good collection of chess stamps. I collect chess stamps and chess cancellations. For instance, during this tournament the Tilburg post office used a special cancellation, *Tilburg Interpolis Internationaal Schaaktoernooi*. Apart from these items I also collect stamps with mistakes and proofs. I am very satisfied with my collection and I think that my chess collection is one of the biggest in the world.'

But there aren't that many chess stamps, are there?
'Now there are many. A couple of hundred, and of most of these stamps there are proofs, at least of half of them, or there exist varieties. And these I collect as well.'

What are proofs exactly?
'Normally speaking, proofs are unperforated stamps and they differ in colour from the ones that were actually issued. For instance, there are proofs of every stamp from Monaco, because that is how they go about it. They make proofs and then they have to get the approval of the Prince of Monaco. They go to him with these pages without perforation and in many different colours and ask him which colour he would like these stamps to be, and the Prince decides that this one will be in red, this one in orange and so on. That is what happened with their chess stamps, too. They had chess stamps in 1967 and they had proofs in many colours. I think I have them in ten different colours, or maybe more.'

They aren't destroyed after the Prince has made his choice?
'No, normally they must go to the National Museum, but I don't know how they come onto the international market. Maybe they see them as a source of income. Maybe they make duplicates and sell them, I don't know. From time to time they are put up for sale. They are rare and they are expensive.'

So, apart from all the chess stamps that ever have been issued, you also have these cancellations...
'Yes, cancellations, first day covers, proofs, and unperforated stamps. (Pauses, then continues) But chess philately did not start all that long ago. The first chess stamp appeared in Bulgaria in 1947 on the occasion of the Balkan games. Then the Soviet Union had three stamps in 1948 for the World Championship tournament Moscow-The Hague. In 1950 Hungary issued three stamps, both with and without perforation. These were the first unperforated chess stamps. This Hungarian set without perforation is very rare.'

But you have it?
'Yes, I have it.'

Is there anything in chess philately that you don't have?
'(Laughs) Because I have almost everything, I have started to collect in blocks of four. And now I have almost the whole collection in singles and blocks of four. A number of very rare stamps you cannot get this way, but this Hungarian set I have in blocks of four, which is tremendously rare.

'The boom in chess philately came between 1972 and 1974 when the African countries began to issue chess stamps on the occasion of the Spassky-Fischer match, the Nice Olympiad, fifty years of International Chess Federation and some other events.'

What did you think when you got the first stamp with your own portrait on it?
'I don't know (laughs almost shyly). Of course this is strange. In 1978 two stamps were issued in the Philippines for my match against Kortchnoi, but there was no picture on them. It just said: "Match for the World Title, Karpov-Kortchnoi". These were the first two stamps. And then, I think, there came stamps from African countries with my portrait. Now there are many. In the Soviet Union they issued an overprint in 1982 or 1983. When you print something extra on a stamp which has already been circulated, this is called an overprint. We had stamps for the Interzonal tournaments, the men's and the women's, in the Soviet Union in 1982, and then half a year later they made an overprint on the stamp for the men's Interzonal, saying: "Karpov is holder of nine Oscars", or something like that.
'But the chess stamps are not the biggest part of my collection. The biggest part is the Olympics. I have a tremendous collection on the Olympic Games.'

How tremendous is tremendous? How many Olympic stamps are there?
'That's hard to say, because again there are proofs, stamps without perforation and so on. But Olympic philately started in 1896, together with the first modern Olympic Games. The first set was from Greece, which is quite rare. I have this set in blocks of four. (I cannot help laughing. Karpov joins in, while he continues imperturbably) And mint. Mint in blocks of four. There may be more collectors who have this, but I only know of two, Samaranch[21] and I. But probably there will be one or two more. Samaranch collects Olympic stamps, too. I have seen part of his collection when we had the Olympic Games in Moscow in 1980. There was a philately exhibition which also included stamps from his collection. And this block of four was there.'

So, Olympics constitutes the largest part of your collection?
'Yes, Olympics. But now I also have another very strong field. Russian stamps. Not stamps from the Soviet Union, I don't have such a good collection of these, but old Russian stamps from before 1917.'

And you are trying to get this collection complete as well?
'I have it almost complete, but again there are many specialities, letters and so on. So you can never say that you have it complete. In my old Russia collection there are three things missing, but they are very difficult to get and very expensive.

---

21 President of the International Olympic Committee.

Not so long ago I was lucky to get an excellent collection of Russian stamps for a reasonable prize. From this I started to collect. It is very difficult to collect Russian stamps one by one. Once you have got a collection you can improve it. I got mine from a big collector in the Soviet Union. He is the only Russian collector who has ever won the gold medal at the International Exhibition. There are World Exhibitions organized by the International Philately Organization where you can earn medals. There are several gold medals, but there is only one big golden medal, and he got it for his Russian collection. Over the years he has bought many collections, and from them he made his own collection. From the rest he made a second one. I could buy his duplicates and added my own stamps. So, at the moment I think that I have the second best Russian collection in the Soviet Union. But it is no comparison with his collection, which must be worth something like one million dollars.'

Is there a reasonable chance that you will someday get these three stamps that are still missing?
'I know people who have them, but they are very rare and very expensive. It depends on how much you want to pay, because they do crop up at auctions from time to time.'

What is 'very expensive' when you are talking about stamps?
'The catalogue I have here says they are something like eight or ten thousand dollars.'

What was the highest price you ever paid for a stamp?
'I don't remember, because I never bought separate stamps, but this block of four was very expensive. If you take the price of singles, the catalogue price of this block of four, without additionals like condition and so on, would be sixty thousand French Francs, a little more than ten thousand dollars. But it would be more, because this is a block of four and in perfect condition.'

You have mentioned your chess stamps, your Olympic stamps and your Russian stamps, but still this isn't your entire collection. You once told me that you had Holland complete as well.
'Yes, I have Holland complete and Luxemburg and Belgium.'

Could you give an estimate of the total size of your stamp collection?
'I don't know exactly, but I think several hundreds of thousands.'

Do you still take an interest in the stories behind these stamps as you did when you were a young boy?
'Yes I do. As far as chess is concerned I'm in the know (smiles). Those stories I know by heart. The history of all those competitions, especially as I played in most of the more recent ones myself. But I also know a lot about the Olympics, and you have to know the where and when when you collect these stamps.'

I also understand that you have quite a nice chess library. Did you start collecting chess books at an early age?

'No, I didn't. When I started playing chess my father bought me this opening book by Panov. On my seventh birthday I got another book, *Capablanca's Best Games*, also by Panov. The first book I bought myself was on the Candidates' tournament in 1959, a very nice book by Gligoric and Ragozin. In the course of time I got more and more chess books. In 1972 I played this tournament in San Antonio together with Petrosian and after this tournament we were very close for a very short time. I infected him with my philatelic virus and when I came to his country house I could see his chess library. At that time I already had quite a good chess book collection myself, but there I saw his collection of chess sets and in 1972 I began to collect chess sets as well (laughs). So now I am collecting everything connected with chess. Chess stamps, chess badges, chess sets and chess books.'

How big is your chess library?
'Now it's about five thousand books.'

Do you have any special interests?
'I prefer tournament books, biographies and selected games of the best players. But I also have many books on studies and endings.'

Did you get chances to buy complete libraries?
'Yes, I did. In Leningrad in 1970 I could buy several hundreds of chess books. These were mainly books from the first fifteen years of the Soviet Union. Some years later I bought a library of some thousand books. But the main part I collected myself, because a few hundreds and one thousand do not make up five thousand.'

Are there particular parts of chess history that you are interested in?
'I am very much interested in the history of chess competitions and in the history of chess itself. But not, for example, in the development of the rules through the ages.'

Is it true that you are working on a new Soviet Encyclopedia of Chess?
'Yes, that's right. We shall finish our work in November and it will be printed next year.'

You supervised this enterprise, but didn't write any contributions yourself?
'No, I didn't. A lot of people worked on it. Our editorial board consisted of fourteen people, and we tried to get as many collaborators as possible. We have been writing to countries like Nicaragua or Mexico to get people there to write about their chess history. It's an entirely new encyclopedia and there are many corrections in it on existing works of reference. This will be the most complete chess encyclopedia to date.'

You said that you also collected chess sets. Do you display them in your house?
'No, I have them in boxes, because I have no space. I have quite a lot of sets already and some of them are rather unique. I don't have really old sets, only two or three, but I have some very nice modern ones. I have a unique set of porcelain, of which there exist only three. And another set made out of a rare variety of stone. Originally this stone was only found in Aragon in Spain, but ten years ago they also discovered it in the Soviet Union and called it Aragonite. They made three chess sets out of this stone. Two are in a museum and the other one was presented to me after a simultaneous exhibition.'

But you haven't become an active chess set collector yet. You don't go to auctions?
'Not yet. Someday I probably will, but as there is no order in my collection I cannot tell what I really need. Only my chess stamps are arranged in their proper order. My Olympic stamps and Russian stamps to a certain extent. I would need a week to arrange them properly. But I don't know where to find the time, as I am playing in so many tournaments.'

Garry Kasparov

Tilburg, September 1989

'I guess that I am continuing Fischer's fight'

2793! Seventeen years after Robert Fischer reached dreamlike heights Garry Kasparov crushes through. The World Champion looks immensely satisfied and with a broad smile he accepts all congratulations. But he will not be tempted to easy boasts. The question if he is now the strongest player in the history of chess is evaded in a way that befits a true champion. 'The only way to prove your superiority over another player is to sit opposite him and to play. If I didn't actually beat Fischer or any other player I can't say that I am better.' Modest words of wisdom, but after Kasparov's World Cup victory, his astounding 12 out of 14 in Tilburg and his formidable new record Elo, his fans can be sure that they hold very strong trumps to claim that he is now the greatest ever.

At this new peak in his career Garry Kasparov granted me the 'lengthy interview' I had asked for one year earlier. In two sessions he talked at length about his achievements and his ambitions. Rousing the reader's interest with adjectives like frank, daring, spontaneous or outspoken, would be completely superfluous. Whether he talks about his hunt for Fischer's record, his fight against FIDE or his severe criticism of the stagnation in Gorbachov's politics, for Garry Kasparov there is only one way. 'I play with all cards on the table. I accept no other game.'

By breaking Fischer's legendary Elo record you have achieved what many people thought was your biggest dream. Was it your biggest dream?
'The first time I thought about it was in Brussels after the Ohra tournament, where I gained ten points and my Elo became 2755. We were discussing it with Ray Keene and probably Leontxo Garcia and they thought I had a chance. I said, "Yes, there is a chance, but you have to win several tournaments with a result between plus seven and plus ten. I'm not sure whether this is possible." Another question is: am I going to dedicate my life to this attempt? I thought it was extremely difficult. Ray even thought about announcing some kind of bet, you know, one million pounds whether Kasparov will break 2800 or not. Right now I think nobody will give a penny for this bet (laughs). My next chance was after the Amsterdam Option Exchange tournament where I reached a really nice score and my Elo became

something like 2765. Then in Belfort I could have broken the record, by beating Karpov or by not losing against Karpov. But it was not my intention to beat Fischer's record. I don't know why. Probably it should be deep down in your mind that you are fighting the record. I got to 2775 and I was stopped and then I realised that I had no real power to do it. In Reykjavik I just fought to keep my rating, which I did fortunately and then in Thessaloniki something very interesting happened. I signed this petition[22], because I'm completely against calculating team competitions, but funnily enough FIDE only made a decision after six rounds. I had played five games by then and had four out of five. It was very unfair that they were looking at my result. After five games everybody realised that my result would be very high. My final result in Thessaloniki would have brought me to 2788. And after Thessaloniki I felt that there was a chance. It's not so unlikely, let's try. The time before Barcelona was very bad for me. I couldn't prepare properly, but still I managed to win the tournament and save my Elo. And after Barcelona I told journalists that in Skelleftea, Tilburg or Belgrade I would beat Fischer's record. Actually I thought that it would be in Skelleftea. It wasn't but the intention was already there, very deep down in my mind.

'I started to play in Tilburg and after four rounds I was optimistic about my chances. When I beat Ivanchuk (slaps his hand) I felt that this was probably my chance. When I beat Ivanchuk I knew that the tournament was already won, so what about increasing my Elo? The critical game for me was Agdestein with black. I said to myself that if I beat Agdestein I must continue to fight for Fischer's record. But it wasn't because of me, because of the high quality of my games, but because of the opponents. They were scared. When you sense that they have this feeling it's much easier to play. They feel your superiority, this pressure and they are scared.

'The game against Sax was terrible. I made two mistakes. Of course f5 should be played automatically. This game showed me that I was very tired. Fortunately that evening I went to see the new James Bond movie[23] and I relaxed a bit. And then I beat Kortchnoi easily, but this I knew beforehand. In my second game against Ivanchuk I made another mistake. I think this was brought about by this game against Sax. After this second game against Ivanchuk I was very very angry. But I decided to win the last two games and this I did very easily.

'One of the best things here was Kortchnoi's prediction that Ivanchuk would win the tournament. And Botvinnik said the same in Amsterdam. This made me furious. They forgot that I can play chess, you know (laughs). It's not exactly impolite, but if you say that somebody will win the tournament when the World Champion partic- ipates, you have to add, "If the World Champion plays badly." Probably they forgot that I can play reasonably well. It was a very timely shock. So I thought, "Everything

---

22 To exclude results at the Olympiad from the Elo-list.

23 *License to Kill*

is bad, the conditions are miserable, I'm alone, I have problems with an ingrowing nail, I'm tired and I've lost concentration. Now it's time to show your ability." I think I did everything perfectly. I left De Parel[24], my first good move, and came to this hotel[25]. Psychologically this was very difficult because I had already unpacked my suitcase. I repacked and went to a very nice restaurant. I had my micro-climate here and I started to play chess. I was working very hard. I had a challenge now, a real challenge. And don't forget that Tilburg 1981 was still in my mind. Since Tilburg 1981, I haven't lost any competition in which I participated.'

Is it a great relief that finally you have the Fischer legend behind you?
'Not a relief. I feel I've done something very important for chess. Fischer's name now belongs to the past. His achievements were great, but now an active chess player has the record, and I'm glad it's me (laughs). It will help the further development of chess. It's a relief for chess. The door is open. Also it's quite important for my country. For the prestige of chess in my country. It was the only non-Soviet chess record.'

Your victory in Tilburg was the climax of a successful period. One month ago you were honoured as winner of the first World Cup cycle. How do you look back on this first cycle? How does winning the World Cup compare with winning the World Championship?
'I think that the World Cup is an important step to promote essential chess events. To spread these events among the players. It has been said that it is elitist, but, come on, the World Championship match is even more elitist. Even in the Candidates' quarter finals only nine players are involved. Eight Candidates plus the World Champion. Right now we have an absolutely honest and fair qualification system for the World Cup, so nobody can complain that it is elitist anymore. If you want to play you have your chance. Regarding the World Cup title I must be modest, but I took a great risk by being one of the organizers and promoters of this new competition. Just imagine if somebody else had won this event. Many people would have serious doubts about the credibility of my title. I think that the World Championship match is the most important competition in the chess world. Everybody wants to know who is the World Champion, who is number one. In a match you can prove this in a very fair and honest way. But I think that in the future the World Cup will become very important. If we get the chance we will improve the system. The World Cup winner will become the second title and I hope that in the end these events will get as much publicity as the World Championship.

'Finally I have no doubts that the first experience was very successful. Don't forget it was our first experience. We were very short of time, there were big troubles

---

24 The bungalow park at a forty minutes' drive from the playing hall where the players were housed.

25 Right in the centre of Tilburg, at five minutes from the playing hall.

with organizers. I have to reject all this criticism from Spassky and other players that the prizes were not so high. Yes, I understand, but you cannot improve everything in one go. My prize-money for these four tournaments of 175 thousand dollars was very nice. Even with appearance fees I could hardly expect the same prize in four tournaments. Of course this is for the winner, but the conditions are improving from the top, not the bottom. I have no doubts that the prizes will be improved in the second World Cup. I'm sure a fifty percent increase can be guaranteed. The criticism was very unfair given the short period of time we had to complete these competitions.'

ROSA DE LAS NIEVES

Garry Kasparov: 'I'm categorically against any attempt to create a professional competition in active chess.'

And the other point of criticism, that the tournaments are too long?

'This is true. This I have to accept. It was a problem, especially with these local players. I think we can't have more than fourteen players in one tournament. Thirteen rounds is more than enough. I have presented my idea to the GMA board and I hope they will accept it. I propose to have 24 or 28 players, let's say 28 players. Six tournaments, everybody plays three tournaments with all three tournaments counting. Then after these six tournaments you have eight qualifiers and they will bring their average score, the average result of three tournaments, to the final double-round tournament. With this system you can increase the number of players, reduce the number of rounds and take away the criticism that the tournaments are not evenly balanced in strength. With this system it is not even necessary to arrange a single tournament with me and Karpov. We can play three different tournaments. There will be a final anyway. The question is how to find a major sponsor and how to increase the prizes. I estimate that for the next World Cup the prize-fund will be between two and two and a half million dollars.'

There is a likely risk that most sponsors will be interested only in the final tournament.
'Exactly, but it is very important to find a major sponsor for all seven tournaments. One major sponsor and then the tournaments can be divided between the cities that will provide the prize-funds. But anyway the final tournament will be much more expensive. The final prize-fund for these eight players could be something like half a million dollars.'

Will it still be a two-year cycle?
'I think the seventh tournament should be played in 1993, because 1993 is an empty year. There's only the World Championship match. It's very good for chess to have at the beginning of the year, let's say in February or March, an event like the Tournament World Championship and at the end of the year the real World Championship. The World Cup has created a new standard for chess. Unfortunately the players were not ready yet to show their worth, to meet their obligations to the tournaments. We must try to avoid short draws and put up really good performances. I don't want to go into a discussion about suit and tie, which is important from my point of view, but unfortunately very few players recognize this problem.'

How do you mean?
'I think that it is important to play in suit and tie. This is my opinion.'

Because of the sponsors?
'Yeah, if you want to find major sponsors, if you want to prove that this is an intelligent sport, not for poor people from the street, you must provide an image of chess players. But first of all you have to provide really high quality games, fighting chess. If you want to get money you have to present something. Many players do not realize that there is a connection. The difference between a World Championship match and other events is quite logical. Because everybody was interested in my matches against Karpov the prizes keep going up, up, up. There was no real interest in the other events and the players did not feel any obligation to create this interest. They see some money coming and they don't seem to think it can be increased, really increased to give them a better living. I can live better even without the GMA, but I think I have a duty as World Champion. The difference between what I earn and what other players earn is huge. I think that it is important that the whole chess world is going up, up, up. This is my moral obligation. But they should feel some obligations as professional players. However, the spirit of professionalism is unfortunately too weak now. Insipid draws are the main objection from the sponsors and the public. Probably we have to create some new ways to approach the public. More comments, more discussions with the press, more TV appearances. It's a long road, we are just at the beginning and we need new volunteers.'

Would you also like to combine these attempts with rapid chess competitions?
'This is an important question. Only to combine. You can use rapid chess for charity events and other public events to create interest, to explain the chess rules, show the spirit of the chess fight, but nothing more. I'm categorically against any attempt to create a professional competition in active chess. Completely against. There are many players who want to encourage this active chess, or blitz chess. Even for example Max Dlugy, a very good friend of mine, has supported it many times. And now Walter Browne has created this Blitz Association. It's very short-sighted. It will destroy chess completely, the system we have been building despite so many difficulties. If the quality is disappearing, what can you expect from chess? You could play any other game on the table. It's no longer chess, it's something else.'

Over the last few years you have been very active in all kinds of chess exhibitions. What are your motives for playing a simul against 89 Minitel-users or a clock simul against the French national team?
'OK, these are two different things. First there are normal simuls and such public appearances I feel are very important. The World Champion has to be in permanent contact with the public, especially in countries like France and Spain where chess is growing. These clock simuls are a different story. I like to play clock simuls against strong teams. When I was nine, in March '74, I played against a grandmaster for the first time. I was a pioneer from the Baku team and in the annual pioneers tournament I played against Tal, Averbakh, Kuzmin, Polugaevsky and Taimanov. In 1975 in Leningrad I played against six grandmasters including Karpov. I lost from a winning position in our first encounter. In 1981, when I was eighteen I played my first simul as a grandmaster. Until now I have played between 35 and 40 really strong clock simuls. Probably I have the richest experience in this kind of simuls. Three times, in 1981, 1985 and 1987 I played against the pioneers and many times I played simuls in the Botvinnik-Kasparov school on five or six boards. Don't forget that my opponents in these simuls were players like Akopian, Shirov, Serper, you know (laughing), Kramnik, very strong players. My pupils. I like this, I can play quite fast and I enjoy the opportunity for combinations. If I make a mistake, well this is very bad, but I'll have a very good move in another game.

'The first time I seriously played such a simul in the West was in 1985 in Hamburg against the HSV team over eight boards. I thought this was a team competition and I was a team so I refused to play eight whites. I had done no preparation and the team was quite strong. I mean, Chandler was on first board. I had just finished my match against Timman, I had annotated a game till half past three in the morning, I'd had a big press conference at Amsterdam airport and within two hours of my arrival in Hamburg I played the simul. I lost this simul. A year ago I returned and won seven to one. Although there was no Chandler, the simul was stronger and I think Chandler made a wise decision not to play. I was in no doubt about the likely result.

'I played against the German national youth team in 1986 and won 6½-1½. I also played against the juniors of the world by satellite with Patrick Wolff playing from America, Conquest from England, etcetera. I won 8½-1½ which is not bad either. I also played against the American national youth team including Patrick Wolff and Stuart Rachels and won 4-2. I was very tired but still the games were very exciting. I lost to Patrick Wolff in a very exciting game. And I played against the Swiss and French national teams – the French team twice. The last result was very impressive, I played very well against two grandmasters and four international masters. I enjoyed this very much. Now my dream is to play the German national team. I don't know whether they will agree. Friedel is trying to provide the conditions – a one hundred thousand deutschmark BMW for me if I win and a hundred thousand deutschmark for four players if they win. Hort, Lobron, Lau and Kindermann. This should be fun. I would like to meet this challenge[26].'

Let's return to the World Cup for a moment, which also must have been a great challenge for you. To my mind Belfort was your best tournament. Was this because the challenge was still fresh?
'I had very bad feelings after Seville. OK, I won the last game, but still I understood that this was a terrible performance, a great shame. Well, not very bad, but very passive. I just wanted to save my title. This was my only idea. When I lost game sixteen I decided only to keep my title, nothing else. This thought didn't give me the chance to play normal chess. After the match my reputation was down. Then I played the blitz championship in Canada, in St. John. Well, sorry, even now I can beat anybody without any problems. I lost to Georgiev because I couldn't play after the first game. I had something like thirty seconds and I made a stalemate with queen and bishop. Having king, queen and bishop against king. It was terrible. My next appearance was in Amsterdam and you remember it was not bad (broad smile). And then in the first World Cup tournament in Belfort I played brilliantly. I think this was my best tournament despite the loss to Karpov. Now I think I have an explanation for this loss. I won five games in a row, against Ljubojevic, Andersson, Beliavsky, Ehlvest and Short. Five games against very strong players. Here in Tilburg I won five games in a row as well. Probably five games is now my limit – I can't win more than this. Then you lose energy. One hour after the game against Karpov I found that I could have played Rook c8. I immediately mentioned it to Yusupov who can confirm this. I am sure that I would have found this move in the game if I had played Karpov one round earlier. But by then I was too tired. It was not because my play was in a crisis. The next day in the final round I played Sokolov and killed him. One of my best games as you will remember.'

---

26 In 1992 Kasparov won his BMW in Baden-Baden when he beat a German team consisting of Wahls, Hertneck, Lobron and Hort 3-1.

Another last round game that attracted quite some attention was your game against Spassky in Barcelona[27]. How much truth is there in the story that you discussed the opening of this crucial encounter with him before the game?

'Aah, that…You have to understand my relationship with Spassky. It's normal for us to make many jokes. We have strange relations. Yes, we have different feelings about each other. The day before the last round we were having dinner together in the restaurant downstairs at the Ritz hotel. When I came down I had first asked Beliavsky what to play, e4 or d4. Sometimes Spassky offers me an opening. For instance in Reykjavik he suggested to me "Let's play a Closed Sicilian". And I said, "OK, let's play a Closed Sicilian." Then before the game, two hours later, he said, "OK, I guarantee you the moves e4, c5, knight c3." He didn't tell me his third move and after Knight c6 he played Bishop b5. So, it's nothing unusual and in Barcelona I told him "I will play e4 if you guarantee me that you will play the same as against Ljubojevic. In his game against Ljubojevic he was better in the final position after Ljubojevic had made a mistake and after the game I said to Spassky, "This line is very bad for Black." And he replied "If you want you can try it." So now I asked him and he said "I have to think about it." Later he came up to my room with Ulf (Andersson) and said, "No, I only guarantee you that I will play Spanish, but not which line." Then I said, "In that case let's forget about it, I will play d2-d4, the story is closed." Well, actually I said that I wouldn't play e4, which means d4, and I played d4.'

While onto the subject of last rounds, you could not have been too disappointed when you learned about Karpov losing his final three games in the Rotterdam World Cup tournament. What did you feel when you heard the news?

'This is very interesting. When Karpov won against Sax, Roshal was sending reports, (in a dramatically enthusiastic tone) "Karpov is coming". I saw the games and realized that they were nothing special. But he was fighting. It is difficult to have this confirmed and Karpov may say, "OK, now Garry produces this story", but at that moment I said that he was fighting too hard. He doesn't have enough energy to fight like this. The game with Salov was crucial and when he lost this game I felt that he would lose the tournament. Karpov is not used to concentrate fully. He has never used one hundred percent of his energy. This was his problem. He didn't play like Fischer. In Rotterdam he tried very hard. He probably felt that it was his last chance, but he wasn't ready to fight to the last bullet. He lost to Salov, then he was winning against Ljubo. But he has lost several games in this manner. There's no win by force, time-trouble, and he loses. And I had no questions about the game against Nunn. No, no, he couldn't fight, no chances. Actually I was a bit upset. The World Cup was over before the final tournament. When Karpov started to win I was preparing myself for a big fight in Skelleftea. I think I loosened up a

---

27 With one round to go Kasparov was trailing Ljubojevic by half a point. Ljubojevic quickly drew his last game, while Kasparov went on to beat Spassky for the first time in his career.

bit after Rotterdam. I was still trying to prepare, but my mind kept telling me, "the World Cup is over, the World Cup is over, the World Cup is over." I just had to try not to lose Elo points and win the tournament. Of course this is very bad. If Karpov had won in Rotterdam I'm sure that I could have won many games in Skelleftea. Just look at the positions in Skelleftea. He can't complain that he was unlucky in Rotterdam, because then I can complain about Skelleftea. There the same could have happened as in Tilburg. The positions were very good. I just had to use them. I could win nine or ten games easily in Skelleftea. In the last round against Nikolic I played very well in the beginning, I was absolutely winning with black. And then I looked at the positions and thought, "Karpov is worse against Ulf, I'm better", and immediately I made a mistake and Ulf made a mistake too.'

What about your relationship with Karpov these days? I gained the impression that you have reached a workable relationship.
'Whether it's workable depends entirely on him, because I think that he was completely unreliable in our GMA discussions. He was too pro-FIDE. First of all he had his own interests, secondly FIDE interests, and thirdly GMA interests. It was very bad. Right now he has changed a little bit. He doesn't care about FIDE anymore and he is ready to combine his interests and GMA interests, which is very good. I'm very glad that he signed the petition[28] and he wasn't isolated. I appreciate that we have this kind of unity. But still I think that Karpov is not really ready to give up some advantages in the interest of the GMA. Which is bad according to me, but which is probably right according to him.'

There was this story you were supposed to have told at a press conference in, was it in Switzerland?, when you were asked about stimulants...
'(Immediately jumps at this) This is very interesting. Where was this press conference? In Switzerland? Now there are three possible versions. The official Spanish press release said that this press conference was in Graz, in Austria. Now you say it was in Switzerland...'

No, I'm simply mistaken...
'Actually, as far as I can remember, this press conference was in Las Palmas. It was a normal question. Can you use drugs, stimulants, in chess? My answer was absolutely normal. I said "You can't. It affects you very badly, because it only has a short-term effect. But you have to play for many months or at least for some weeks. So, there's no use." Then they asked, "We heard rumours that in the first match Karpov probably used them." And I said, "Probably, but it's better to ask Karpov." This was my answer, but the transcription was different. Then Karpov wrote an official letter

---

28 The consensus reached between the Candidates' semi-finalists and Kasparov about the further proceedings of the current World Championship cycle.

to the GMA and said that Kasparov should write an explanation. My reply was very simple. First of all the fact that they mentioned Graz instead of Las Palmas indicates that it's just rumours. Secondly, if Karpov wants to seriously accuse me he must get the tape or a confirmation from this Spanish agency or newspaper. A newspaper with rumours is not enough for me, I'm not going to reply. I think that in the end we more or less managed to solve this problem. I understand he was insulted by these publications, but sorry, it had nothing to do with me. A newspaper reversed my words and insulted another player. I can help this player to accuse the newspaper, but I'm not going to defend myself.'

Much of your energy is spent away from the chess board. This year was again a very busy year. You helped organize the Moscow GMA qualifier, found a sponsor for the GMA qualifier in Palma and at the same time you continued your fight against FIDE and did your other work as president of the GMA. On which of these activities do you look back with most satisfaction?
'The Moscow tournament. Yes, this was a great success. Not only for the GMA. After this tournament we were also able to create an independent chess union, which is now the official opposition to a non-existent federation. I was very happy to get this going. If you know the situation in my country you will understand that it is very difficult to organize an independent competition without official state support. I found some good friends among officials, I received support from a trade union organization and from a cooperative enterprise. Very intelligent, very bright people who knew how to approach sponsors, how to find money. OK, I can tell you, we spent nine-hundred thousand roubles and about two-hundred thousand dollars for the tournament. Nobody could complain about the quality of the tournament despite all the stories. After the first GMA qualifier in Belgrade many people didn't want to go to Moscow. They didn't believe in the tournament and thought the conditions would be miserable in the Soviet Union. I think it was a decisive win over the conservative mentality of many players and sponsors.'

What are your expectations concerning the third GMA qualification tournament in Palma?
'Oh, Palma will be a great success. The latest news I received from Palma is very good. Everything is running very smoothly. And the Balearic government agreed to open a Kasparov chess centre. They will give a hundred million pesetas, which is about nine-hundred thousand dollars, for the building, for accommodation, and we will launch the academy in December. In the middle of next year we will start the first sessions for young western players.'

Can you tell something more about this project?
'Again it's my childhood impressions. When I was ten years old I was invited to the Botvinnik school and I felt very happy and lucky to be among his pupils. I learned a lot from him and other great Soviet players. It's a kind of tradition, a spiritual tradition in our country. The new generation profits from the experience of the

older generation. When I became World Champion I felt that it was very important to re-establish this tradition, because nobody paid enough attention to it. I helped Botvinnik work on this school and now it's my school. Some time ago I conceived the idea to create one united academy for the whole Soviet Union. I couldn't find financial and political support, nobody cared about it. Now the time is not right in the Soviet Union. So I failed and then I realised that it's much better to move this academy to the West. I got a very nice reception in Palma. In February we talked about it and in June we signed the protocol of intention and I hope in December we will open this academy. It will help to improve chess throughout the world. We also plan to open a special faculty for national coaches. I can bring ten or fifteen Soviet coaches, but this is not enough for the whole world.'

Aren't you afraid there will be problems with the Soviet authorities?
'No, no, no. We are planning to create a special academy in the Soviet Union under the supervision of the independent chess union and this academy will send coaches. But it will also operate in the Soviet Union. No, we won't forget our people, our kids. The problem is that it's a very bad time for chess in the Soviet Union. But Soviet chess won't suffer. We really want to help them, although it's extremely difficult. Because you have the old chess organization, you have these national controversies. If you want to help you need people who will let you help them. That's not so simple for us.'

In Brussels at the World Cup prize-giving you asked Bessel Kok to stand for president of FIDE. Do you think that this is the only way to avoid a split in the chess world?
'I'm sure, and I hope that many people share this view, that we need two organizations. We need a professional organization, let's call it the GMA, probably it will change in the future, and we need FIDE. Let's call it FIDE, anyway a general organization which should cover the development of chess such as these academies, these schools, everything. The GMA is going in the right direction. Within FIDE everything is wrong. I don't want to repeat that it is corrupt or that it is ignorant, but everything is absolutely wrong. I want FIDE to survive, but in order to achieve this they must first of all change the people and then the structure. The only chance is to get rid of Campomanes, all these corrupt people, terrible people like Ghobash, Toran and Makropoulos, and to replace them by normal people. I believe Bessel is the only person who can save FIDE, who can give FIDE a real chance, not only to survive, but to be reborn, to get a second wind. The current FIDE leadership can't accept the GMA as it is, but if they want to fight us they will be destroyed in this fight. There's no doubt about that. They don't care about FIDE. I care more about FIDE than they do. Because in the future all these academies should be under the supervision of FIDE. I'm only the World Champion. I can't spend my whole life organizing these centres. If they want to fight, then they will be killed. We have so many trumps and so much power in our hands now. But I repeat, we don't

want to fight and we did send this peace proposal. I think it is much better not to deal with Campomanes, but still we sent this peace proposal. They rejected all our peaceful proposals. I hope that the FIDE delegates will realize this and will kick Campomanes and his mafia out themselves. Because this is a real mafia. We don't even know under which law they are operating. Nobody knows, it's a secret.'

Not under Philippine law?
'No, come on, nobody knows. Probably the organization is illegal. They can't exist. If they don't realize it, well, that's their bad luck. The only way Campomanes can help and promote chess is by resigning now and taking all these people with him. As FIDE president he is destroying FIDE. If it is necessary I will fight till the very end. Apart from a powerful organization, apart from public opinion, apart from everything we have in our hands, I have the World Championship title. Right now I also have the best Elo ever, which probably is helpful too.'

In view of your fight against FIDE I have been wondering about your world title. Is it yours in a legal sense?
'Nobody knows, but I'm sure there's no legal ground for it. But just let's go into history. What's my number?'

Thirteen.
'Thirteen. So who was the first World Champion? Steinitz. Steinitz, Lasker, Capablanca, Alekhine and Euwe. They became World Champion without FIDE. I would be number eight if it's a FIDE title. This means that the title can't belong to FIDE, because officially I'm still number thirteen. Everything about the organization of the World Championship match by FIDE was so amateurish that nobody cared about the legal standing of the world title. But in the public opinion I am the thirteenth World Champion and the only legal or legitimate way to become the fourteenth World Champion is to beat me. He can't appear without beating me.'

What do you think will be the next step in the negotiations between the GMA and FIDE?
'I think war is inevitable. The last crusade of FIDE. The GMA will provide professional conditions. We need GMA performance ratings, a new system. We need professional team competitions. This is my dream, to have professional team competitions sponsored by multinationals. I would like to see sponsored teams with regular salaries for the players. Fifty to sixty real professionals. They have to be professionals because their salary will depend on their behaviour.'

You mean something like Kasparov playing first board for Hamburg and Karpov playing first board for Rotterdam?
'No, no, Kasparov playing first board of... eh... Crédit Lyonnais, and Karpov playing first board of, I don't know, Mitsubishi. Fully professional teams. This will be the

last step to create a professional chess world. This is my dream. It will be done in the next two or three years. I guess we can start with ten teams, six, seven players, probably including one woman. But women, this is the Polgar problem. An absolutely unprofessional story.'

What's wrong with the Polgar story?
'They are spoiling the professional chess world with their conditions. If the organizers provide such great conditions for potential talent this is very bad for professional chess. Everything should have an objective value. In a professional chess world you wouldn't give somebody more than he deserves. But in our chess world this happens. You can offer one sister more than you offer Kortchnoi and nobody cares. Which is very bad. But this is another story. Probably we will have to include one woman.'

And once you have realized this you can look back on your work as a satisfied man?
'Absolutely satisfied. Then we will have everything and it will be the beginning of professional chess. My job will be over. I will have completed my duty. I guess that I'm continuing Fischer's fight. In his days it was hopeless, because it was too early. He did a lot. At least he gave a very good example of how to fight against bureaucracy. His task was hopeless, because the time was wrong, the public wasn't ready and he had no real support from players and sponsors. Somebody has to sacrifice himself for the success of the future generation. It was because of Fischer's sacrifice that they couldn't disqualify me. FIDE couldn't use the only weapon they have against the World Champion. By preserving my title I could continue Fischer's ideas and now I guess I have achieved almost everything he wanted. Probably the World Championship will be independent from FIDE, that's exactly what he wanted. We've got the World Cup and there's the idea I just told you about. He would be very happy.'

Of late you haven't limited your criticism to the wrongs in the chess world. In the November issue of Playboy you severely criticized the stagnation in Gorbachov's politics. What changes do you think are needed in the Soviet Union?
'It's not a matter of what changes. The point is that there should be changes. Right now we have no real changes. There are some changes in the Soviet Union, but they are caused by the situation and not by the government. I guess that Gorbachov's government has a limit and they've reached that limit already. They are not in control and now they are being threatening. Like yesterday. There was a meeting of delegates and they claimed that they needed a fifteen-month ban on strikes. It's like a dictatorship. I don't think they realize that there's no way to repair this rotting regime. Because it was not only rotting during the stagnation period as Gorbachov calls Brezhnev's time, but it is rotting still. Now that it's too late they want to use strength. The people are very unhappy and they are

completely against this kind of politics. The government is going to lose if they insist on using strong measures.

'It's important for me to talk about this. Perhaps I am making a mistake, I don't know, but if you want democracy you need different opinions. I'm World Champion, I'm well-known in the West, in the whole world, and people can listen to me and compare these different opinions. It is very bad if you only want Gorbachov's opinion. I don't understand the bulk of the western press because they still continue to make these comparisons between liberals and conservatives in the Communist Party, ignoring completely the real strength of the country, the Soviet people. I think the people don't care who are going to win, the liberals or the conservatives in the Communist Party. They want to see food, they want to see agricultural and industrial changes, they want to see human rights, they want to see normal salaries, normal living conditions. And I think that neither the liberals nor the conservatives are able to give them these.'

Aren't you afraid that publicly pronouncing your opinion will bring you into trouble?
'Well, I have many friends, for example Yuri Afanasiev, who take really serious risks. You know, somebody has to speak. Somebody must be the first. I feel that I have this chance. If I don't speak, if I leave my country, if I live in the West, this would be a very bad example for the Soviet people. People say, "If Garry didn't do so many things in chess politics or in general politics or in business, he could be even more successful." Yes, OK, but without the organization of the tournament in Moscow, without Palma, without this fight against FIDE, I couldn't become Kasparov. I have gained strength by fighting against the system. At first I was fighting against the domestic federation in Azerbaijan, then against the Soviet national federation, then against FIDE, then against the Sports Committee of the Soviet ministery. By now I have to challenge the system itself. Don't forget that ever since my childhood I've had this slogan "If not you, who else"[29]. I mean, if not me, who else?'

What part did Vladimir Vissotsky play in all this?
'I think he played an extremely important part in the formation of my mentality. I don't know how, genetically or from books, I got this strong feeling that something was wrong in my country. Vissotsky's songs and his life gave me a new impression, a new vision of life. As I understood him better and better I came to the conclusion that the lives of people like Vissotsky should be continued. Their dedication to us changed a lot in our souls and somebody has to continue this. And if I feel the strength, why not me? Yes, I can do it. I have very good relations with his widow, Marina Vlady, we are very good friends. Probably she feels that I have the same kind of mentality.'

---

29 A line borrowed from the poet/songwriter Vladimir Vissotsky who died in 1980 at the age of 42.

Despite the fact that you are still very much the same Kasparov, who relentlessly continues his fight and keeps playing great chess, I get the impression that lately you have become calmer, less impulsive.

'Yes, this is true. First of all there is age. I'm getting older, wiser, more experienced. On the other hand I can now see the result of my fight. When I started my fight I was almost alone and I felt like a raider, dropping explosions and bombs in the enemy camp. This is all very nice, but you can't win the war in this way. You can create a big mess, but you won't win the war. Right now the character of this war has changed completely. Now my side is on the offensive, we've got the initiative, we're moving forward to the enemy's camp. I have troops behind me and we occupy the centre. There's a big difference between these two fights. Having real strength behind you makes you calm. The war of three years ago couldn't continue without these impulsive actions. But this fight in Dubai, against FIDE, alone against the whole organization, against my own national federation, against everybody, this fight started the GMA.'

And now you're looking back and there's no regrets.

'No, I have no regrets. Certainly, I made mistakes, but if you play a risky game and you have everything on the table, you can't avoid mistakes. And I accept only this kind of game, with everything on the table. I was very lucky, and I think that many people can't forgive me such luck in that I was never seriously punished for my mistakes. I was given enough time to rectify these mistakes and I always rectified them.'

Garry Kasparov

Linares, March 1992

'Something strange is happening in chess'

Just when an increasing number of pretenders to the throne audaciously questioned his superiority, the emperor struck back. For Garry Kasparov his landslide victory in the tenth Linares tournament could not have come at a better moment. On the day of the prize-giving the World Champion took his time to answer my questions. The unchallenged winner looked remarkably relaxed. 'I've found my place and I feel quite comfortable.' Yet, as always he was bursting with new plans, such as a challenge to the American team to be played in Caesar's Palace, Las Vegas. And he remained adamantly determined about his new position in the chess world. 'If FIDE is helpful, fine. If the GMA is helpful, fine. If they're not helpful, that's their problem.'

I take it that you didn't mind too much that Round 13 was played on Friday the 13th?
'(With a happy smile) Oh, no, I was very happy about that. My problem before the thirteenth round was whether I should play big chess or secure myself with a draw. But Ljubo made my life much easier. After his mistake in the opening I was forced to fight. By the way, I was encouraged by the score I have against Ljubojevic. I played several games with White and I won only one, besides four or five draws. As Black I played eight games, including the last one, and I won six (laughs loudly). I didn't look at Timman's game[30]. Actually I didn't think that he would win, just as I didn't believe that I would lose. When I decided on ...d4, I followed the position's demands. I couldn't let him play d4, because then the position would have been equal.'

In my New In Chess report on Reggio I wrote that your result and play there seemed to call for a period of reflection and preparation.
'Yes, absolutely. Before this tournament I had a period of reflection and preparation of more than ten days. Even more important, as I told you in Reggio, is the fact

---

30 Timman still had a theoretical chance to catch up with Kasparov if the latter lost and the Dutchman won his game.

that my life has been changing. Many commitments I cancelled. Not only because I wanted this myself, but also because political life in Russia is getting quieter. There is no longer this big fight against Communism. We still have some political conflicts, but the current situation leaves you time. Time to breathe, time to work, time to travel around the world. Or time to spend on chess. In fact, it wasn't a proper training session. I spent ten days together with Shakarov and Makarychev just moving the pieces. Watching games on the computer. No special preparation. Just looking at the French Defence, the idea I used against Anand. Some King's Indian ideas. I was refreshing what I knew about chess and I looked at some new ideas. And I felt before the tournament that the preparation would have some effect. I was not in great shape, but still in much better shape than in Reggio. I don't say that I reached a limit, but still it was a very good performance. I think it was even much better than Tilburg. Here I was more solid.'

This is a general evaluation. What about the individual games?
'Looking at the tournament, I can say that I got a plus-seven score without any substantial luck. The drawing of lots was quite interesting. I played Timman, Karpov, Ivanchuk, Anand and Gelfand, five of the strongest participants in the first five rounds. My game against Timman was complicated. I played it very riskily and maybe Jan would have been better if he hadn't made this mistake, Bishop d3. But still... if you want to win with Black you have to be prepared to take risks. Then I played a very good game against Karpov, probably one of the best games in the tournament. In the third round Ivanchuk introduced a novelty and I was pressed to defend, which I did very well. In time-trouble I even missed a chance to get an advantage, a probably decisive advantage. If I avoid the exchange of his bishop against my knight, leave his stupid bishop on c6 and play Knight b6 in time, his position is very dangerous. But I was happy, I played a good game. Then there followed a disaster against Anand. I didn't have enough energy after my game with Vassily. The same thing happened later on against Salov, after I had played a very difficult game against Yusupov. Against Anand I played a very strong novelty and played a very good game up to the point where I missed a forced win. Then I won against Gelfand, not very convincingly, but at least I showed some very deep analysis from the last match. He didn't defend the endgame very well, but probably it was lost anyway. Then I had a crisis, against Speelman and Bareev. These two games I didn't play well. Against Speelman I got an advantage out of the opening. I made a mistake and lost it again, and then Speelman played some dubious ideas like Bishop e3 and I got an almost winning position. Instead I made two mistakes culminating in c5, a move that loses by force. Speelman could have won by Rook b8 instead of Bishop c6, but we were both in time-trouble. One and a half minutes each for six or seven moves.

'In my game against Bareev I was lost again. I couldn't find normal counterplay in the opening and I was lucky. But then I played a good game against Short, and a normal easy draw based on home analysis with Beliavsky. After that I had a very good straight finish, starting with wins over Illescas and Yusupov. That was a very good game. Against Salov I also played a very good game, but unfortunately I missed the win. That is why these two games in which I could not complain were balanced out by these two games in which I clearly missed chances. So, I don't think that it would be fair to call me lucky.'

From your last three games against Karpov you have scored two and a half points…
'I have a psychological advantage now. The comparison I like to make is one that I read about after the first or second match I played with Karpov in Moscow, when someone compared us to heavy-weight boxers. What these heavy-weight boxers do better than other boxers is that they don't miss the chances they get to deal punches. And they know how to protect themselves. Karpov is definitely a heavyweight boxer in chess. But you know, he is pretty old now and even when you're a heavyweight you should move around the ring. He's not moving at all. I am still moving. For me it's easier, while I can still protect my face, to get him from different angles. Basically he is getting old, he's not moving, if you accept my comparison.'

Do you nevertheless think that he is going to be your challenger again?
'No. I think that he has a good chance, but I would actually bet on the three others against Karpov. If you give me the three others and you take Karpov, I accept equal bets. He has probably better chances than anyone else, but he is now in such a form that he can lose to anyone. Here he even managed to lose against Timman, the player he had been beating for ten consecutive years. I don't think that Short is in very good form, but still I think that the match is very unclear. Not because Short can win the match, but because Karpov can lose it.'

And what about Timman-Yusupov ?
'I would bet on Yusupov. He is more stable. But this tournament proves that something strange is happening in chess. It's the psychological pressure. The pressure arising from all the available computer information. The players make many mistakes and the mistakes are getting unpredictable. You see a loss of stability. Karpov is losing his stability. Maybe only Ivanchuk and Anand are pretty stable, but then again, it is not a high-class stability. They both lost their last games in Brussels[31]. They don't show very stable high results. But still they are better than the others. Look at the other players, phew, going up and down. You might say that it's a lack of class. But this is not the fact. They are good players. So, it must be the pressure they cannot sustain.'

---

31 At the SWIFT. Candidates' Quarter Finals in the summer of 1990.

Isn't that quite a worrying idea? If this is the result of the faster time-schedule and we are about to see the introduction of one-session games and knock-out systems?

'Yes, but this is a magic circle. What can you do? You have to make chess more attractive. Plus, the interference of the computer forces us to avoid certain adjournments that can be decided by computers. My opinion is that we need some experience now. With one-session games, with some other time-controls. We have to have some experiments to understand what it's all about. I don't think we have to move without any experiments. But something is definitely going wrong. Just look at the players. They all have computers, they all know theory and yet all of them, except maybe for Anand, spend one hour on their first fifteen moves. Which is total nonsense. Why? I'm in favour of experiments. We should find the best between what we can afford and what the public can take. (As if to stress the Champion's words, there is a knock on the door and in walks FIDE President Florencio Campomanes to hand Kasparov a Shogi clock[32]) I think that we should have some experiments with this kind of clock and I appreciate it that Timman and Speelman supported this idea as well.'

Obviously you take a keen interest in such new possibilities. What other activities have kept you busy recently, apart from the tournaments and exhibitions that people could read about?

'Oh, but I just told you in Reggio that I was in the process of a big change. I'm no longer involved in big wars anymore. I established my position. No one is challenging me in my area. I think I've found my place and I feel quite comfortable. It's a quiet atmosphere after three years of marriage. The situation in Moscow has improved, I fixed my position in the Democratic movement. Again, it doesn't take too much time or energy anymore. I feel much better now and I will have more time to concentrate on specific chess issues. Like my own tournaments, the chess academy, chess promotion in the States. Actually I'm going to the States from here.'

How are things going in the States?

'Very well. I hope that in April or May at the latest, they will have a title-sponsor for the match. There are some negotiations right now. I believe that more money will be raised than the amount required for the World Championship match. They publicly announced that all money will go to chess. There are several programs. One of the key ideas is to use the money of sponsoring companies that have a specific interest in certain African countries to send grandmaster teams to these countries. To improve the image of the sponsor and to develop chess there. I think we can raise quite a decent amount of money to do this. And there are some interesting programs in America itself. The organizers are accepting all my ideas including my

---

32 During the Experts Commission talks that morning the possibility had been discussed to experiment with this type of clock, which some believe has given Fischer the inspiration for his clock.

professional league, which you know is my old dream. If that proves itself commercially viable, chess will have a very good chance in America.'

You know the reactions of many American grandmasters. Trying to make chess big in the United States is like banging your head into a brick wall.
'True, if you do nothing you can save your head, but nothing will happen either. I still disagree. I think that nobody ever tried to do such a thing on a professional basis. This is the first attempt. Ted Field, who is so enormously rich, that he doesn't care what will happen afterwards. He simply wants to support chess. But these Intermark guys, they want to build up self-financing chess in the States. I think that the chances for chess development are pretty high. If you are familiar with American chess life, you may know that there's been some progress, but the major progress will be 1993. We're about to start campaigning, and that will be the key for the media coverage.'

Don't you think that it might just as well be true that the sponsors want to sell the product Kasparov rather than the product chess? That's what people often said about Fischer. Everyone was fascinated by Fischer, but few of them cared about chess.
'The product Kasparov is not a problem to sell. You can sell that in whichever quantity you want. I could just as well play some exhibitions, but for me the target is to sell this product to stimulate chess education. That is the only way to make chess really popular. To have it included in the curriculum. I believe we have fairly good chances. They're not very high, but don't underestimate them. Also here in Spain, in Galicia, there is a fair chance that chess will be included in the curriculum at the end of this year. I believe that the situation in the States is much better than three years ago or than one year ago. We have experience, I have a good team of people, I made good contracts now, and there is money. It's just the beginning of a process. I think that in three or four years' time I will have achieved the most important goals, i.e. to make chess professional, and to include it in the educational system.'

When you were talking about selling the Kasparov product, I was thinking about other sports and the trends that leading personalities in these sports tend to set. Such as Agassi who convinced many young people to wear cycling shorts under their tennis shorts. Or the typical gestures of soccer stars after they have scored a goal. You've also introduced certain novelties outside chess theory. For example, let's call it the Kasparov flick. When you capture one of your opponent's pieces or pawns you pick it up with your right hand and in one go throw it to your left hand before you put it next to the board. Or, when you're analysing you push your pieces towards the intended squares, there pick them up again and with a short bang put them down again. Is this something you developed on purpose or that gives you pleasure?
'(With a smile) No, that's just habits. Habits that any person develops no matter what he plays. These are just automatic movements for me. I only know that I've been doing this for many many years. I don't know why. Just like I also have the

habit of putting the knights with their heads turned to the left. That's the way I think it should be. I think that the importance of these things is increasing now. Professional chess life is becoming very tough. And we need to have good conditions. That's a categorical demand. We don't want to have something like Reggio Emilia[33]. There should be no disturbances, everything should be fixed. If the organizers and the public demand great games, big fights, a full sacrifice of energy, they should offer very good conditions in exchange. That's the only way to help us cope with these tough conditions.'

What struck me was that both in Reggio and here you had lunch very late, in fact immediately before the game. Not so long ago you preferred to take a nap between lunch and the game. Have you changed your views in this respect?
'I am trying to adjust to the World Championship match. I sleep before lunch. I think that is better. The game is very long and you're getting very hungry if you eat too early. I always had breakfast, then I went for a walk, then I had some sleep and then I had lunch.'

Starting a game immediately after lunch doesn't make you feel drowsy?
'No, no, I'm just fine.'

What about the Experts Commission's meeting today? You called it a constructive meeting.
'Yes, it was a constructive meeting. What we discussed today was prepared by the agenda in Tilburg. The key problem was the two or three-year cycle. My point of view was simple. It would depend on the financial viability of the match in Los Angeles[34]. I actually offered to go for a two-and-a-half-year cycle. Not to fix the date for the next match, but to have it somewhere between December '95 and May '96, again depending on the financial result.

'There are some other problems. Actually some unusual problem was raised by Anderton when we discussed the FIDE/GMA agreement. My point of view was and Anderton developed that from FIDE's point of view, that there was a contract between the GMA and FIDE, a contract which is based on the assumption that there was a players' organization representing the majority of the players. That did a lot for the players. That's why it needed some money from the World Championship match. From the next match this 8 per cent is some fifty thousand dollars. I think that the current GMA record is not very impressive, not really enough to get this money. Nothing is happening. I had many

---

33 Where plastic pieces and the absence of a special toilet for the players were only two of the imperfections that filled Kasparov with anger.

34 The city that was the intended site for the 1993 World Championship match. LA withdrew their bid after severe race riots had convinced the City Council that the money would better be spent on social issues.

complaints from my former compatriots, from the Commonwealth grandmasters. They are saying, "Fine, but what is the GMA doing?" Not one single serious tournament has been organized since Murcia. OK, I don't want to go back to this discussion. I think it was a wrong decision. I think the GMA had the upper hand. We could dictate our rules to FIDE. They wouldn't accept this, fine, the decision was taken.

'The result is that now the GMA is not functioning as it was before. We can have another look at all these major tournaments organized by the GMA and just ask ourselves, "Who was actually the organizer?" But, again, even if we forget this past rivalry, what is the organization doing now?'

They will need these funds to start new projects.
'Yeah, very good, but where are these new projects? I explained my position and I feel very uncomfortable. I still have the ability to raise money. I'm asked by many grandmasters, average players that feel very upset and that feel lost now that nothing is happening, to do something. OK, I don't have any ties with FIDE[35]. Some top GMs they can say whatever they want. I have no ties with FIDE, I have no relations with FIDE, I have no intentions to have relations with FIDE. I'm not fighting them, because they can't hit me and I can't hit them. I have no official ties with the GMA either.'

Would you still be inclined to help them?
'On what basis? The organization just took the wrong direction. They just thought they could do whatever they wanted, but they were wrong. I still want to be active, but I want to understand what the GMA is doing now. It seems that the organization is not functioning. What is the point of its existence? And I'm curious about the money. I could do something, but then I will need this money to start some projects.'

That's how you feel at the moment. That you're completely independent...
'Absolutely. Yes, I'm absolutely independent from anyone. We have our own organization in Russia now, the National Chess Union, but we're not connected with anyone.'

Did you ever discuss the past with Mr Campomanes?
'No, no, no. I don't think we have anything to discuss from the past. I think we have to give Campomanes credit for the fact that he was clever enough to understand that we are opposite-coloured bishops. We're operating on different diagonals. I can't do anything inside FIDE. I gave up all these attempts in '87. Then it seemed that there was the GMA and that the GMA would take over the cycle. The

---

35 Rumours that started after Kasparov met with Campomanes in Moscow.

GMA refused to do it. Fine, I established my own position and I'm totally independent now. My decisions do not depend on Campomanes or the GMA. I can do whatever I want and I am ready to work with any organization that is helpful. If FIDE is helpful, fine. If the GMA is helpful, fine. If they're not helpful, then that's their problem.'

There is one question that I should not forget to ask while we're talking about your activities. Last year here in Linares you announced a book on five World Championship matches. Are you still working on this book?
'I will just tell you what happened. My problem in '91 was that I didn't have any time to do it. Right now I don't think I have enough time to write really good commentaries on the last two matches. What I am doing now is working on a complete collection of Kasparov games. From my very childhood and with new comments. Dvorkovich has almost finished the first volume containing games up to 1982 or 1983. I'm writing some comments on the very early games. What the young Kasparov was thinking during these games and what the World Champion now thinks of these thoughts of this eleven or even ten-year-old boy. I think that will be quite interesting. But again, I will definitely cover the world championship matches. But I need time, because I want to make good books. I perceived some psychological resistance when I thought about writing about the last two matches in Seville and New York/Lyon. I don't know, maybe it's something I want to have behind me. But still, it's my obligation and I will definitely do it.'

Would you also rewrite material that you did with Nikitin ?
'I don't know. Again, it's a time problem.'

Two days ago I talked to Karpov who suggested that your books on the matches were written by Nikitin. Is this accusation too ridiculous to answer to?
'I don't want to answer to that. First of all, if you know anything about literature you can check the style. All books were written by me personally, by my hand. You can ask all people that printed it, typed it. The first book was written in twelve days. In '85. I started at the end of November and finished on December 11th. I wrote it by hand. Shakarov and Tsaturian actually helped to work it out. For twelve days I worked day and night. This was just before the match with Jan (Timman) in Hilversum. The Soviet authorities stopped the book for five months, because of the little introduction that was considered scandalous in 1985. They actually sent it to Pergamon in May. Because of these four or five pages of introduction. The second book took me three months. I spent more time on it and apart from that Game 16 took me ten days of analysis. Actually there are some mistakes in it. I don't know whether anyone went over all this analysis, but I looked at it with Azmaiparashvili and we found one mistake. Not a very principal one, but still. Maybe there are many mistakes.'

Let's return to your promotional activities. In January you played a clock simul against the German team...
'(Enthusiastically) Oh, we were just talking about Kasparov products. I think that this match had the biggest impact on chess in Germany ever. Did you see the German press afterwards? There were fifteen hundred people in the hall. It was a big chess celebration. I prepared very well for this. I spent four days, eight hours a day, in front of the computer together with Friedel. Actually for me this was a great training. I was very happy with this event. I spent a lot of energy and the public in the hall was electrified. I think that was important for German chess. I saw in your magazine that you talked to Khalifman and that he said that it would have been wrong for him to play. I think that is a wrong concept of professionalism. Professionalism implies that you go for an event that is well paid because of public interest. If the public demands me to play in a simul I might do it. First, the prize-fund is very high. Secondly the public wants to see this. If you are a professional you should accept the challenge.'

I think he was reluctant to take the place of one of the German players.
'So what? Now, you know, I sent a challenge to the American Federation. I know that Seirawan was very negative about it. I think this is very, very wrong. This match will be held in Las Vegas, in Caesar's Palace. With a betting line and covered by American TV. Can you imagine better promotion for chess? Plus, the prize-fund will be one hundred thousand dollars per night. And you know the conditions, the winner takes all. I accepted this and I think it's great. No one can accuse me of asking for a high extra. Each player can win twenty-five thousand dollars for one night. I think if you're a professional you should go for this. The organizers, the people from Intermark, only want native Americans. There will probably be a conflict with Russian Americans. Obviously they want to present an American American team. Like Seirawan, Christiansen, Fedorowicz, Benjamin, or Wolff. This is a much stronger team than the German team. I think I'm going to lose the match, but so what? You have to go for it if you are a professional.'

Any other team you would like to challenge?
'No, the American team is the last team you can challenge. But there are several other forms of chess. You can play consultation games. I can play against the British team consulting each other. What I am just talking about is taking such exhibitions seriously. These are challenges, first for publicity's sake and then for the money. You must do this if you consider yourself a professional. Forget about the result. You convey chess and the excitement of the chess fight to the public. Then definitely they will want to know more about chess and they will go for chess. Plus, it might give a new lease of life to the old tradition of playing simultaneous exhibitions. When there was a thirty-board simul and the person who lost had to pay. The grandmaster, too, had to pay when he lost. I think we should use all types of chess as long as it doesn't affect the classical form of chess. And it doesn't.'

Don't you think that with all these spectacular exhibitions, knock-out systems and super-tournaments, hard times are approaching for the players who are not in the world's top twenty?
'I don't think so. If you have big exhibitions there will be need for more players. If for example in America you have big events and everyone is going for it you have ten players to satisfy New York and Los Angeles, maybe Dallas. But what about the other states? If there is an interest in South Dakota, or Wyoming? Someone else will play there. My rough estimation is that within three years chess will give a proper job to between one hundred and one hundred and fifty players. It will be like in tennis.'

You're obviously fascinated by the prospects of chess in the United States. What about chess in Russia?
'Now there is nothing much to say about chess in Russia. Chess in Russia finds itself in fairly difficult circumstances because of the economy. We hope that we can just save something. I organized a group of coaches, we set up our academy near Moscow and we hope we can offer young Russian talented players the opportunity to be trained. We're trying to make use of the year 1992 which is the centenary of Alekhine's birth. We sent a letter to the Russian government, and there will definitely be a positive reply from Yeltsin, in which we asked to give tax deductions to any private company that will finance Alekhine memorials in Russia in this year. What we need is money. I will raise this money, several millions of roubles to finance the activities of the Russian Federation. Plus we now need financial means to send a team to the Olympiad and to organize other teams to establish connections between the Commonwealth countries. It's a very complicated process. Nobody wants to play for roubles. We organized several tournaments where nobody played, but then we organized a speed chess tournament with a prize-fund of two thousand dollars. First prize was one thousand dollars and thirty grandmasters were playing in the Central Chess Club. I would be very happy if we could just save some islands of the chess activities that existed and then develop them slowly. It takes time. There is no state support at all. The Russian government announced that they will only support big sports. At the moment chess is out in Russia.'

Garry Kasparov

Linares, March 1993

'I'm not going to compromise'

On the final day of the annual elite gathering in Linares, Garry Kasparov expressed his views on the creation of the Professional Chess Association and the impact he expects it to have on the chess world. Fully confident the World Champion summed up the ingredients that to his mind begged for some pretty good cooking. One week before the new bids for the World Championship match between Kasparov and his challenger Nigel Short were to be opened in London, the eager chef de cuisine still cherished good hopes on a settlement between FIDE and the PCA.

What were your thoughts or feelings when Nigel Short phoned you?[36]
'I didn't really expect it. I had my own thoughts on how to deal with the situation. I had no doubt that the World Championship cycle in this format doesn't work and that the system was doomed. Obviously, after my match with Nigel (Short) I was going to do something drastic. No doubt about that. I mean, you cannot go on with all this nonsense. With FIDE taking all decisions. Maybe theoretically FIDE could be reorganized. But FIDE was spoiled by having too much power. They had unlimited power. It was not a body used to fighting for survival. They used to get a World Championship match and took the money out of it. They're too lazy and too fat. Before this they were very bad, they represented evil. Now they are simply inefficient. Campomanes did nothing specifically wrong this time. It's just the inefficiency of the whole body. Even if they are trying to be very polite and cooperative. They cannot raise money. And if they cannot raise money why do we need them? They can bring no money for the professional circuit. So, we need something else. I am not going to raise money for the World Championship again. I made that mistake once. That should be done by Campomanes. And this should be done on a professional basis. Not a bit here and a bit there. It should be done regularly and it should work.

---

36   Short phoned Kasparov suggesting to play their World Championship match outside FIDE, which would lead to the creation of the Professional Chess Association (PCA).

ROSA DE LAS NIEVES

Garry Kasparov: 'I hope that FIDE has enough common sense to recognize that it's time to make a deal. To get some financial settlements and to go out.'

'Thinking about this I came to my own conclusions and suddenly when Nigel called I thought, "Hey, we can use this match as a vehicle to promote all these ideas." Because we will definitely have a venue, we'll have the English-speaking press behind us, and the fact that I have Nigel with me will definitely reduce the criticism of western players.

'Probably we have different motivations for this decision. There are great differences in our positions. Difference number one is that I believe that for Nigel it is one shot. For me it is not one shot. I want to professionalize the chess world. The second difference is that I think that Nigel is highly suspicious about managers in general. I think that without professional managers like IMG you cannot move. I will not lie and don't say that I didn't have any dealings with them already.'

You had already been playing with some ideas?
'You need somebody to do it professionally. I can play chess professionally, but the players cannot participate in the organization. We can definitely dominate the decisions they take and we will probably have the seal of approval, but we should not be involved more. There should be a commercial arm. I think there will be problems as to what this commercial arm can do. I think that Nigel definitely has his own ideas. But here I have very strong ideas too, and I am not going to compromise. I see clearly that the differences will come up and we'll have problems to deal with. But whatever happens, I said "yes" to Nigel to bring my own agenda that I had had in mind for many years. I think that now is a good chance. Within five days we will know whether we'll have to do it separately or whether we can find some compromises. But no compromises on the idea as a whole.'

You mean with FIDE or with FIDE and the GMA or...

'No, the GMA is not a player anymore in the situation. I mean that I am not going to compromise on the whole idea that the World Championship cycle, the professional World Championship, will be played outside of FIDE. You can like it or dislike it, you can say whatever you want, but there's only one World Champion. It doesn't matter how many titles you provide. Five, six, ten. As long as I am the strongest player and as long as that is recognized by the public, and as long as the money is here, who cares? As for the players, whatever their doubts, they will go for the best deal. Imagine the worst comes to the worst. There is no agreement, no compromise and FIDE runs its own cycle. What do you think the best players will do? You have one cycle where Garry Kasparov is World Champion and there is a prize-fund of a couple of million bucks. And you have another cycle where the prize-fund will be ten times less. You have any doubts what Anand will do? And Ivanchuk, Kramnik and the others? It happens automatically. I want ideology outside of chess. I want professional rules, commercial validity. And I hope that FIDE has enough common sense to recognize that it's time to make a deal. To get some financial settlements and to go out.'

When I saw you on German television after your exhibition match with Hübner and you were speaking so negatively about the sponsor appeal of a match between you and either Timman or Short I thought, 'What is he trying to do? To get a prize-fund as low as possible to indirectly kill the GMA who depend on their percentage and to play a really big match against Anand afterwards?'

'No, listen. I made some bold statements, because I just believed that unfortunately this match does not have big value. I thought that I would win the match and definitely knew what would be my agenda after the match. To start a new professional cycle. Now I think this match can help us to start a peaceful transition. If Campomanes has enough sense to understand that there's no way back. FIDE cannot run it. Full stop. If you want to have Timman and Karpov play your World Championship you will destroy your organization totally. If you want to see reality you have to negotiate, to get your money. But no influence. That's what I wanted from the GMA and that's what Bessel Kok rejected in 1989. To offer FIDE a financial deal, but no power.'

So, this match still doesn't have too much chess importance, but is mainly a vehicle to...

'Yes, absolutely. I did not, I do not and I will not have any doubts that I'll win the match. My target is not to retain the title, but to play great games and win convincingly. All conditions are very good to create great attention. I am playing a foreigner, not a compatriot, and we'll play in an English-speaking country. To succeed we need a huge audience. Ten times more than now. This audience has no idea about FIDE, the GMA. Maybe they heard about Kasparov, Fischer, maybe Karpov. Probably they mix up Kasparov and Karpov. Their knowledge of chess is very limited. They will buy the story you sell to them. That's why you need a new deal. That's why you need IMG. That's why you need TV. You need all these guys to set up the commercial arm. Who'll say, "We'll sell the story." That's what was done with tennis and golf. Chances we'll succeed in chess are fifty-fifty. If I believe I have a fifty per cent chance, I think I have to go for it.'

Do you think these chances can be negatively influenced by circumstances such as Short first calling you names and then embracing you, his dealing the GMA, the organization of which he was president, a lethal blow? There are people who see immoral aspects in this.
'From my point of view I feel very strongly about immorality. I didn't do anything that could be considered immoral towards any of my allies. I did everything in public, I explained all the reasons for my acts. As to what Nigel said about me... Well, when I was in England I got the same question. "Do you feel chess is like boxing now, where people make statements to raise interest?" And I said, "Yes, Nigel is doing a great job. He is making the match much more exciting for the public." I think that for the public I am talking, the millions of people, such things are irrelevant. They have no idea what happened in the past of chess. Unfortunately, chess history belongs to a very limited group of people. You know, I know, chess fans know, but we want to reach millions of houses. For them it will be a fresh start, a new beginning.'

Is the atmosphere where newspapers rejoice in abuse and insults an atmosphere the chess world should look forward to?
'I think Nigel had some problems in the beginning. He didn't know how to define himself as a challenger. Because (laughs) his score against me is minus-ten. Or minus nine, I don't remember exactly. A very very bad score. Obviously he was trying to get equal by finding some wrongdoings in Kasparov's career. Outside of chess. I don't blame him for this. I just think it was silly, it was stupid. I could have reacted strongly. I didn't. Because I didn't think it was relevant.'

When I spoke to Nigel Short before I came here I was surprised to learn that apart from Anand he had not spoken to any of the other players. Have you spoken to the others. I mean, is it relevant to you what they think?
'I don't think it is relevant what they think about it, if the money is behind us. At the same time I believe it's necessary to talk to them. I was a little bit upset that Nigel didn't speak to the players. With many players he had better relations than I have. I spoke to some players here. Maybe apart from definitely Karpov, Kamsky and Timman, I spoke to anybody else here. I think I got their understanding. They listened, even Ivanchuk, and they understand that if it's a good arrangement, they will like it. They're not going to do anything about it. But the idea they like very much. They'll go for the best deal. They have much less to lose. I have a lot to lose, because I am changing the rules basically against my interests.'

Do you feel isolated in these matters? You try to get things done and the others just sit and wait?
'I have been World Champion for almost seven years. I learned a lesson. The World Champion will always be isolated. This is a rule. And if you want to be the greatest you will be twice isolated (laughs).'

You hope to set up a new qualification system starting with the next cycle. Will this wreck the Biel Interzonal?
'It could take place in Biel also. I prefer a smooth transition. I hate wars. They are not very constructive. Now we have a chance to bring big money. If we're obliged to fight there is no problem. I feel very confident now. As a chess player and as someone who brings this new concept.'

What does the creation of the PCA mean for your International Chess Union?
'I can't say now. Maybe we have to amalgamate it with the PCA. Maybe there is a way to amalgamate it with the GMA. There may be a solution. I don't know right now. But we're definitely going to do something. I mean, we have many ingredients now for good cooking. But much depends on our quality as cooks.'

But I take it that you will be the chef de cuisine?
'(Broad smile) Yes, this result in Linares gives me some authority to be chef de cuisine[37].'

---

37 Kasparov won the 1993 Linares tournament with a 10/13 score.

Anatoly Karpov

Monaco, April 1993

'Kasparov, Short and Keene, a nice company'

'You have rules and at a certain moment you must use them.' In the serene quiet of the Monaco Metropole Hotel, the sumptuous venue of the second Melody Amber tournament, Anatoly Karpov is his usual laconic and confident self while commenting on FIDE's determined reply to Garry Kasparov's and Nigel Short's 'World Championship match hijack attempt'. While he admits that the current chaotic situation is not that bad for him, the former FIDE champion does not pull his punches when he expresses outright indignation about the foundation of the PCA and concern about the possible long-term effects. And he welcomes his unexpected FIDE World Championship match against Jan Timman. An encounter that may prepicipate another clash with an even more familiar ring to it. 'It's quite clear that I should play a match with Kasparov.'

What were your first impressions about the foundation of the PCA and the ensuing developments?
'It didn't come as a complete surprise to me. For me it was just another farce. Of course, it is quite clear that this idea has nothing to do with politics. This is purely a financial matter. Between the lines of this dispute with FIDE you can read quite easily that Kasparov and Short don't want to finance the GMA. They don't mention this explicitly, probably because they were both president of the GMA and they are ashamed. They don't want to pay to the GMA the percentage they negotiated when they were president. They know full well that by declining FIDE's authority they automatically deny the agreement between FIDE and the GMA. So, they don't have to pay anything to FIDE and not to the GMA either. Next, just to save a little bit of face they must do something for chess, mustn't they? – they created in theory an organization to which they promise to pay ten per cent of the World Championship match prize-fund. But in this organization there are just the two of them. Two grandmasters, Kasparov and Short. And, if I understand correctly, Keene as treasurer. (With a mocking laugh) So, this makes a very nice party[38].'

---

38 In a letter to the editor Raymond Keene denied that he had ever held a post on the PCA board.

Their breakaway from FIDE caused quite some chaos. Are Kasparov and Short the only people to be held responsible for this?

'From a moral point of view Kasparov had not even one point to complain about. It was he who caused the chaos about the venue for the World Championship match. He persuaded Campomanes to accept the offer from the United States, which was not supported by a bank guarantee. Then he insulted the Moroccan people and the Moroccan organizers, so that Morocco withdrew their bid and we had no choice but to accept the American offer, which failed completely. So, it was one hundred per cent Kasparov's fault.'

Of course, Kasparov could not foresee the riots in Los Angeles.

'No, but I remember what he said at a meeting in Tilburg. You may ask Timman or Ljubojevic. They were present as well, as was, I think, Barbara (Schol). We had lunch and there Kasparov said, "It doesn't matter that they don't present bank documents. If something fails I will pay with my money." Then I asked him to put this on paper (grins). Of course, as in many other cases, this didn't happen. Kasparov was absolutely convinced and even made this statement. Like he did many other times. He was always saying, "OK, but then I pay my own money." Which never happened. This is his normal way to force people to accept his proposals.'

Or maybe a way of expressing his self-confidence.

'Yes, but only recently at a meeting of our chess federation there were complaints. They said that he had promised many things, but that he had failed to fulfil them. Then he explained his theory or his view on life. He said, "Yes, I try to do a lot of things and in some of them I fail. But that doesn't matter." So, you can never be sure when he is serious or when he is cheating you. That's why I don't think that Kasparov had any moral grounds to complain.

'For Short it is different. He is a newcomer. He was complaining that they didn't consult him on the choice of the venue. But actually, according to the rules, FIDE has no such obligation to consult the challenger. In the latest version of the rules, which was accepted by Campomanes and the GMA, and Kasparov in his capacity as president of the GMA, they removed the rights of the challenger to be involved in this matter. Before it was the World Champion and the challenger who made known their preferences and sent in official documents. Now you no longer have any articles on this. Only the World Champion and FIDE decide where the match will be played.

'When this was decided I didn't take part in the discussions and I protested against this decision in the GMA. But nobody wanted to listen to me. Their way of reasoning was like this: two years before the match the challenger is not yet known. Still, we have to start working on this match as early as possible. That's why we cannot wait for the challenger. To which I replied that the main idea should be that the World Champion's and the challenger's position should be as equal as possible.

Especially in this respect. Which means that the World Champion should not be involved either. So, just take the bids, examine them and then decide yourself which is the best offer. If the World Champion is involved and the challenger is not, their positions are already no longer equal. Nevertheless they made these rules, which do not give the challenger any rights. As I said, this was done when Kasparov was still president of the GMA. They made these changes before our match in New York and Lyon.'

Were you highly surprised by Short's move?
'Yes, absolutely. What I don't understand is that he took this huge risk to damage his image. They are talking about a lot of money, but in the end the difference between the Manchester bid and the new one is not so tremendous. Let's presume he will lose, and if nothing extremely strange happens he will lose this match. Then, after all deductions have been made, all taxes have been deducted, he may make one hundred thousand dollars more. Maybe even less. Not millions of dollars. One hundred thousand dollars is not enough to risk everything you have got in your life for. I was absolutely surprised. I don't think Short had good advisers or that he spent a lot of time thinking about this.'

Kasparov's story is that he had planned to break away from FIDE anyway and that this process was only sped up by Short's telephone call. His main desire is to have professionals run...
'No, I don't believe this story. First of all I believe that the motor behind this was Keene and this group. Secondly, I cannot believe that a declaration like the one they issued on the 26th of February was written after just a few telephone calls. You must work on this. We know Short's schedule. He was at the GMA board meeting in Cannes on the 20th of February. Then he made a trip on a boat, when he could not be reached by telephone. This means that they prepared all this much in advance. The last occasion was when both Kasparov and Short were in England. On the 15th of February I was flying to South Africa. On the same day Kasparov left for London.'

This premeditated action is what Short firmly denies. He says he got this idea on the spur of the moment and soon afterwards he phoned Kasparov.
'And when did they prepare this declaration?'

It was only one page.
'Still, such a declaration... To decide on the right phrasing, for that you must spend hours on the telephone. I don't believe this. I was involved in many negotiations with Kasparov. He is very careful about any word that is put in writing. For instance, when we prepared the declaration on the rematch, when Kasparov didn't want to play and we had negotiations and he agreed, we worked on this, after previous discussions, for three or four hours in Lucerne. Just to put every word in the right place. You cannot solve this in three telephone calls.'

You cannot really compare this. Your personal conflicts were much bigger.
'Personal conflicts did not matter. We had already come to an agreement. We only needed to put it in writing in the right way. Here we are talking about a big scandal in the chess world. OK, they are on the same side, but still they had to be exact on many things.'

To my mind the entire document made an improvised impression. It didn't look like something that had been worked on for days.
'Well, then it's not serious. If Short just had to read what Keene had prepared. This is even worse (laughs).'

What do you think of Kasparov's conviction that professionals should run the World Championship cycle and that FIDE has proven completely incapable of doing this?
'FIDE made many mistakes. I have been complaining several times, especially about the unequal conditions in my matches with Kasparov. According to the rules FIDE must keep an eye on the organizers, inspect the venue, see that everything proceeds fairly during the match. Both in London and in New York the conditions were unequal. In Lyon the conditions were absolutely different for the World Champion and the challenger. In Lyon it was really bad. I am not talking about the houses and all the other things about which you can argue, but in Lyon Kasparov got a house at a five-minute walk from the playing hall. I had a house, and this was the only one that had been proposed to me by the organizers, at a fifteen-minute drive by car. Because of traffic jams, quite a common phenomenon in Lyon, I was sometimes late for the game. They didn't even supply a police escort, as I asked. According to the rules they must do so.

'FIDE didn't want to interfere. Actually, if you calculate this, every day it took me fifty minutes more to get to the playing hall and back. So, during the entire match I spent maybe thirty hours more in my car than Kasparov spent on his walks. This is a big advantage, about which I complained.

'I think that FIDE must tend to their duties. At the end I suggested, just to find a correct solution, that if the conditions are not equal, there could be a drawing of lots to decide in which place you stay and live during the match. In that case the organizers would be more careful about the conditions they propose. Because their favourite might end up with the bad conditions they prepared for the challenger.

'Well, we wandered away from the question a bit, but I think that FIDE must fulfil the duties they have. Of course they have problems with the Candidates' matches and with the Interzonal. I don't think that professional chess players can afford to organize the whole cycle. The main idea of Kasparov and Short is just to... OK, Short, I think, is just temporarily in this business, but Kasparov just wants to make his own choices. To play with one player and not to play with another. If he doesn't like Kamsky, he doesn't play him. And if he likes Kramnik or, I don't know,

Anand, then he plays Kramnik or Anand. This is easy. To organize only the sweetest part of the World Championship cycle. The world title match that brings money and public interest. But to organize a whole system and to be correct to every chess player at the top? This is something different.'

You don't agree that he has a point when he says that FIDE are not up to their task of staging the World Championship match and that it is high time professional managers take over the commercial aspects of the match?

'Maybe the commercial aspects could be done better. As for that I don't want to argue with Kasparov. At the same time I can say that over the last years FIDE managed to increase the prize-funds quite considerably. Let's have a look. The match Fischer-Spassky was one hundred and sixty thousand dollars and then an additional ninety thousand dollars. So, two hundred and fifty thousand dollars. My match with Kortchnoi in '78 was, I think, five hundred and something thousand dollars. Then the other match with Kortchnoi, in Merano, was approximately the same, six hundred thousand dollars. With the matches against Kasparov the prizes were going up.

'Of course, I am not talking about the matches in Russia, because they had no prizes at all. They just announced some official amount to pay this twenty per cent to FIDE. To us they didn't pay any serious amounts. When we played outside the Soviet Union it was different. I think the last time it was three million dollars or about three million dollars in New York and Lyon. And it was two million and something in Seville. So, it wasn't so bad, I must say.'

Do you give full credit to FIDE for these amounts?
'No. At that time, in New York and Lyon the GMA was involved. But Seville was just the organization of FIDE.'

The current situation doesn't seem to look that bad for you. First you can play a FIDE World Championship match with Timman and in case you win you might...

'Actually I am not glad with the whole situation, because I think it will hurt chess life and the chess world. It can bring chaos. Nowadays the World Championship match is just the tip of the iceberg. If you remove it the whole iceberg might break apart. If you destroy the whole system as we have it, this can hurt the chess world tremendously and affect the lives of many grandmasters. Not all federations have the dream to get a World Champion. Many federations want their chess players to become Candidates. Or to become participants in the Interzonals, you know. For this they organize tournaments and chess schools. For this idea. If you destroy the whole system then probably one day most grandmasters will no longer be able to get any money from their federations, because there no longer will be this interest. You just have the top of professional life and then nothing. Nothing at the level of villages and cities.'

What changes were called for? If they hadn't created the PCA, should they have worked with the GMA or...

'In principle I do not understand why Kasparov put so much effort in organizing the GMA, just to betray it and then set up another professional organization. If he had some deep ideas... Especially in the first years he got full support from Bessel Kok. All his ideas were supported by Bessel Kok. They had absolute influence in the GMA. If they had wanted to have, let's say, an association of the twenty best grand-masters, it could have been done.'

But this collapsed on this personal controversy.

'No, it collapsed because Kasparov was forcing Bessel Kok to the limit and then Bessel Kok decided that he had to show his position, because otherwise he would be like a servant of Kasparov in this organization. So, they started to have fights. But in these first years they could have organized it the same as, what do they call it, the PCA. Actually we had the idea to support professional chess, so I don't understand the deep idea behind this new organization. Just to bring Keene as a treasurer of this organization? Maybe. Maybe this is the deep point (smiles mischievously).'

You think that the role of Keene is much bigger than most people suspect?

'Of course. You may ask any grandmaster who knows Keene. Everything he is involved in is based on personal interests.'

Which in itself need not be bad.

'But very deep personal interests (laughs).'

You and Timman have agreed to play the FIDE World Championship match. What validity has this match?

'According to his results it is quite clear that Kasparov has been the best over the last years in tournaments. He is much stronger than Short. From a sporting point of view a match Kasparov-Short may not be so interesting as my match with Timman. The final result of a match between Kasparov and Short is absolutely clear for most people in the world. But when something is beneficial for you, then you use FIDE rules. For instance in '87 in Seville when the match was drawn Kasparov used FIDE rules to maintain his title. When they are not beneficial you throw out the rules. In the last six years Kasparov played two matches with me. In Seville it was a draw and in New York and Lyon it was plus one for Kasparov. We don't talk about the quality and the chances. Because I missed many chances. So, in the last six years Kasparov won by one game. Forty-eight match games and he won only one game more than I did. If he wants to crush me as he declared in New York and in Seville... On the other hand, for the last ten years Jan Timman has been one of the best chess players...'

But he has a horrible score against you…
'Yes, but in our match in Kuala Lumpur he was in very bad shape. Tournaments are different. This has nothing to do with matches.'

Like your score against Kasparov over the last five tournament games is 1-4 or something?
'Yes, yes. But you may remember that I lost against him on time in Amsterdam with three pieces up. And I didn't win a game on time where I was a piece up. That makes a lot of difference in our tournament score, you know.'

Is actually what you are saying that if Kasparov beats Short and you beat Timman, there may be a much more interesting match between Kasparov and you?
'Yes. Yes. It is quite clear that for the last few years our matches were the most exciting and interesting ones from all points of view. As sport events, from a theoretical point of view. We brought a lot of interesting ideas to modern chess.'

Would you be prepared to play such a match outside of FIDE?
'Eh, no. No, I will not play outside FIDE. (After some thought) There may be an agreement to play this match. But it will not be inside the PCA. I will surely not join this organization. Just like many other grandmasters as I understood in Linares and also here in Monaco.'

Out of necessity this match would have to take place outside the normal FIDE structures.
'It cannot be played within the FIDE structures, because there is no place for such a match. It could be organized under special conditions. But not under the auspices of the PCA.'

This is in fact what I meant when I said that the situation is not that bad for you. Of late you have been playing very well and more than once you confirmed your position as the second player in the world. You might find it a pity to go through the entire cycle to get to another Kasparov-Karpov match?
'Yes, but (starts laughing) this is a difficult question. On the one hand, yes. I am the second player and it's quite clear that I should play a match with Kasparov. But I lost to Short. OK, I was in very bad form. I don't know why. But you have a competition system. And if you don't win, you must wait. What to do?'

But you would rather not wait?
'Yes.'

Would you mind being called the FIDE World Champion if you win this match against Timman?
'We will have so many World Champions, that it doesn't matter what you call me. Fischer is World Champion… Actually, (laughs) the main point is who is the best player. This can only be decided in a match.'

This intermediate step wouldn't be too reminiscent for you of the situation in 1975.That again you would be declared FIDE World Champion with this other guy in the background?
'Oh, but Fischer was always behind us. Behind Kasparov, behind me. What can you do? OK, you have this reproach, but if in the soccer World Championship Maradona makes a decisive goal with his hand he says that it was the hand of God and still he is World Champion. What can you do about that?'

True, in soccer it is much easier to become World Champion without being the best team.
'In other sports, too. But what kind of solution would you propose? For instance, the European champion in basketball, Saloniki, was banned for two years. They won the championship in Turin, but their fans ran riot and the club was disqualified. They may keep the championship cup but they cannot participate in the next championship. Being the best team. But you must do something, otherwise you have complete chaos. Or take the British soccer clubs. It was quite clear that some years ago they were among the strongest clubs in Europe, but because of the disorders and riots in the stadiums they were banned from European competitions for two years. What to do? You have rules and at a certain moment you must use them.'

To your mind Kasparov and Short have placed themselves offside because they didn't play according to the rules.
'I think so. Actually, when I played Kortchnoi in Merano and then a second time in 1985, I suggested that FIDE freeze half of the prize-money of the World Champion and only pay this amount the moment he starts to play another match and defends this title. In this case Kasparov would still have one million dollars frozen in his account and if he doesn't want to play without there being any serious reason, if he hasn't had an accident or has fallen ill, then this money could be used for another match. And it would be goodbye one million dollars for Mr Kasparov (laughs). You would have a situation in which you not only control the moral side, but you also control the situation financially.

'We discussed these things in the GMA. Kasparov and Ljubojevic wanted the GMA to take full control in professional chess. We discussed this and decided that it is not correct to let FIDE organize everything at the bottom while you take the top. If you want to do everything, OK, then start from the Interzonal. When we discussed this we decided that the whole system is the property of FIDE. Which also means that the title has two owners. The first owner, known to the whole world, is the World Champion. But he is so according to the FIDE system. Because you can have another system and probably have another champion. Not so many chances, but it could be. Which means that the holder of the world title is the owner of this title, but so is the organization which created the competition and set up the whole system. So, you just breach the right of ownership.'

Timman expressed his hopes that your match would give a new lease of life to the GMA. On the other hand one strongly gets the impression that FIDE only wants the help of the GMA now that they are in trouble, whereas there were strong suspicions that they had no intention to pay the GMA their World Championship match percentage. What do you think? Is this a real chance for the GMA to come back to life?

'Of course. I must say that if Kasparov is not involved this is even better, because always we had these stupid discussions about personal influence and ideas that had pretty little to do with the other professional chess players. For instance, right from the first meetings I wanted to bring up for discussion the rights and obligations of both the players and organizers for private tournaments. Many cases are known of misunderstandings and violated promises from one side or the other. I proposed to discuss this and draw up a professional contract for tournaments of category twelve and higher. Both sides should sign such a contract, the organizers and players. To avoid situations where an organizer invites a player and then cancels the tournament. Or where players agree to play in a tournament but withdraw their participation one month or even one week before the tournament.

'But we never got to discuss this, because we always had these talks about the relations between the GMA and FIDE. Instead of discussing serious professional problems.'

You think there is still ample room for the GMA as a trade union for the professional chess players.
'If the GMA is constructed with serious representatives who start to discuss professional issues, then this would be the organization which I wanted to be involved in and which I had in mind in '86 when I started as a vice-president. This organization would be top professional and improve the lives of the grandmasters and protect all grandmasters who are in trouble. Just like a trade union, yes. In reality we failed completely, because we spent too much time on (briefly looks for the right word)... nonsense.'

Pierrette Kok-Broodthaers has announced her resignation as legal adviser of the GMA. Her open letter to the grandmasters paints a picture of a cynical chess world full of opportunism. What do you think was the most cynical aspect of the recent developments?
'Something I heard about the last GMA board meeting in Cannes. Short was very upset because of attempts by Keene to get involved in the organization of the Manchester match. In Cannes they spent a lot of time discussing this point. Short wanted to be protected from Keene and his influence and participation. Pierrette, as a lawyer, was giving him advice and she promised him full support. Then, only three days later he entered an organization in which Keene is one of the main officers. Probably she was upset by this. She recognized that she had spent a lot of time just for nothing. This was the last drop. It was terrible that she was adviser of an organization that was betrayed by two out of three of its presidents. I can under-

stand her move. I think that she had tremendous patience. In her place I would have resigned much earlier.'

You support FIDE's sanctions against Kasparov and Short. How determined should FIDE's attitude be in general? Should they ban PCA members from FIDE events?
'No, this is always very bad. To ban players. We also had these discussions in the GMA when we started. You remember the opposition we had for this rapid World Championship. Kasparov proposed to morally condemn the players who participated in this. He even managed to get a vote on this and achieved a majority in the first vote. This could have been the end of the GMA and a split in the world of the top professionals. But then we had some discussions and agreed that it was very bad to forbid something or to ban somebody. If you want to bring people to your side, just offer them something better. If you can do something better, people will come to you. I think all this banning is very bad. It's a relic from the Soviet Union. Not to allow people to go outside the country, so they cannot see how people live outside their country. A very bad habit.'

Is there a chance that Kasparov will be another undefeated World Champion? That he might end up isolated from the rest of the players?
'This is his problem. His way of life.'

Finally, what about your match against Timman ? Are you confident that you will win that match?
'Of course, if I start to play I feel that I can and must win. Otherwise you cannot play a match. If you're not sure. When you start to play you must believe in your force. If you say "Maybe I'll win, but maybe he's stronger", then you should not start this match.'

On the basis of recent results you are clear favourite.
'That doesn't matter. In a match your personal opinion is the most important factor.'

Garry Kasparov

Linares, March 1994

'I don't think that a match between me and Karpov is of any interest'

Silence has descended on the Himilce restaurant. The Linares clientele stays away on Tuesdays and many players skip lunch on the day of the closing ceremony. Ruminating cheerfully about his first win over the strongest player in the world, Joel Lautier is having lunch[39]. Then, in bursts Garry Kasparov, walks up to Lautier's table and inundates him with streams of lines he has just found that might have saved his game. Pointing at imaginary squares Kasparov radiates the fervour of a kid who has just discovered a marvellous new game. Is he trying to analyse away the disgust of defeat or is it the chess animal inside that has gotten the better of him? After lunch we asked him.

'It's not out of disappointment. I just like chess a lot. I felt that there was a great potential that had not been realized in this game. At first I didn't want to look at the game at all, but when I had a brief look anyway I thought, "Gee, what a situation". And I called Kramnik and I called Lautier. I believe it's a unique position. A position that happens maybe once a century. Why shouldn't we look at the position? The game itself was very poor in general. Because of White's extremely poor play Lautier had this trick 20...c2, which is probably a wrong move, because I could probably draw, and we reached a unique position. A position that increased our knowledge about the game. Definitely my knowledge about the game. The practical problems that might arise after 21.♘c5 may even put Black in danger of losing. You have too many possibilities. As Kramnik put it bluntly yesterday, "You have half an hour left. The first fifteen minutes you are looking for a direct win. Until you realize that there is no forced win and that there are dangers. You panic and then everything can happen."'

---

39 In the final round the Frenchman beat Kasparov with the black pieces. Anatoly Karpov won the tournament with the incredible score of 11 points out of 13 games.

Linares 1993 was pure chess for you. All your days were filled preparing, playing and analysing. Was it the same this time?

'Yeah, it was the same. But you may remember '91[40]. This year was better, but it wasn't such a good year either. I think that after the World Championship kind of crisis, there were too many other crises. Some may know that I was too active in other areas plus that I have major private problems, personal problems. And you can't isolate yourself. It was too much. Frankly speaking, I didn't work enough on chess. I was eager to do some work, as there was great chess potential waiting, many novelties. The problem was that I couldn't concentrate on this work. Then there was another problem. Here we spent a lot of time looking at some chess lines, but sometimes things don't work. If the opponent doesn't play the right openings, if you make mistakes. It just wasn't the right constellation to make everything fall in place.

'I could not get myself into the right mood. After what happened in my game with Karpov I understood that it was almost over. You know, it's madness. Something doesn't work. People talk a lot about the luck strong players have. Strong players always have luck. Because they are fighting better. Usually it's luck after you fight, but here, for the first time I saw luck without a preceding fight. Karpov's opponents did something wrong, including myself.'

You were White against Karpov and came close to losing.

'After 13... ♗a3 I probably could have resigned. It's madness. I had a few ideas against Knight d7. The main idea was what I played against Kamsky. We didn't spend less time on this position than Karpov did. After my game with Gelfand we looked at the position again. Suddenly I saw this game Anand-Epishin, and the next day I changed my mind. Why did I change? Something was definitely wrong here. My mother told me[41] not to spend any time on preparation and just go there and play. Before my game with Shirov I was looking what I was going to play against 1.d4. And Shirov played 1.e4. During this tournament I made many psychological and strategical mistakes. The main problem was that I couldn't mobilize enough resources. When I saw Karpov making six out of six... Ivanchuk losing a much better position, Illescas is losing, Lautier is losing, Bareev is dropping his rook, everything... To overcome this and play Game 7, I needed a lot of strength. Which I didn't have apparently. Before my game with Lautier I was thinking about Amsterdam already. I thought Karpov would play there. I discussed things with Makarychev. We were not preparing for Lautier, we were preparing for Amsterdam.

'Other incidents that added tension, even though they were no main factors, were this story with Polgar, these rumours before my game with Kramnik, and

40 The year Ivanchuk finished ahead of Kasparov in Linares.

41 On the phone.

then this story with Beliavsky which also upset me a lot[42]. These are little factors that I could have fought separately. I could have fought them all, but only under much better conditions. It was an extremely negative combination. I cracked down under the pressure. In some games I felt my strength, but... (After a slight hesitation) I believe that I am now about to go to a different chess level. This is a very painful process. I am rebuilding a lot of things. As I did in '91, when I switched to 1.e4 and changed my repertoire and my style. Now I have to do the same. because we have to adjust to the new time demands.'

You mean new time-schedules?
'No, in general. You can't work with all the available information. That's impossible. You have to find a way to deal with quantity. I think this is one of the secrets of Karpov's success. He is best adjusted to the new developments. He is playing with minimal resources and doesn't spend much energy. He takes the shortest way. He is not cracking under the pressure. Many players I see cannot cope. They lose in the quality of their preparation. And they are suffering.'

At the same time, if you look at the games that were played here, you can only come to the conclusion that chess is very much alive.
'Yeah, it is alive, but in my opinion we have to go further to reach a better quality in chess. For instance, if you look at the FIDE matches in Wijk aan Zee. Black did much better. For me there is only one explanation: lack of preparation. White is believed to be the stronger side. White is supposed to be playing for a win. But if you have not enough preparation this is not an advantage, but a disadvantage. You are trying too much, risking too much, and it works against you. It will take maybe a year or two for us to again adjust to the new times. You have a lot of tournaments and a lot of ideas and it is probably too much. But I continue my way of playing and preparing. I still believe in serious analysis and your own systems. I believe I will come back with some very nice ideas. I think it is very important for somebody to develop chess and not just try little moves here and there. I don't think that Karpov can survive with the Knight d7-system (in the Caro-Kann) in the World Championship match for more than three games. It is extremely difficult to survive with very solid openings in a serious match. In a tournament you can, but not in a match. There the real problems will be revealed.'

Which did you think were Karpov's best games here?
'I think there is only one reasonable game. Against Kramnik. It was a good game with an important novelty, and it probably refuted this line. Played solidly and

---

42 In his game against Judit Polgar Kasparov was suspected of having changed his 36th move after he had already released his knight on c5. Before his game against Kramnik a strangely inquisitive person came to his room to verify the rumours that Kramnik had agreed to lose to Kasparov. Similar rumours before his game against Beliavsky made Kasparov so furious that he went up to Mr Rentero and announced in true Linares idiom that he would fight to the death.

really well. Classical Karpov style. I don't think any of his other games here could be considered as proper games.'

What about your best games?
'I am very happy about my game with Anand. A high-quality game, with some tricky move orders. In the opening you have to calculate where the king is better, where the queen. And I think my game against Ivanchuk was a good game, because I was facing a novelty. My game against Anand is too much a game for professionals. There are some really hidden finesses in the opening that can only be judged by a professional. A conceptual game. And I liked the ending with Polgar very much. The winning combination after the time-control I calculated very precisely. Move by move.'

You referred to the Polgar incident. How do you see it?
'This story was raised during the tournament and revived especially before the end of the tournament. I don't think it shows the chess world in a good light. Particularly if you look at the person, Mr Toran, who raised it. Obviously, the purpose was to put some pressure on me. They succeeded, because I was very upset.'

Why couldn't you convince Mr Rentero to show the video of the game? This would have been within his power, of course, and would have put an end to all speculation.
'Rentero didn't want to have any more complications with this story. That was his principled decision. I was satisfied with his press release, which in my opinion put an end to the story.'

What will you do if they finally show the video and it appears that you did release the piece?[43]
'So what? I mean, I didn't do it on purpose. I believe I didn't do it. The arbiter was there, so sorry. I don't know. My conscience is clean. I don't think I left the piece.'

Did you discuss the matter with Judit Polgar?
'I don't want to talk with her at all. In fact, she just said publicly that I was cheating. That will be on her conscience. I think a girl of her age should be taught some good manners before making such statements. This afternoon she told me in the lobby that I had been cheating. She came to me smiling and said, "How could you do this? You released the piece. We saw the tape and it's clear." I said I didn't see the tape. And that I didn't think I released the piece. And she said, "I trusted you", and went, "You were cheating us." So I said, "Fine. If you think I was cheating, we're not talking anymore." She was there. Her sister was there. Her mother was there. After the game we analysed. She didn't have any single idea. What the hell, she could have asked it immediately after the game.'

---

43 Which was what actually had happened that same afternoon.

How annoyed are you by this result? Is it one of the bigger shocks in your career?
'It's the worst performance in my career. I mean, I'm not in such a bad mood. If it happens, it happens. It is quite annoying that it coincides with Karpov's best performance. Probably the best performance ever. That even I will never repeat. I think it is impossible to repeat this without such luck.'

It must hurt. Last year when we were talking you rightly called this the tournament of the players. Where we can see who is who in chess.
'Yes, but I will come back this year. I can take it. You have results. There are good results and bad results. So what? I can't win all tournaments. The only negative result from this tournament is that it creates more complications in the chess world. It is not going to serve any purpose. In my opinion. There will be some wrong ideas about what is going to happen.'

Let's do some stocktaking, as we did last year. See who is who. Where is Karpov at the moment?
'I don't know. It might be that he's nowhere. Because he is out of the legitimate cycle in my opinion. The legitimacy of the World Championship match depends on the World Champion. That's what chess history says. And not what a couple of bureaucrats say. I won my match. Short won the cycle. I played Short. That's it. Now some people follow bureaucrats and exclude themselves from the real cycle. Because this cycle is there. The moment the PCA put together the cycle there was only a minor historical change. One organization, which could not organize it properly, was replaced by another organization, which organized it much better and raised a lot of money. Since Groningen I don't think there is anything to discuss. Because we have our legitimacy. The legitimacy of the thirteen World Champions, including Karpov. Who didn't beat Fischer, but Fischer refused to play. Fischer didn't play the challenger. I did play the challenger. Who also beat Karpov. Short was the legitimate challenger. I was the legitimate champion. So, what's the difference? That FIDE is not there? Who cares?'

Where is Karpov in a chess sense? Last year you said he was enjoying an Indian Summer. It doesn't seem to end. He had a tremendous year.
'Surprisingly he didn't show his best quality chess, but it was his best year. I saw Karpov playing much better. I don't know. I still believe it's an Indian summer. You can't continue forever. He just proves he's a great fighter. He keeps his ability to fight and saves enough energy. The problem is the real opposition in my absence. He is just going from tournament to tournament and just gets it. Here it was really big.'

Does his result emphasize undeniably that whoever the two of you are playing, in the end the inescapable truth is that you are simply waiting for each other?
'Yeah, but Karpov lost to Short. I don't believe Karpov will beat Short in a match now. It will be an equal match, but he has very good chances to lose. Matches are different.'

People might have good grounds to call his loss against Short a one-off result.
'The fact that Karpov is not playing in Amsterdam shows that he stays away because of Short[44]. It shows that it is probably not that simple. I know something about chess. I predict that, if the FIDE-cycle lasts, Karpov will even have big problems in these matches. In a match you need a lot of energy that he is lacking now.

'Personally I don't think that a match between me and Karpov is of any interest. It would be an easy fight, because he doesn't have enough energy. There will be a lot of excitement and after ten games there will be no excitement. Different preparation, different... I think that Short didn't beat Karpov by luck. He has an extremely strong character. I felt it in the match. He was almost destroyed and still fighting till the end. I didn't play well in the second half, but still he was there. Short, Anand and Kramnik, I think these people can fight. A match will be more complicated for Karpov. In a match you have to waste a lot of energy. That's Karpov's problem. He is a great chess player, he can find great moves, but if it requires a lot of energy...'

You mean that in tournament play Karpov can apply his energy very effectively?
'Exactly. In a match you have a great fight every day and always the same opponent. I think that now he has to prove something... If he beat me and Nigel Short in these small matches you would have to review everything and say, "Now it's time for a match."'

OK, but he will not play in Amsterdam.
'He understands perfectly well that it's not simple to play six games against me and Nigel.'

I think that he'd rather play a big match with you.
'Yes, but then we return to this big chaos, an absence of any order. These people that accused me one year ago that I am destroying the existing system, now want to completely destroy the new system. Now that the money is there for all stages of the cycle.'

You don't see any interesting opportunities now that FIDE has decided that their champion can put his title at stake at any given moment?
'The FIDE champion doesn't have any legitimacy from my point of view. Karpov lost to Short.'

---

44 Karpov withdrew from the Amsterdam VSB tournament after Anand had been replaced by Short. Karpov argued that with Short the tournament had taken on a completely different character. To his mind such a FIDE-PCA clash demanded a special kind of preparation that did not fit in with his schedule.

Garry Kasparov and Anatoly Karpov at the 1994 Linares tournament.

You keep pinning everything on this one loss of Karpov against Short, while he had such tremendous other results.
'Yes, but he lost in a match. He also came very close to losing to Anand in a match. You can win many tournaments, but when it comes to a match you have to prove that you are the best fighter. He beat Timman in a match. Not a big deal. Not the biggest deal.'

So, you're attributing hardly any significance to tournaments...
'No, no, no. This result is absolutely great. But it is something separate. There are few champions that won many tournaments during their reign. Karpov and I are the exceptions. Nobody doubted that Botvinnik was the Champion, although he hardly won a single event. I think that the match is the only way to find out who is the best fighter.'

Alright. Where is Kramnik at the moment as far as chess is concerned?
'I still think his chess talent far exceeds anybody else's. He is really a potential challenger. He still has many weaknesses and he is struggling with his life now. Trying to find out where to go. There are too many problems that he cannot not solve easily. It's probably too early for him to make big decisions. But from the way he thinks, the way he plays, the way he analyses... Kramnik and Anand, they have some... Anand is more mature, but he also has some clear weaknesses. Kramnik doesn't have any clear weaknesses and he is extremely pragmatic. I think that in a match Karpov-Kramnik today, if Kramnik has two months of prepara-

tion, I would take Kramnik. An equal fight, but I would prefer to take Kramnik. He is making progress. The crucial question for him is whether he can make the step from the top top-player straight to the highest mountain. I believe he can.'

You are saying that Kramnik has bigger potential than Anand. And also that Kramnik has equal chances in a match against Karpov. On the other hand Karpov has good chances to lose against Short. Does that make Short the second player in the world?
'No. A match is different. In a match Short is probably very dangerous to anybody. You can ask Gelfand. You can ask, maybe Jan (Timman). Nigel's win wasn't a one-off win. To win the cycle is not that simple. It takes a lot of stamina. But Kramnik's potential is much higher. No doubt about it. There is another great talent, Shirov, but his instability... Players like Shirov bring a lot of excitement. That's very good.'

Isn't Shirov the living example of the unfairness of judging a player only by his match results? Perhaps he would lose many matches because of his risky play, but he is such a great player.
'It depends on what we want to find out. Tournaments are very important, but they cannot identify the best player.'

You might be a great talented player but simply lack the talent to play matches.
'That means that you miss the stamina, the ability to fight. All of which are very important. If you look at any World Champion, we have the combination of all these factors. If somebody can't fight, tough luck.'

What about next year's Linares tournament? I understand you had a talk with Mr Rentero. Did you discuss specific changes?
'I suggested that we do away with adjournments. To have four rest days. After Rounds 3, 6, 9 and 12. We play six hours. And then I suggested to change the clock. To a digital clock with, whatever you call it, the Shogi or Bronstein or Fischer way of counting time. The same clock and time-schedule we want to use in Novgorod, in our PCA Classic tournament. A six-player double-round tournament in August. A classical tournament. The end of the game is played like in Active Chess. It's a fair decision to change the clock to avoid some unfair results. In situations where somebody might play on a rook down because his opponent has no time left and so on. That was our proposal that I gave to Rentero and he said that he would accept it. But first he would talk to the players. In fact, I spoke to most of them and they liked the idea.'

Would you support Rentero's candidacy if he ran for FIDE president? As he intends to do if Campomanes doesn't run.
'That's not my business. I hope that one day FIDE will be a proper organization that will take care of their functions and will sign a contract with the PCA that will allow us to overcome the existing difficulties.'

If this is your wish you will need the right person to talk to in FIDE. Could you imagine Mr Rentero in that position?

'The good thing in Rentero is that in my opinion he has respect for the players. For real players. He loves chess. And he doesn't earn anything from chess. That's different. Normally we have little bureaucrats who try to get little pieces from everywhere. Rentero, I believe, would do most of the things in the interest of chess. But he also has his liabilities. Like some of his close friends. Who might give wrong advice. It might be a change for the better. Because he likes to do things in the interest of chess. I don't think he will change as president. He will be the same guy. It's FIDE's problem to find their place and to fulfil their functions and to recognize that there are new realities in the chess world that they should accept sooner rather than later.'

You don't think that at the moment Karpov's position is a new reality?
'From what point of view?'

Well, from the point of view of points.
'There is this double standard adopted by FIDE and also by Karpov. When they publish rating lists they don't count Kasparov and Short. We are just not there. But here, without my rating Karpov's rating wouldn't be that impressive. They added my rating just for the purpose of the average rating. It's a classical double standard. You do whatever is useful. Again, it's a great pity that Karpov is not there in the cycle. But, so what?'

Anatoly Karpov

Linares, March 1994

'Now I can say that I am the best player of the moment'

Looking back on his stupifying explosion Anatoly Karpov remembers that it was actually Don Luis Rentero himself who first hinted at a super-score. Gratified by his first two victories he wondered why Karpov could not win his first six games. Karpov duly obliged and finally finished with an unprecedented total of nine wins. Yet, he declines to see his FIDE-title in a different light. 'I don't understand this obsession with the World Championship. Who is FIDE champion and who is PCA champion.' To Karpov's mind we need a new approach. A World Champion he will always be. The only accolade he claims after his resounding victory in Linares is 'The Best Player of the Moment.'

After Tilburg you took a break that was almost similar to the kind of break you usually take before a World Championship match. Except for a friendly match against Morovic that you won 5-1 you virtually stayed away from chess. Was this Linares tournament that important to you?
'No, I didn't have any special preparation. My good fortune was that after my match with Morovic I spent five days away from chess. Away from anybody. I went to the south of Gran Canaria and was just lying on the beach in the sun, alone at the ocean. This was very good for my nerves. I left there five days before this tournament. This was a very important part of my preparation. Just to do nothing. As for my chess I mostly relied on what I did last year. When I played all these tournaments and especially when I prepared for my match with Jan (Timman). So, evidently we did some good work.'

When did you get the feeling that things were going even better than you could have expected?
'It's interesting, but I had a clear feeling at the drawing of lots. Normally you are a little bit disappointed if you pick a number in the second half. This means one extra black game. Moreover, I drew the black colours against Kasparov. So, two negative emotions during the drawing of lots. Still, I had no bad feelings. I was neither disappointed that I took a number in the second half nor that I had to play Black against Kasparov.'

Why?

'I don't know. I was looking at the list and immediately saw the good news that I would get Kasparov's opponents one round later. This is good, because he gives them a hard time (laughs). And then the next day I play against them. Of course, Shirov was in the best situation in this tournament. He met players who had just played Kasparov and me. Actually he proved how good this position was.

'The first game against Lautier I played quite well. I had pressure and under this pressure he made this big mistake. People just reported that I was lucky in this game, but it was not as simple as that. It was no coincidence that Lautier made this last mistake. He felt uncomfortable in many variations and then he overlooked the simplest one. This may happen when you defend a position for a long time. Suddenly you don't like one continuation, then another, and finally you make a move that loses even faster. This was a good start. In my second game against Bareev I had a long fight and then in time-trouble he made a mistake.

'Already two out of two was a very good start. Then Rentero approached me in the lobby. Many people were around. He is always very emotional about victories. He said if you can win two games, why can't you win six games in a row. He was the first who said this. I won my third game and my fourth and then six. In fact, I even could have won more. I got some problems when I had played Kasparov and beat Gelfand. I got a little bit tired and missed these easy wins against Shirov and Kamsky.'

Somebody who observed you in the early rounds said that it looked as if you were surprised by the ease with which you scored your points. As if you were looking around you thinking, 'What has happened to my opponents? Is this Linares?'

'No, I didn't have this feeling. I was just playing. Actually I was the hardest worker in this tournament. I played all my games to the full and had two adjournments. Many games of five hours. Probably I spent much more time at the board than anybody else.'

Were you ever overcome by fear that you might collapse like you did in the Rotterdam World Cup when after a tremendous start you inexplicably lost your three last games?

'Yes. Even now I cannot explain what happened in Rotterdam in those last three games. Probably my nervous system collapsed. There was one moment here that I thought about this. When I missed the win against Shirov. Then I got the feeling that I must remain very alert so as not to repeat Rotterdam. I had these thoughts and I was more careful in my next games when I was calculating variations. And more careful in spending my time.'

People often suggest that sportsmen should stop at the peak of their careers. You regained the FIDE world title, you beat Kasparov in one of the strongest tournaments in history. What drives you on?

'I don't know. I like chess. It is very easy to decide for somebody else. It would leave an emptiness in my life. I like to play chess. I like to see people in the chess world. So, why stop? Of course, this would be a great moment to stop. Just to say: "OK, goodbye, (laughs) I don't want to see you anymore." But this is not true. I like the chess atmosphere.'

Do you also need this chess atmosphere? The tension of tournaments. The kick of winning them?
'If I stay away from chess for one month I feel that I miss something. I want to play. If one day you decide to stop completely, life is over.'

Does it surprise you that you have been playing so well in the past year? Is there an explanation for what people call your second youth?
'I don't know. Yes, last year was extremely successful. I only lost this decisive game against Kasparov in Linares. I was too active in this game. I felt I had good chances to win the tourna-ment, I had White, so I took risks.

Anatoly Karpov, king of the 1994 Linares tournament.

Then I lost the game. Otherwise I won almost all tournaments with very big scores. Dortmund, Dos Hermanas and Tilburg at the end of the year. One of the most successful years in my life.'

Are you especially motivated by the current situation in the chess world? The rivalry between FIDE and PCA?
'Maybe. (With a telling smile) Maybe this also creates some additional motivation.'

The other day in the press room Ljubojevic was comparing the current situation to the one in 1975. He argued that the moment Karpov gets a world title for, let's say, free he feels a tremendous urge to prove that he indeed is the World Champion.
'Mmm, mmm. Of course, the situations can be compared.'

How long did it take before you really felt World Champion after Fischer refused to play? When did you prove it to yourself?
'I felt that in the absence of Fischer I was the best. I proved it. It was not my problem that Fischer stopped playing. What could I do? If somebody stops playing he can't claim the title for himself for the rest of his life. Immediately when this match didn't happen in April, I played in Ljubljana/Portoroz in June and I won

211

nicely. Next I played the Milano tournament in August. In this tournament almost all the best players played. When I won this tournament everybody stopped talking.'

How were your feelings this time? Did you feel World Champion after the last game in Jakarta?
'No, but this is not the right approach to the problem. I think that only in chess you have this strange discussion about the World Championship. It would be better not to speak about the World Champion, but about the best player of the moment. Once you got the world title you have it forever. In history you are World Champion, like you are president of the United States. Nobody says ex-president of the United States, Richard Nixon. Or ex-Olympic winner Mark Spitz. It is Olympic winner Mark Spitz. And it doesn't matter if it was '72 or '76.'

People do say former president Nixon...
'No, normally they just say president. As they say Olympic winner Mark Spitz. Nobody says ex-Olympic winner Mark Spitz. This sounds stupid. You must speak of the best player of the moment, of the year. As Fischer became World Champion, Botvinnik became World Champion, they are World Champions. Botvinnik is not the best player now, but he is still World Champion.'

You mean he is a World Champion.
'Yes, and apart from that you can talk about who is the best player. The best player of the moment. When I won in Jakarta I could not say to myself that I was the best, because Kasparov was still there. Now I can say that I am the best player of the moment. Because I won this tournament where everybody participated. Now it has been proved. Of course, in Jakarta I could have said that I was one of the best. Kasparov and me, we were the best. It was still an open discussion who was the best. Now, because I was playing much better here, it's quite clear.'

How long do you remain the best player of the moment?
'Till the next possibility occurs when we play. We might play a match, I don't know. But for the moment it's quite clear.'

This whole question of FIDE and PCA World Championships doesn't really bother you?
'Not too much. How shall I put it? I'm not jealous. I was always saying that Botvinnik is World Champion. That Spassky is World Champion. Fischer is World Champion. What is the problem? Kasparov is World Champion. This is not a problem for me. I never said that only I am World Champion and all the others who are no longer active are stupid. This is not a problem for me. I don't even have the wish to explain this to anybody. I am World Champion in the FIDE system and Kasparov World Champion in the PCA. I think this is just ridiculous.

'I don't understand the discussions, you know. You have two systems. One is the winner of the one system, the other is the winner of the other. In other sports you can find many such examples. For instance, at the Olympic Games in Barcelona, Sergey Bubka, one of the greatest pole vaulters, failed and another one won the Olympic title. He was the best, even though Bubka had all the world records. Still this other pole-vaulter was the winner. So what is the discussion about?'

You mean the world title is comparable to an Olympic medal. If you win it it doesn't necessarily mean that you are the best.
'Right.'

This deviates from the idea that always existed in the chess world. People have always been obsessed by the idea that the World Champion should be the best player.
'This is not necessary. Why? This was not always the case. For instance the last years that Botvinnik was World Champion. In tournaments Keres was better, Tal was better. And many others were better. Botvinnik was just more successful in matches. He was regaining the world title, because of the matches. In tournaments he was weak. He won many Soviet championships, but in international tournaments he was weak. Another example. Spassky lost the match to Petrosian in '66. But from '66 to '69 he won almost all tournaments he played in. Petrosian won maybe one or two strong tournaments. So how can you say Petrosian was the strongest in '68 when Spassky won everything? Even with Fischer. He took the title, but then he stopped playing. Can you say he was World Champion in '73, '74 and half of '75? Of course not. It's a discussion without end. But not a very serious one (laughs apologetically).'

In Jakarta you said you didn't feel the urge for a unification match or whatever one might call this. The one who needed this match more was Kasparov.
'(Broad grin) Now he needs it even more.'

To what extent do you need it?
'I just wait, you know. I await serious proposals. Now he needs it much more than after Jakarta. This is quite clear.'

Which did you think were your best games here?
'I won a very nice game against Topalov. This was probably my best game. And my game against Kramnik. The final position is easily winning. That's why he didn't know what to do. He was trapped. He looked at the clock and saw that his flag was about to fall. Then he looked at the position, but he couldn't find a move (laughs).'

And which did you think were Kasparov's best games?
'Kasparov's best game? Probably against Anand. But Anand told me he didn't play well in this game. He shouldn't take the bishop on h5. Then, I must look. (Takes the playing schedule and sums up Kasparov's opponents) Maybe his game against

Ivanchuk was good. Illescas, not good. Kamsky played very badly. Bareev was in the first round. OK, possible. Not a very good game, but possible. I think his games against Anand and Ivanchuk.'

Last year Kasparov said that Linares was the tournament of the players. The tournament where the players take stock. Could you give an assessment of who you think is who in the chess world after this tournament?
'At the press conference after last year's tournament Kasparov said that this is the real world championship.'

Well, he called it the unofficial world championship.
'Yes, yes (laughs). It would be interesting to ask him again this year. How he feels about this tournament. This tournament showed that Kramnik and Shirov are already real top players. Of course, like everybody, Ivanchuk is disappointed with his performance here. This is not his level and not his style. He must have collapsed in the first rounds. After he lost to Kasparov with Black and to me with White. Then, it's clear that Anand is one of the top players. So, in this tournament the ranking is as it should be.'

What about Kamsky?
'In this tournament he didn't play his best. He lacked confidence. For him it's not easy, because he is alone. Probably he lacks the right approach to work on chess more successfully. He needs guidance. When he was still in the Soviet Union he had no real trainer or good friend to help him. He left the country at the age of fifteen and he is absolutely alone in the United States. Working on his own. Probably because of that he has his problems from time to time.'

And Judit Polgar?
'Judit Polgar didn't show her best, but this was her first experience in a very strong and tough tournament. Here you have to work every day with full energy. In the other tournaments she played you may have your occasional short draw or weak opponent to have some rest, but here you have no weak opponents. She could feel it right from the first round when she lost to Illescas. And then she collapsed after her game with Kasparov. She lost four or five games in a row[45]. Probably this incident demoralized her completely.'

What do you think should have been done about this incident? Do you think the organizers should have shown the film rightaway?
'I don't know. These things are difficult to prove. Maybe we came to the best solution in Gijon, when I had a similar case with Yudasin. He claimed that I released the piece. I was absolutely winning. Five pawns up or something like this. But in rapid chess it's easier just to stop all this arguing. We just agreed to replay the game.

---

45 She scored half a point from her next five games.

There were players who said that I hadn't released the piece and there were two journalists who said I had released it. Most players said I hadn't. And then Yudasin and I had the same idea almost at the same time. He said, "Why don't we play another game to decide who is the winner in this situation?"

'Here they had videos, so they could prove it. But the situation is very difficult to solve, because they were both in terrible time-trouble. If you interrupt the game this will always be to the advantage of one side. Of course, the arbiter should be more careful and strong. But then... It is my conviction that in chess the arbiter is not sufficiently protected. It is not good that players can dictate to organizers who should be the arbiter of a tournament and who cannot be. Then the arbiters always depend on the players, especially on the top players. Could you imagine Falcon stopping the game and saying, "Mr Kasparov, you left your piece, you must lose the game?"'

You insinuate that he could not do this. That this conflicted with his interests. Why couldn't Mr Falcon step in and stop the clock?
'He is the chief arbiter of the PCA. What do you think of his PCA activities (starts laughing) if he had stopped the game and said, "Mr Kasparov you made a terrible mistake but you must execute the move you made."'

Do you find that you can say these things openly?
'Why not? I have had many such problems in my matches with Kasparov and I talked openly about this. In London, in New York. When the arbiters didn't want to act according to the rules. In London there was this problem with the rest rooms. When Kasparov passed through the press room on his way to the rest room. In New York we had this problem with this non-existing flag of Kasparov.'

Suppose it is proven that Kasparov didn't release the piece. In that case there would not be any blame on Mr Falcon.
'If it is proven that he didn't release it, then OK, then he was right. But it was the opposite. Some journalists said they saw the video and they also saw photos from the video of the moment. It is quite clear.'

Why don't they show these pictures?
'They want to sell them. They showed them privately and I think they also showed them to Rentero. They don't want to show the tape publicly because they want to sell it (laughs heartily).'

Your conclusion is that there are too many mixed interests in the choice of arbiters. Just like when Kortchnoi did not accept Baturinsky here as an arbiter in '89.
'I think that arbiters should have a commission of arbiters, just like we have a commission of players. FIDE should pay much more attention to these problems. As the arbiters are not protected they cannot act according to the rules. They act

according to the wish of one of the players. If one of the players is more noisy or more famous the arbiter will serve him.'

Don't you think you sometimes exaggerate your suspicions. Like yesterday, in the last round but one, when you finished your game and I asked if you had seen Kasparov's position against Beliavsky. You said, 'I don't need to watch because the result of that game has been known from the very first move'. Do you regret that you said this?
'No, I don't regret this. I think they were waiting. If I would not have cases against Kasparov, clear cases when he got points, I would not say this.'

Nothing happened yesterday. The game was drawn.
'Because it was a hopeless situation. I made a draw. If I had lost to Anand it probably would have been another result. If the game had ended in a draw before my game I would have had no suspicions. As it happened after my game I still have suspicions.

   'It's better not to have such situations with seconds playing in the same tournament. Even if nothing happens it is very unpleasant psychologically. There is always this possibility. You know which people are absolutely correct and never make any special results. Most of the top players are like this. But still it's better not to have these situations.'

It's a difficult subject. In Dortmund both you and Epishin have been invited. In the eyes of others this also may look like asking for trouble[46].
'No, in most cases, like when I played with Furman, I mostly made draws. We never played one game. We made only draws. Normally I make draws with my trainers. Only against Balashov I always played. We agreed on this beforehand. We always played but we would not play variations on which we had worked together. If you look at our games when we were working together you will always see some variation out of any world championship program or other. Because this was our agreement.'

You briefly mentioned that in case of a good offer you might consider a match against Kasparov. Would this be a good solution to the split in the chess world?
'It is not possible to have a final solution yet. Because Kasparov wants to destroy FIDE and wants the PCA to be the only organization. I am not a big apologist of FIDE, but still we need an international organization and the PCA cannot replace FIDE. The PCA is only for a few grandmasters. Not for all players in the world. Kasparov will never make a programme for children, for women. He will never organize zonal tournaments or team competitions. They aim for just a very narrow area of chess activity in the world. They pretend to be the main organization and want to kill the others. But they have no program for this.

---

46 In Dortmund Karpov beat Epishin, who was in poor form.

'The approach of the press is also very strange. That the PCA can replace FIDE. Never. Maybe FIDE's structure could be changed into another organization. But it still would be an international organization like FIDE. If we didn't have the experience of the GMA I might be more optimistic about the PCA. I know too many stories of the GMA. How it was acting and what happened with the organization. I have big doubts about the PCA. Why they exist and whom they would serve (with a meaningful smile).'

You're thinking of one particular somebody?
'Yes. No, maybe now there are two (laughs). I think the PCA started to make big problems and we should not stay silent about this. They organized their events to clash with traditional tournaments. This means they don't want to coexist peacefully. They want to fight. This is very bad. Now they have got this money from Intel for a rapid chess circuit and, I don't know, maybe for a World Championship match. But with this money they want to kill traditional tournaments. Perhaps next year Intel says, "OK, it was a nice experience but now we are no longer interested in chess." And we will be without Intel and without traditional organizers.'

Are you intending to use your prestige as a leading player to fight this?
'I think that it is absolutely urgent and necessary to have negotiations to clarify the position of the PCA. If they intend to continue like this or not. Most important is that every grandmaster understands what he wants. What he wants and what is the danger. If most grandmasters don't feel any danger they may play PCA tournaments and traditional tournaments, but next year their calendar may be empty. For the average grandmaster conditions are getting worse. It's not easy to be number forty, never mind number eighty or ninety.

'In the PCA this gap between top chess players and middle level chess players will only widen. They have some good prices in these rapid tournaments, but if everybody plays most of them will spend more on their expenses than what they get back in prices. Their situation will only get worse. You need some brains to see through the present situation and to understand what the consequences will be. Unfortunately grandmasters don't have time to use their brains to understand real life. Only when they start to get less money do they feel that something happened (laughs).'

It's funny that you too have a rather low opinion of your colleagues' understanding of these matters. Kasparov told me yesterday that 99 per cent of the chess players did not understand what was going on in the chess world.
'Unfortunately that is true.'

So finally we have found a point on which the two of you agree.
(Laughs consentingly, but carefully avoids to give an affirmative answer.)

Young and Challenging

At many chess tournaments it is common practice among the press to bet on the outcome of the most important games of the day. In a similar vein, journalists and other assorted chess experts never tire of appointing the 14th chess champion who will one day succeed to Garry Kasparov. Predicting the next World Champion is a hazardous undertaking that reminds me of a wonderful remark I heard on Dutch television this summer. A regular feature in the endless stream of soccer World Cup broadcasts from the United States was the unavoidable question: Who would win the World Cup? The answer that appealed to me most came from a former Dutch international who could boast some seventy caps. Solemnly looking into the camera he said, 'First of all, let me get one thing straight; we all know an awful lot about soccer.'

I must also confess that over the years I have correctly predicted the outcome of numerous matches and tournaments. Yet, I would be reluctant to announce Kasparov's successor for several reasons. One reason is that we may not even know his or her name yet. We should not forget that when Kasparov was rising to the top, it was clear for everyone to see that sooner or later he would challenge and beat Karpov. Right now such a player is not around. Another reason may be the authoritative example that Kasparov has set with his rapidly changing and erratic predictions. In 1991 he opted for Gelfand and Ivanchuk. As if on clue they both got immediately kicked out of the cycle. Kasparov's next protégé was Vladimir Kramnik, the wonderfully talented heir to the Botvinnik-Kasparov school. I still remember Jan Timman's joking remark when he heard about Kasparov's new favourite. 'Poor guy, so much for his chances.' This year Kramnik first obliged Kasparov by beating him in Linares and a second time by knocking him out of the Moscow PCA rapid tournament. Then, however, he managed to get eliminated from no less than two world championship cycles.

Perhaps it is Viswanathan Anand's good fortune that Kasparov has never publicly recognized him as a threat. This silence may indicate that he is really worried about him. It may also indicate that he shares Kortchnoi's view that Anand's is a limited talent. Anand himself loves to tell the story of the already legendary remark Kortchnoi made about his play after a rapid game in Monaco. At a certain point in the analysis Anand opined, 'I must be better here, but I don't see a plan to continue.' To which Kortchnoi exclaimed in utter amazement, 'A plan? You don't need a plan. You only play for tricks.'

I do not think that the moment is near when Kasparov will relinquish his throne. But when that moment has come there may be a player ready to challenge his superiority whose name we already know. If it is not good old Anatoly Karpov, I would plump for Vladimir Kramnik or Viswanathan Anand.

Kramnik couples a magnificent understanding of the game with an immense encyclopaedic opening knowledge. Talking to Kramnik is listening to explanations like, 'I know that line quite well. It also happened in a game between Gelfand and Shnapshinovsky in the Under-12 USSR championship in Kuybychev in 1978. No sorry, 1979. Gelfand won, because Shnapshinovsky did not know that he could have freed his position with knight e4.'

Kramnik's main handicap seems to be his frail health. When I spoke to him after his first major international successes I had to laugh when he kept repeating that he had had health problems before or during the tournament. It sort of sounded like a joke to stress that he could even do better. Later, especially after his misadventures in the Candidates', I began to understand that he had not been joking at all. Likewise I understood why in our interview he had emphasized that you cannot do anything without energy.

Anand's great strength is the fortunate marriage of an absolutely unique feeling for the game and a versatile and agile mind. The Indian quicksilver might be the ideal ambassador to spread chess to a broader audience. He is well-behaved and looks accessible while he remains an enigma. One of my favourite Anand stories happened at the end of the 1992 Reggio tournament, his first victory ahead of Kasparov. As we were looking at one of his wins, a journalist for the famous Italian sports newspaper *La Gazzetta dello Sport* knocked at his door to ask a few questions. Initially the pressman's interest was focused on a rendezvous Anand was supposed to have had with a local girl. Although Anand explained that the girl he had had dinner with worked at the tournament and that she was accompanied by her fiancé, the journalist much preferred the romantic rendezvous version, as we could read the next day. When this subject was closed, his interest in chess also turned out to be a highly personal one. Speaking slowly he looked at Anand and asked, 'Hanand, gwich is your favourite piece?' Baffled, I chewed over this question in my mind. Why had I never thought of asking it? Anand, however, wasn't ruffled at all. As if he had answered the question a thousand times before he quipped, 'Well, I've lost most of them many, many times in my career, so I've learned not to get attached to any one of them in particular.'

Anand's main concern for the near future seems to be his bad control at crucial moments. A lack of solidity that cost him his Candidates' match against Kamsky after he had built up a decisive lead. As I received the news about Kamsky's stunning resurrection I recalled the words Anand had spoken to me a couple of months earlier. 'Many people just say, "Ah, he is going to win the tournament, he'll win the match, he'll make a draw easily." But only the player himself knows the demons in his head.'

Vladimir Kramnik

Amsterdam, May 1993

'In chess the most important thing is having energy'

'It was logical that Botvinnik and Kasparov were giving me advice when it was necessary. When I was still young and unexperienced. Now I have already been playing for quite a while and I can judge things for myself.' Vladimir Kramnik, the apple of Kasparov's eye, is seventeen years old. Yet, these self-assured observations are formulated without a tinge of immodesty. There's only this friendly expression on his face that reads, 'Let's look at the facts'. Impressive facts, for sure. Less than a year after he burst on the international scene scoring 8½ out of 9 for the Russian Olympiad team in Manila, the prodigy from Tuapse already played as one of the old boys in Linares. Shortly he will celebrate his eighteenth birthday with a 2700+ rating. In Amsterdam, where shaky play nevertheless yielded him shared victory with Anand and Short, we talked to this affable giant in the much appreciated company of Genna Sosonko who acted as interpreter.

A good few years ago news started to filter through from the then Soviet Union that a fresh young 'K' had appeared on the chess scene, an extraordinary talent called Vladimir Kramnik. Another young 'K', Gata Kamsky, has often complained publicly about the problems he encountered in his early Soviet days when hordes of Kasparov supporters were allegedly making life difficult for him. How were your junior days? Did people help or stimulate you or did you have similar experiences?
'No, I didn't. I cannot say, as Kamsky related about his case, that anyone frustrated my development as a chess player. On the contrary, a lot of people have helped me. As a junior I got ample opportunity to play tournaments in Krasnodar and the neighbouring region. Things got even better after I had won the under-15 junior championship of the Soviet Union when I was twelve years old. I scored nine and a half out of eleven, an excellent score. After that result Botvinnik invited me to his school, which he was leading together with Kasparov at that time. Both Botvinnik and Kasparov helped me to find some tournaments to play in. I could not name anyone who blocked or hindered my progress.'

At what age did people recognize that you had an exceptional talent for chess?
'You would have to ask others. I learned to play chess when I was five and then my father took me to some local amateur club. There was a coach at this club, an

unknown player, perhaps of first league level, possibly even weaker, who instructed the young kids who came to this club. Nothing professional, just out of his love for chess. There were some ten boys and he showed us some elementary stuff. When I was seven I had already reached first league level. That was quite precocious. From that moment onwards two masters from Krasnodar helped me and gave me lessons. But to be honest, these sessions were not very frequent and most of the time I was studying alone. As is still my habit. I prefer to work alone, which I find much easier than working with someone else.'

Was there anything out of the ordinary that impressed or struck your teachers at the Botvinnik-Kasparov school when you first went there? Any remarkable feats you performed?
'(Smiles) Yes, there was. I had a very original style for a boy of my age. I was very fond of the endgame and liked to exchange pieces. Of course, Botvinnik found this fantastic. This came as a complete surprise to him. At that time already I had a good understanding of which squares I should put the pieces on and which plan I should go for. I remember that when I was ten years old I studied *My System* by Nimzowitsch, a book which contributed a great deal to my chess education.'

In what manner? You say that you already had this natural feeling of where to put the pieces. What did Nimzowitsch add to that?
'No, I did not mean that I had such a natural feeling. Now I would say that probably I got this feeling from reading this book and that I later developed this further.'

Did you have easy access to chess books?
'I can say that my style may be explained by the fact that my favourite book was Anatoly Karpov's *Sixty Best Games*. I played through these games over and over again and this probably helped form my style. I only had very few chess books. There were not many chess books in the local bookshop. In fact, it would be more accurate to say that the books chose me than that I chose the books (laughs). It is quite possible that my style would have been completely different if my first book had been a games collection of Kasparov. But this was just the way it went.'

As I understand you are from an artistic family. Your father is a painter, your mother a musician. What kind of influence did this have on you?
'It may very well be that just like my parents I have some artistic talents. As far as my chess is concerned it is difficult to tell whether this talent stems from my parents.'

In any case they may have found it easier than other parents to understand that you did have some artistic talent, this unusual gift for chess? And subsequently encourage or help you?
'I think every parent thinks that his or her child is special or has some brilliant talent. My father certainly did not teach me to play chess hoping to discover some special talent. It just turned out that way. Of course they were enthusiastic about

Vladimir Kramnik: 'Only a Russian can understand another Russian.'

my successes. Then, as now, it was not so easy to accompany your child to tournaments. This travelling cost a lot of time and money, but still they helped me. But as I said, without the thought at the back of their minds that they were stimulating some career.'

Did they hope that you would learn to play an instrument as well?
'Yes, on several occasions my mother tried to teach me to play the piano. She said that I had an ear for music, but I wasn't too fond of it.'

Was it already at an early age that you decided that chess was everything for you?
'(Smiles) I don't think I ever thought that. Nor do I think this today. At first I was attracted to chess as a game. Just like any other game. Cards, backgammon, you name it. For me there was no difference between chess and any of these other games. With the arrival of success I started to like it better and better and I began to work more seriously on chess. I did go to school, but from when I was fourteen I only played chess. I finished school and I became a chess professional. I have some hobbies, but the only thing I take serious is chess.'

The other day Anand said that for him chess was first and foremost a sport. You may try to play the best moves, but ultimately the only thing that counted for him was the result. Do you have a similar approach?
'For me chess is eighty per cent sport. Other chess players may say that for them it is an art or a science or whatever, but in the end I think that for every chess player it is in the first place a sport.'

At the moment you are playing an awful lot of chess. Apart from numerous tournaments you even play in three different national team competitions. Do you do so purely because you long to play chess or is it also because you are not too eager to go home these days?
'I can mention several reasons. In the first place I like the atmosphere at chess tournaments. I have many friends there. That's the most important reason. I cannot say

that I always long to play chess. Especially when I play a lot and get tired I am not really dying to play chess. The second reason is quite simple and natural. I want to make money by playing chess. I think that goes for every professional chess player. Others may be reluctant to say so because it sounds too cynical, but I think that is reality. However, this is an attitude that apparently you shouldn't express too often. Let me give you an example. Some time ago I played three games in the Austrian team competition and in an interview I was asked why I had done this. My answer was that of course I did it for the money. At that the journalist said that he preferred to write down another reason, as he found my explanation too negative. So he wrote something else. I found this very strange. Of course, creativity and all that is most welcome but whenever a chess player plays a tournament his main concern is money. A special incentive why I have been playing quite a lot of late is that I intend to buy a house or a flat in the West in the foreseeable future. That is the main reason.'

By playing a lot you increasingly get used to the more luxurious life in the West. Does this make going home less and less attractive?
'No, there is no such problem at all. I even find it pleasant. I like the people in Russia and their characters. I enjoy the contrast. Even more than that, I would find it very difficult and boring to live in just one country.'

Which are the things that you miss most when you are at home in Tuapse at the Black Sea and vice versa when you are away from home?
'Honestly speaking the thing I miss most in Tuapse is intellectual contact. Of course, there are my parents and my brother, but them I have already known for a long time. You must understand that the town where I live is in a certain sense just a big village. There are hardly any or maybe no people who have travelled and have something interesting to say. That is certainly something I miss a lot. But I am a Russian and when I am in the West I may miss the company of other Russians. Only a Russian can understand another Russian. That is the feeling I miss most when I am in the West.'

Do your parents or does your brother think that you have changed a lot, either in a positive or a negative sense after your travels?
'(Laughs) I didn't ask them, but I feel myself that I have changed. They will feel that as well. Perhaps you should not call it a change. It is rather a matter of feeling yourself enriched, I have experienced a lot of things. My soul hasn't essentially changed, but I feel more mature and enriched.'

Did you ever take your parents or your brother with you to a tournament?
'I took my brother on several occasions. My parents are not too eager to come along. In the first place they don't speak any languages and secondly they have been born and bred there and just don't have this ambition. The only thing my father would like to do abroad is to visit museums. That is what fascinates him and this is

his dream. My brother certainly enjoyed travelling a lot. But you must understand that for a Russian to travel abroad is comparable to a Dutchman going to the moon.'

One more question about your artistic background. What kind of paintings does your father make? Any Soviet Realism?
'My father was a sculptor in Lvov and also taught this subject. Later he moved to Krasnodar where he was the leading painter. In fact his position involved mostly a lot of administrative work. About his style I cannot say too much, because I am not an expert in this field. It was not Soviet Realism. A rather classical style, I would say.'

How big is the contrast at the moment when you go home? Or more bluntly, how is the situation in Tuapse right now?
'Some ten years ago there was no denying that my father was one of the richest people in Tuapse. He got many commissions and made something like seven hundred roubles a month, which was comparable to the income of a director. The average salary at that time was one hundred and fifty roubles a month. So, you can imagine that there were no financial problems at all. We would go on holidays at regular intervals. But every year things got worse and worse. If he still had to live on his earnings he might be just about able to make ends meet, but certainly not more than that. There is simply no work for him anymore in such a small town. In Moscow or somewhere abroad he might make a decent living but he wants to stay in Tuapse. But he hardly works anymore.

'The money I make is more than sufficient. My mother makes something like fifty dollars a month and my father something like one hundred dollars. Several times I have said to them, "Why go to the trouble for such amounts?" They both answered that they understood what I meant, but asked me to understand that their work was part of their lives.'

You say that you play such a lot because you want to buy a house. I take it that Botvinnik would not be too happy with the number of games you play. Are there any people in your surroundings that urge or advise you to play less?
'There are no people in my surroundings who could give me such advice. From time to time I see my trainer Tseshkovsky. He may give me some advice, but nothing more than that. He would not exert any pressure on me. Anybody may give me a piece of advice, but in the end it is I who decides.'

Kasparov never suggested to you to play a bit less?
'I wouldn't know why he should. When I went to their school Botvinnik and Kasparov might have said that I should not play so much. They simply gave me advice. This school doesn't exist anymore, by the way, but I see no reason why either Botvinnik or Kasparov would tell me something like that. It was logical that

they did so when it was necessary. When I was still young and unexperienced. Now I have already been playing for quite a while and I can judge things for myself.'

How did your relationship with Kasparov develop? Is it only based on your mutual interest in chess?
'We have reasonably good relations. We talk and say hello during tournaments. But we never worked together.'

How did you feel when Kasparov began to herald you as the next World Champion? Did you just take it as a compliment or did it also disturb you?
'It doesn't help me and it doesn't irritate me. It's just what he thinks. It's his full right to be of that opinion. As for me, I don't care about it at all. Other players may say that I will most certainly never become World Champion. I don't care. If that's what they think.'

Do the conversations you have with Kasparov have a clear influence on your chess?
'Of course, when I was in his school and I was called forward to show my game on the demonstration board and we discussed my game that was a very useful experience. And of course when we analyse our game at a tournament like in Linares, that is also very impressive. But that is all. For every chess player it is something special to play against Kasparov. Playing him is an event for any chess player. I would gladly play a match against him without any remuneration just to learn from him.'

When I asked Kasparov whether he thought that you could bring something really new to chess he answered that in fact what you brought to chess was more of the same. You work in the tradition of the Botvinnik school and as a consequence it is more of the same kind of chess. Do you think that you can bring something new to chess?
'That is hard to say. For the moment I don't think so. I just play chess and I don't think that I demonstrate anything special. Perhaps I may in the future, but for that I will have to deepen my chess. In chess, to my mind, the most important thing is having energy. What I do feel is that when you're talking about understanding chess, then the difference between me and Kasparov is enormous. On the other hand I don't see any real difference between my understanding of chess and that of players like, for example, Nikolic or Salov. But to repeat, my main asset is having energy. Which you may also call the privilege of youth. I may add that after every strong tournament I have played I have the feeling that I understand chess better and better. If I continue to play in strong tournaments I will understand chess better in a few years time.'

Of course it is not only energy. A couple of days ago Anand expressed his admiration for the enormous amount of new ideas you have. Do you work hard on this or do these ideas come naturally to you?
'That is true. Apart from my energy the source of my successes is my working hard. Particularly on the openings. I have many ideas in the opening.'

You said that you like to work alone. However, you also work together with Shirov, a collaboration that may seem a bit strange to the outside world as your styles are quite different.
'I can tell you that I have never in my life spent two or three weeks training together with anyone. As for Shirov, we may meet at tournaments and spend one day on a certain position. Or we may call each other by telephone and discuss a variation on the phone. But there has never been any question of systematic collaboration. I never had a permanent trainer. Just as with Shirov I've been in contact with many people and have profited a lot from these contacts by finding out how they think. Their views. They did not even have to be strong grandmasters. Also masters might inspire me with their way of thinking and their understanding of chess.'

Could you mention any names?
'People like Gelfand or Khalifman, but these are well-known names. I can also mention lesser known players, like Tseshkovsky. He has a very deep understanding of chess. Or Ibragimov, a very interesting chess player. Or Khenkin, another grand-master. There are many people. I always felt attracted to people with a personal way of thinking. That's how I, too, always wanted to look at chess. I may mention once again the name of Tseshkovsky. His way of looking at chess and his understanding is completely different from mine. That makes it extra interesting to work with him. Let me give you an example. After this tournament I started to think about the following phenomenon. If you take the Sicilian, there are three types of players who play that opening. First, players who just play the Sicilian. The second category of adherents to the Sicilian *feel* this opening. I fit in this second category. I have been playing the Sicilian ever since I was six, so I *feel* this opening. The third type of player is someone like Tseshkovsky, a player who *understands* this opening. This is not easily attained. Except for Tseshkovsky I can mention the names of Kasparov and Short. They *understand* this opening. The others *feel*, or even worse, *play* this opening (laughs). I might look at a position and have the feeling that it's slightly better for one side. I would show this position to Tseshkovsky and he would wonder why I wasn't so sure and say, "What are you talking about? Of course it is better." '

Did people ever define your style in a manner that gave you the idea, 'Yes, this is how I think about my style'?
'Hard to say. I try to have a universal style. It is difficult to pick out certain aspects. Obviously I have my weaknesses and my strong points, but those I would rather not discuss.'

In the September 1963 issue of Chess Life *Robert Fischer analysed a game he played against Hans Berliner at the Western Open. At the end of this highly illuminating analysis Fischer wrote, 'It is difficult to find one particular game that is typical of my "style". This comes close.' It was a seemingly simple, straightforward, crystal-clear game. Which of your games do you think are representative of your style?*
'(After a short think) My game against Ulibin in Chalkidiki last year. Against Ivanchuk in Linares this year. Kamsky in Linares. Seirawan in Manila. And John

Nunn in Manila. I could name other games, but these were games where at certain points I showed interesting ideas, something deep. I cannot say that I always play very deep games and that's why I am very happy when occasionally I play a game that can be seen as an entity.'

Who amongst the younger players do you feel some affinity with as far as style is concerned?
'That is difficult to say. I might mention Sakaev. Not for his style, but because of the way we approach chess. There are a lot of positions that we understand and evaluate in the same manner.'

Any older players?
'I have the same with Khalifman.'

And even older?
'So far I haven't had too much contact with others, but if I look at the games of Ivanchuk I get the feeling that we have many things in common as well. If you take Gelfand for instance, just to give a contrasting example, he is something completely different. In my opinion Gelfand loves difficult, extremely complicated positions. That's the kind of positions he steers for and the kind of positions he plays very well. I, on the other hand, prefer positions with very clear positional reference points. Hard to define what that means. It's something you simply feel.'

You just mentioned Ivanchuk. Before you appeared on the scene he was the Soviet player most often mentioned as a possible next World Champion. These days it is generally thought that his weak nerves are too big a handicap. You, on the other hand, seem to be extremely cool. How nervous were you when Kasparov managed to get you on the Russian Olympiad team? Your rating was encouraging enough, but even so you were only a FIDE master at the time.
'Initially I was nervous, yes. I understood full well that if I played badly, everything was going to be bad. It was one big adventure. Frankly speaking, I already was quite a strong player at the time, as I confirmed in Manila. But I was still only a FIDE Master, a unique situation in the history of the Russian Olympiad team. They were always grandmasters. Just imagine that Russia had not won and I had only scored plus two. Everyone would have wailed, "Why Kramnik?" Before the Olympiad I understood very well that if I played badly I was going to be the scapegoat. Even if I and someone else had played badly, I was going to be blamed. Not by the players, but by the officials. So, there was great pressure, but I was in excellent shape. In all respects. From a chess point of view and also mentally and physically. I remember that when I was playing my games at the Olympiad I forgot all these secondary things. Perhaps I was helped by the fact that many other countries thought that I was the weak spot on the team and tried to get a point on my board. (The interpreter and the interviewer were both in Manila and look at each other in utter disbelief) At least, that was the feeling I had because everyone played very aggres-

sively against me. With the exception of Seirawan. I am convinced that he came to this game to get a point. He remained true to his style, got a slightly inferior ending and then tried to win the game anyway. Of course, when I had scored five out of five or six out of six, I don't remember exactly, they began to understand that I was not as weak as I looked. But, just to give another example, I had already scored six out of six when I was playing Olafsson. He was Black and offered me a draw in a slightly worse position. He was obviously convinced that he was the better player.'

In general you make a cool impression. It doesn't seem too easy to upset you. After Linares you stunned me by saying that the tournament hadn't been that strong because you had a worse result in Pamplona. What's this?
'(Laughs) Before I went to Linares I was expecting hard times, because as far as chess understanding was concerned I was weaker than almost any player in the field. Everyone told me that I might have had a good result in Manila and might have won all kinds of tournaments, but that in Linares I would see something different. But I didn't (laughs). In none of the games, with the exception of my game against Salov. That was his type of position, his type of chess and I was outplayed. Most of the players considered me to be the weakest or one of the weakest of the participants. Ivanchuk told me that before the tournament he had been thinking against whom he was going to win and the first one to come to mind was me. Nevertheless, and this may sound a bit arrogant, apart from this game against Salov I was never outplayed or shown something spectacular.

'On the other hand I would not say either that I played so brilliantly and that the others were outplayed by me. It was more or less an equal fight. I think there were two reasons for my good play in Linares. First because I worked hard before the tournament and as a result had many ideas and, as I said before, I had a lot of energy. In fact I missed many points there. One and a half points at least. I was winning against Karpov, even at the adjournment. Really unbelievable that I did not win this position. Against Timman I was winning. Against Yusupov I had a decisive positional advantage and he was in terrible time-trouble. And against Shirov I was a rook up (laughs). The only game, to mention some compensation, where I had a really bad position was against Ljubojevic. I invested a lot in this tournament and it has given me a lot of self-confidence. Or as the Russian proverb says, "You don't have to be a god to do something special". In other words, after Linares I understand that I can play and fight against the strongest players of the world.'

You say that energy is an important aspect of your strength. Are you never afraid that your smoking and your partiality to an occasional drop of cognac may be detrimental to this energy?
'No, I am not. I feel that when I am at home I build up such a surplus of energy. Every day that I spend at home I get such a portion of energy. I am just ripening with energy, getting fit from energy. After two or three weeks at home I am completely ready to play a tournament and I feel that I have ample energy for all aspects. My

worst tournaments I play when I have not been at home for one or two months. At a certain point I feel drained, empty. Take Pamplona for instance. I was just lying in bed, no energy, absolutely empty. My only wish at the outset of the games was to finish them as soon as possible. And, true enough, these games were generally very short. I would offer Spanish players draws, etcetera.'

Should we see your partiality to a glass of cognac in the light of a Russian tradition or are you simply a seventeen-year-old boy who is so strong that he can handle everything?
'It is not part of a Russian tradition but one of my character traits. Russian mentality, if you want. It is nothing to do with drinking, it is a matter of mentality. The way you look upon life. Not only to do what is useful, but also what is pleasant.'

Even if this has negative sides.
'Yes. I know that it can affect your play and therefore I have become more careful lately. I used to do this more frequently. A year ago I used to drink more. I may drink something after a lost game or at a closing ceremony, but I don't think I drink more or do whatever more than other chess players.'

In Linares you told me that you don't have absolute goals like winning the World Championship. You take tournaments as they come. Does the Biel Interzonal nevertheless occupy a special place in your tournament agenda for the coming six months?
'When I am playing in the Interzonal my only idea will be to qualify. I find it quite nonsensical to think of the World Championship match when you're playing the Interzonal. All my strength and energy has to be focused on this one event.'

Ultimately this may lead to the FIDE World Championship match. Would you rather play the FIDE World Championship match than the PCA World Championship match?
'I don't know. If the PCA continues to exist, and Kasparov told me that it was an excellent project, then of course I will play in the PCA. I think that if this continues all strong players will join the PCA and then of course I will play there. What use would it be to play a FIDE World Championship match if this is a surrogate match? If everyone joins the PCA and Karpov wins the FIDE title, then he will still be the second player.'

Your attitude towards the world around you comes across as very down-to-earth and matter-of-fact. Don't you cherish any secret dreams?
'I can tell you this absolutely honestly. I live in the chess world, where I have my work, which is also my hobby. Still, this is a far cry from the most important things in my life. The most important things in my life are the normal things in life. Personal contacts, my relatives and friends, my private life.'

Viswanathan Anand

Wijk aan Zee, January 1994

'They say the Emperor is in Beijing. But there are mountains'

Viswanathan Anand's streamlined course in the PCA qualifier in Groningen and his superior disposal of Artur Yusupov in the FIDE matches in Wijk aan Zee confirmed once again that the Indian quicksilver is World Championship material. Although he agrees that Kasparov may be waiting somewhere down the line, voluble 'Vishy' prefers to go step by step. 'There is a line between confidence and overconfidence that I try not to breach.' How was the raw talent polished to a gem of a player? In Wijk aan Zee we looked for an answer and got an interview in the fast lane.

Obviously you're quite delighted to be one of the lucky three who are still in the race for two World Championship cycles. Could you imagine your misery if you shared Shirov's predicament and were out in both cycles?
'I'd feel pretty miserable. You can overdo it. It would feel like the end of your life until you realized that it wasn't the end of your life. It would last a while and then you'd decide that your life is more important than your results.'

How essential or pivotal are these two cycles for your chess career?
'I imagine they're very important. But one good way to deal with it is to realize that and then stop thinking about it. I don't constantly tell myself, "If I'm not in these two cycles it's the end of my dream." I wanted to be in two cycles, I qualified, so I don't want to think anything more about it than that. You have enough pressure upon yourself without adding to it. I don't see the point of dwelling on it and making it worse for yourself.'

To an extent your situation was comparable to that of Shirov after you had been eliminated by Karpov in Brussels in 1991. Many people had high hopes of you and now suddenly you had to wait for two or three years. How did you cope with this disappointment?
'It wasn't so much of a blow then obviously. I simply lost to Karpov. Maybe if I had lost to someone else it might have been worse. For me just breaking to the Candidates' was good news then, bringing you a hell of a lot of good invitations. It gave me a chance to play all kinds of exciting things. Of course the second time around you like to go a few steps further.'

To my mind the progress you have made over the past two years has been the most crucial advance in your career. You confirmed the promise that you are made of World Championship material. Where do you see the changes yourself?

'Clearly I have become more experienced. Maybe that's all it is. Maybe I was immensely talented but there is no way of knowing it unless you play the right people. After I played Karpov in a match, after I got to play all these guys so often, and did well, you allow yourself to entertain some thoughts. I can't say I changed my lifestyle, just little bits. I've been adding. For instance these days I often spend some time training for these matches. Obviously in the years when I was playing these tournaments I hardly did any training at all. In that sense I am working harder. I'm thinking more about chess. But you cannot concentrate in a vacuum. You need something to concentrate for and these matches are a sort of a tool that force you to concentrate on a goal. The ultimate goal is to improve your chess. To the point where you can play tournaments, matches, everything better.'

Is it as abstract as that? I cannot imagine Anand having improved his chess and being happy with a tenth place in the world as, alas, some guys happened to improve their chess more. I think you're more ambitious than that.

'Yes and no. Yes, I am ambitious, but I've always been convinced you should do things one step at a time. At least at every stage I keep telling myself that I will believe it when it happens. Then I'll go to the next stage. Now I scored 4½-2½ against Artur (Yusupov). A couple of years ago I'd be delighted, extremely surprised. Now, since I've had all these good results, I just take it in my stride. OK, it's good to know that I could do that, but I sort of expected it. Though Artur is such an immensely strong player. Still, through all these results I believed it could be done. Beyond that you shouldn't dwell on this too much. Or at least you have to get to the stage where you think that what people think good results are just normal results for you. That's the only way you can get accustomed to going even higher. Beyond a point it doesn't pay too much to think beyond the next stage. There is also a danger of slipping into overconfidence. There is a line between confidence and overconfidence that I try not to breach.'

Part of your maturing process must have been an deepened understanding of the game in aspects other than the purely technical ones.

'I start to understand the psychological aspect of the game more and more. Maybe a few years ago I thought this was some sort of big joke the top players would talk about. Now I understand how in a match psychology is very important. It's kind of abstract. I cannot put into words how exactly this has changed. Overall I start to feel more and more comfortable in top chess. Certainly three years ago, when I qualified in Manila, my chess was very raw in that sense. Of course, I knew the openings and that sort of thing, but a lot of psychology was missing. For instance these days I understand there are two kinds of equal positions. Equal positions you like to play and equal positions you can't stand the sight of. These are important aspects in top chess.

'When you play a top tournament you get insights from playing your games, from your own observations. You have to view these top tournaments and Candidates' matches as some kinds of laboratories. Where you get to test your theories and everyone is feverishly making notes on what these theories are and how they work practically.

'To be honest I must say that I am not dwelling too much on the fact that five years ago there was this little boy who was doing this and now I am doing that. I don't like to look back. I'm happy the way it's going. It's nice to see some old games, but beyond that I don't want to dwell on what happened in your life. I think you should start doing that much later.'

At tournaments you make a very serious impression. You don't let other people interfere with your tournament rhythm, don't hang out with the boys...
'Yes, but this has more to do with the fact that I simply don't drink. I'm not much of a party animal to put it mildly. A discotheque once in a while is fine, but I like to be by myself quite often. And I simply make time for this. During tournaments between ten and eleven I simply like to go to my room and watch TV, do something inane. Something really stupid, like watching some meaningless television. The idea is to have some time for yourself. To lock up my room and be in my own area. I can't say it's part of a strategy, but it's worked well. It's what I feel comfortable with. I know that when I am comfortable with myself my results will tend to be better. Occasionally I may go for a drink or something, but I don't see the point of punishing yourself and staying away beyond twelve or one just because the others are doing it. It's pointless. You have to understand what's good for you and what's not. And what's good for you is good for your tournament.'

It's been said that a crucial difference between equally talented players is the way they adjust to hotel life, travelling a lot and being away from home. Has this always come easy to you?
'I try not to think of the alternatives too much, which helps. Up to a point I just like hotel life. There's no point not liking it. You simply have to do it. If there's some aspects I don't like of being a chess player... I mean, there are a lot of people who think that part of being a chess player is going out for drinks at night. I try to be social with the other players but I recognize that for me there's a limit. Call it culture, call it habit, whatever. But a lot of people find quiet niches. For instance, Jeroen (Piket). I find very often he is very impressive in this. He creates his own atmosphere and he works with it. Goes out for drinks with the boys and whatever is necessary, but he seems to be in control of his own life. In a sense that he doesn't do something because the others are doing it. He does it because he wants to do it.

'You always find people who do this. Gonzo[47] in his own way does this. Very much in control of his own life. To the point where he almost doesn't associate with other players. If he doesn't think it's necessary, it's not necessary. This is not to say that what works for me is specifically good for everyone. For some people maybe partying out every night is the best. For me it's the wrong thing. I assume they have tried partying out till six at night. It seems to work for them and they stick to it. Fine. If you travel a lot you see lots of people and lots of different lifestyles. There isn't one disciplined lifestyle for everyone. A discipline is more a state of mind how you adapt to your surroundings rather than what time you go to sleep.'

Viswanathan Anand: 'You shouldn't start planning when you retire from chess. That's a very bad way to play chess.'

Is your curiosity to go to places bigger than your desire to be in Madras?
'O yes, for sure. But this is connected with my desire to play chess. In Madras there's not that much chess going on. It's nice to go back to Madras and relax. Madras is for family and relaxation. All those good things. You can always think that the grass is greener somewhere else. On the other side you have to think if you want to do something else, "Do I want to go to college? Or something else?" And then I think, no. I can't be bothered by all that. I want to be a chess player. Once you've made this decision you take the lifestyle that comes with it. And you train yourself to be comfortable. I am very comfortable with the chess player's lifestyle. I recognize that this may not always be the case. For every chess player there comes a moment that he maybe has to stop, or has to realize that he is not getting any higher. When the moment comes I hope that I will recognize it.

'I feel comfortable with the chess player's life. The partying life is just one tiny aspect that doesn't attract me so much. On the other hand I love sleeping late. You

---

47 A nickname of Garry Kasparov's, particularly popular amongst Western grandmasters.

know it's a luxury. I notice that chess players often don't care which day of the week it is. Because they can't be bothered. That's a luxury many other people don't have. Sunday is special to them. I couldn't care less, because almost any day of the week can be special. There are very nice aspects to it. A lot of free time, lots of time to explore, lots of time to yourself. I don't know too much about philosophy and so on but I can imagine that sometimes when you work in a job your security is higher and so on. But you also think that your life is passing you by, because you have Sunday and then you're too tired and then it's back to Monday to Friday. Of course it helps that I'm doing well at chess, when it's much easier to accept that it's a great lifestyle. '

What kind of profession is chess for you? Do you intend to play chess for some ten more years and then retire or...
'I don't think about this really. You shouldn't start planning when you retire from chess. That's a very bad way to play chess. If you start thinking that you have ten years to make money you probably make much less money than if you just forget about this aspect.'

You are a chess pro who often expresses his concern about the status of the chess player as a professional.
'Let's put it this way. I think it's important for instance that chess be organized in such and such a way. Beyond that point I'm not a martyr. If I think that chess should be run in a certain way and it's not, I'm not going to quit chess and do something else. Obviously I am deeply concerned by the state of chess. I think it could be vastly improved. There are also signs that there are lots of people who share this view.'

Which are the first things that need to be changed?
'It seems to me first that something like the Passion Public tournament in Paris[48] is a good place to start. We must start attracting a larger audience. Chess players tend to be quite defensive about their world. Sometimes I think we should open up a bit. I can't give you a specific thing. It's a whole attitude. The general image of chess is not very high worldwide. It's good in a few isolated pockets, but not worldwide. I don't know what turns on spectators. It seems to me that rapid chess attracts them, but this seems a bit simplistic. It may for a while and then it may prove a passing fad and they move on. But we won't learn unless we try.'

Is the general image of the chess player a serious handicap. As they were immortalized by Fred Waitzkin as a 'ragtag group, badly dressed, gulping down fast food, defeated in some fundamental way'?
'No. I don't think a sport should be promoted mainly by how you dress. This is an important aspect for image, but it depends what is necessary. First of all Fred

---

48 The Immopar Trophy.

(Waitzkin) looked at a very narrow group of chess players. There are lots of chess players who are not ragtag, who don't eat hamburgers all the time. But he is right. There is a group like that. But this also has something to do with the state of the sport. You have to stop seeing chess players as some static individuals. They are also adapting all the time. You saw for instance that the same players who dress in tennis shoes and jeans looked quite differently in Passion Public. They transformed themselves very quickly. You can compare it to college students who once they get a job clean up their room. I don't know how many hippies from the sixties run big companies. It would probably shock them if they went back and spoke to themselves in their youth.'

Is this what your hopes concerning the PCA are pinned on?
'That is one aspect. But even at the Passion Public tournament my impression was that it did not get a hell of a lot TV coverage. This was very impressive at the London match. Forget the way it was organized. Forget the way it took place. I don't know the details but I heard bad stories. For a moment let's even forget about all that. Ninety per cent of the people who watched these broadcasts only saw some select aspects. And they only will remember select aspects. But, at least in Britain, it managed to break onto television in a big way. It's been done. I don't know whether it will continue, we shouldn't start making very optimistic projections, but there is certainly scope for improvement.

'One of the things I noticed is that the PCA are often accused of not interacting with the players very much. I hope that this is a sign that they spend a lot of time talking to television companies or whomever and trying to get them involved. Once they come in all these players will dress very well. They will make an effort to present a nice image. Once they see some connection between the money they earn and the image they project. And also the connection between the money they earn and whether they give value to the spectators. Once that connection is made chess players will be like everyone else.'

Is selling the product chess complicated by a clear lack of charismatic chess players? The number of players you can sell worldwide is very limited. You got Kasparov, Judit Polgar, Karpov and you. And perhaps or of course Bobby Fischer.
'First of all I don't know what constitutes charisma. Second, insiders in the chess world often tend to like people other than these four. Once you get to know these chess players people often have other favourites than Kasparov and Karpov. I can easily see that once chess players are exposed to a wider audience, they will find their fans and their supporters and whatever. Now you just don't have much of an audience and that's the point. Initially when you're introducing the players you have to introduce those who have the largest appeal. Good or bad, Kasparov has an image. People know him as this or that and they can argue if he is good or bad. But most of the chess players people can't associate with anything.

'But appeal is not necessarily connected with your results or looks. Appeal can often be connected with how you behave, how you present yourself. I can imagine someone like Yusupov can be very popular to an audience who knows what he is like. Audiences often support modest decent people. Who like to project a very modest approach. The most charismatic players are not necessarily the babes.'

Do you care a lot about your own public image?
'I haven't given any thought to it till now. I try not to get in anybody's way. Not say anything rude or stupid, and hope my image will take care of itself. I don't know much about this. I'd be fascinated to meet someone who knows a lot about the subject. It's two kinds of images you're talking about. One is the kind of image of what you are. But you have to realize that TV is a very superficial medium. Often you just look for one second. And if you're a nice person and very intelligent, but not photogenic, often you will not come through on TV. Also magazines like *Time* or *Newsweek* are likewise very superficial. Very rarely they will give you an interesting perspective on the news. You can see this from the way chess is reported in the news. It will be on a very bland level, because they have to present it to a general audience. Often you will find that very many interesting aspects of a player, which I know because of my association with them, have not made it to the mainstream press.'

Do you have an advantage in this sphere, being the dark guy from India who plays fast? Does this make things easier?
'It's possible, yeah. In a way I'm in a unique situation. But these things work in funny ways. You're often surprised who becomes a superstar and who doesn't. I'm often surprised in any way. For instance in tennis I used to like Courier a lot, but I found that Agassi was always the big superstar. To some degree I understand in major sports hype and marketing come into it. Then it's not so much your image as how much print space you achieve. It's a strange world and I'm not sure we'll all be very happy in it. It could be uncomfortable. But it is connected. We all want better incomes.'

Does it bother you to be always presented as the fast playing young man from India who beats all these players who grew up in more traditional chess countries etcetera?
'No, it's partially true and people like simple labels. For ninety-nine point nine per cent of the people, chess is simply not a part of their lives. It will be interesting for us to access them in a commercial sense. For the most part chess will have to be presented in very simplistic terms. There will be lots of levels, but the superficial level will always be the largest group, of course.'

Through your travels and the magazines and newspapers you read you have become very much globally orientated. How Indian do you still feel?
'This is an interesting question. In very many areas there is coming a global culture already. For instance the whole of Europe and the United States. They are culturally

different, but you go to a supermarket and you will see that they are absolutely the same. There is a lot of levelling going on and very few aspects survive this. I feel completely Indian of course, but the difference is less and less all the time. For instance in a chess sense I'm not Indian at all. In chess I am just an international chess player. I can't think of any Indian aspects to my chess. But in a general sense, of course, I feel Indian.'

When you're at home, do you play the Pet Shop Boys or do you play Indian music?
'I play Indian music sometimes, but I like the Pet Shop Boys as well. There is also a global pop culture which that is a part of. I've gotten to like a certain kind of Western pop music. You also find lots of things through your travelling. For instance, in Linares literally the only entertainment available to human beings is that radio and that one radio station they have (laughs). Now I know or vaguely recognize a lot of Spanish artists and songs. You get exposed to a lot of cultures. I don't know how much I am taking in and how much I am keeping out.'

You also like to go to the movies. These will be mainly American movies. Do you also go to Indian movies when you're at home?
'O yeah, sure. When I'm in India I watch a lot of Indian movies. I can't watch them outside India. Outside India I only watch American movies. If your only language except for my mother tongue is English there is no choice for me but watch American movies. Inevitably I have become less and less, I won't say an Indian, but someone who is following, for example, Indian news. For many months I am cut off from it totally. Completely cut off, because out here you only get the most irrel-evant titbits. I do care about this, but to a point it is almost impossible to find out.
    'In these days the world you live in tends to be your profession, not your country. Especially if you're a traveller. For me this is my world, the chess world. It's chess news which I'm always interested in. Chess gossip, chess news, what chess players have to say, what's going on in the world of chess. This is the news I follow most of the time.'

Is it correct that despite your international chess life your parents expect you to let them choose a wife for you according to Indian tradition?
'(Clearly not welcoming this question) In some aspects I remain an Indian, of course. Which is not always the case with other Indians. A lot of Indians tend to break loose of their roots. The only question is to what degree. If you travel a lot, you will have to change your lifestyle. The only question is how much you change. (Still reluctant) The honest answer is you can't control your life. If it happens it happens, but let's say, normally my parents doing this for me is a default option. Unless something else happens this is what will happen. It's just traditional. Normally speaking I will follow tradition unless something happens which I cannot control. But my parents are not sitting in some cold room and sort of deciding it. They are

also looking at me. It's not like one day they are phoning and say "OK you have to come back and marry". But it's true. In India we do tend to arrange marriages.'

Another problem I could not fail to notice at many occasions is the problems people have with your vegetarianism. You win a prestigious tournament like Reggio and at the closing dinner they are completely at a loss what to do with this guy who doesn't eat meat.

'Yeah, in some countries it is bad. In my case it is mainly beef which I don't eat because of my religion. Why I don't eat the other things I don't know. It's partly not really wanting to be cruel. But beyond a point I am not so confident about my faith. I mean, you also have to accept that in nature animals kill animals. You survive or somebody else survives. It's not exactly that I believe that everyone should become vegetarians. I just feel more comfortable with it. To survive I have started taking fish occasionally. If you go to a country like France or Spain this helps, even though I'm not very comfortable with fish either.'

Let's talk about chess again. It seems as if 1994 and 1995 are going to be key years in your career. Is the image of Kasparov much more on your mind than it was before?

'No, actually not, would you believe. If everything goes well he is like three or four stages away. I notice that you keep asking me if this is my key year. Even if it is I see no point of telling myself that it is. By telling you it is crucial you also tell yourself that if you screw up it doesn't matter what happens in the other year. You just play as if it is a normal year and if it goes well you will tell yourself later that it was a crucial year.'

Let's put it differently. For most of the chess players Kasparov is some kind of a demigod, way way above their level. He is the touchstone for excellence. For Karpov he has inescapably become part of his life. What is Kasparov to you?

'He's the best chess player of my time. Or at least he has been World Champion for nine years, or eight years or something. He's there. It's like in China. They say the Emperor is in Beijing. But he is far away. There are mountains (laughs). It's that sort of thing. He is there somewhere and every year in February I see him. But my thoughts are not on him. Obviously I understand that if this year goes well and the next match goes well, I'll meet him somewhere. When it gets a bit closer I can start worrying about him. At this point competing against somebody you're not going to see is not the point.'

Many people think that you are about the only one who might dethrone him. Do you feel this as a responsibility?

'No, if he was an evil tyrant who went around killing everyone I might feel this as a responsibility. He is the World Champion of chess. If I don't get there the chess world is stuck with him. No, I see it as my responsibility to try my best and to accomplish whatever I can. You have to do this for yourself. Of course I can't pretend that I haven't noticed what everybody says. Lots of people talk about me being the next World Champion and so on. From time to time the thought is there. But first I see myself with all these other strong grandmasters in the cycles. I haven't eliminated them yet. I think it is irresponsible to think what I am going to do against Kasparov or somehow seeing myself getting there. I am not saying this as some speech, I also try not to think about it so much.'

On the other hand these days there is an increased amount of, let's call it sporting aggression in you when you speak about Kasparov. As if you're psyching yourself up now that he's getting closer.
'Maybe. I haven't thought about it in those terms. I believe there are lots of good things he has done and lots of bad things he has done. And when I think he has done something that is not beneficial I say as much. I don't make it into a big deal. I'm not one of his most outspoken critics. I find him quite an acceptable World Champion. On the one hand he actually tries to do a lot for chess. I appreciate this. But there are certain things about him that nobody likes very much. That's clear.'

I also mean that this is part of your way of looking at things realistically. You don't want to look at him as a demigod, but rather as someone who can be beaten.
'O yeah, for sure. It's also clear that people are still scared of him.'

Are you scared of him?
'Well, even if I was, I wouldn't tell you, would I?'

I don't know.
'(Smiles and briefly reconsiders the question) Well, I don't think I am. But he is a strong player, what can you do? You can sometimes wonder what to play without being scared. It may be a chess thing. What the hell do I play against him? I am not sure what I can tell you here. To be honest I simply try not to think about it that much. It's not just diplomatic. It's also practical. It's very nice for the chess world to assume that you're stronger than the other Candidates, but your reputation doesn't help you too much at the board. Take a player who is leading by one point before the last round. Many people just say, "Ah, he's going to win the tournament, he'll win the match, he'll make a draw easily." But only the player himself knows the demons inside his head. Until you qualify it's almost frightening to think about what will happen when you qualify.'

And Linares? Is it just a strong tournament or does Kasparov come in somewhere?
'No, he doesn't actually. It's not a tournament with much at stake except prestige. Last year I finished second-third in Linares. A very good performance. What did it mean to me? Absolutely nothing. If I hadn't drawn Epishin in Biel, and Gurevich hadn't lost to Lautier and blablabla, I wouldn't be playing in the Candidates'. There

wouldn't even be a chance that I play Karpov at the end of the FIDE cycle. There are important tournaments and there are other tournaments. Linares is nice. People call it the unofficial World Championship, but unless there is some sort of official recognition people can talk as much as they want. If you become World Champion, or *a* World Champion these days, and you screw up every tournament you play, people still call you World Champion. Maybe a sloppy World Champion, but they call you World Champion. You win Linares once and you make two mistakes in the next months... People don't call you World Champion when you win Linares ahead of Kasparov. They get excited. That's all.'

You wouldn't give up one of the cycles to win Linares?
'O, no,no, absolutely not. That goes without saying.'

Still, you would like to see a different kind of World Championship. Could you imagine a tournament like Linares to be the World Championship once every two years for instance?
'It's a possible format. Of course, it's too small a group of people. If you are going to have a World Championship that is slightly less snooty than it's now. Now there is so much of the surviving as Larry (Christiansen) put it[49]. Crossing the Amazone and climbing Mount Everest. On the other hand you don't want to make it a farce. It's obviously an important event. But an annual event will not have the same aura that a three-year event has. Linares is a possible format, but it can also be a rapid tournament. Or a knock-out like Tilburg. It could be a tournament followed by a match. Also it could be simply a matter of your overall performance rating. I don't think that's such a bad idea. I don't see the need for a *de facto* World Championship. It does not seem to me a bad idea to make you play consistently through the year.'

You find that the current World Championship takes away too much money from other events?
'Well, yes. Or rather, it has an existence that has nothing to do with other events. The rest of the chess world can suffer, the rest of the chess world can do very well. Lots of attractive tournaments, lots of sponsors or no tournaments and no sponsors. I wouldn't even say this event takes money from other events. It has an existence on its own. For two people. For the other chess players there is hardly a connection. They don't make much money out of it. Ninety-nine per cent of them will have been eliminated within the first three months of the cycle. Can you imagine? Ninety-nine per cent of the people are eliminated within three months of a three-year cycle? Why do you need two years to separate the other one per cent? That's basically the point I am making. And it's a World Championship that heavily favours one guy, the incumbent. He just sits there three years waiting for his opponent. He has a good time...'

---

49 In New In Chess 1991/5.

Occasionally he reads about some guys who crossed the Amazone...
'Yeah. That sort of thing. He's half way across the Amazone? You mean, he's past the crocodile bank? He's past the crocodile bank? That's interesting. Well, there's still the alligator. He will get him.'

Suppose you become World Champion by beating Kasparov. Would you be willing to give up your privileges to restructure the chess world according to your present views?
'I guess so (smiles). It would be better to do it before. You're much better off persuading a guy to give up privileges he's not acquired yet. This is simply my understanding of human nature. Again, it's not something I feel comfortable talking about. But let's assume that I did become World Champion. If I got a guarantee that the next World Champion would not re-assume these privileges and so on and it was actually a creditable system...
   'The reason why the World Championship goes on as it does is simply that you can't argue with success. It does raise three or four million dollars. No organization can argue with that kind of money even if it benefits only two people. If a restyled other World Championship could raise a reasonable prize-fund, like a million, that's nice. If it raises nothing, that's pointless. If it could be done well, I think that I wouldn't find it so difficult to give these privileges up. At least at the moment. But I cannot say this with certainty. (Smiling apologetically) I'm trying to be honest.'

Is money the measure of all things in the chess world?
'Money is not the measure, but people do measure the World Championship by the amount of money it gets. If it gets good money it's seen as a realistic championship. Why do people think Kasparov-Short is more important than Karpov-Timman? Because Karpov-Timman struggled to get sponsorship. The money gives you credibility and some sort of legitimacy that the world recognizes you as the legitimate event. Money may not be the only measure, but it is a very important measure.'

In the case of the PCA it was important enough to determine most chess players' decisions. Do chess players simply go where the money is, steering clear of possible ethical considerations?
'I don't see why people think of this as an ethical question at all. If I'm in India and India goes to war and I decide to go where the money is anyway, that's unethical. But FIDE is not a country. It's like a company. Is it unethical to quit a company if you get better paid elsewhere? Maybe the original act of Nigel (Short) breaking away, maybe that is unethical. But for the rest? Where's the principle involved? We go where the conditions are better. (Rather indignantly) Who on earth doesn't do that? The question of ethics or principles doesn't exist as far as I'm concerned.'

OK. Final topic, Kasparov.
'Surprise, how did we get to that?'

Over the past few years, no matter what he does or what he wins, people have been saying from time to time that Kasparov is past his prime. That he has had his best years or that he is no longer the Kasparov he was, etcetera. Quite often he himself too laments about his failing strength. What is your view in this?
'It is difficult to tell this on the basis of results. He still has some very good results. Except for '91. In '92 and '93 he had some spectacular results. He plays much less. This is one of the things with the World Championship. Once you become World Champion there is no incentive to play. It gets boring. It's much better travelling the world like some ambassador of chess. And just play the World Championship. What he does play in he wins overwhelmingly, but in some sense I think the gap has been narrowing. Simply because when he was very young his approach to chess was new to everybody else. People had not been used to studying the openings that way. Now everyone's preparation has improved. The world may be catching up with him rather than he getting past his prime. Perhaps he looks past his prime. He looks much older these days. He still seems to have his energy, but for instance he puts on glasses from time to time now (laughs). In that sense... He starts to get some white hair and talks about it all the time how he is getting old. And you can't escape the impression that there is some truth to that. But as I already pointed out, your prime is more that your youth. He seems to have compensated what he lost of his youth with his experience. He is a very experienced player. His knowledge of theory has expanded enormously. Well, like it always was. And his understanding of chess has improved. He's learned a lot from playing with Karpov. Karpov was a very good trainer for him. Incidentally he was a very good trainer for Karpov as well. In the same sense you can say that Karpov's results are even better now than they were before. As World Champion he believed in winning a tournament by half a point. Nowadays he goes for more.

'On the basis of results these guys are still doing quite well. On the other hand mother nature is working on them. Eventually they will slow down. They're getting older. Kasparov doesn't give the impression of someone who's bursting with energy, although he still has a lot of energy. I didn't know him very well earlier, so I can't tell you, but you hear stories from his opponents then about him being this dynamo. Of course, if you get wiped out in twenty moves you tend to describe your opponent in superhuman terms. I don't know. I can't give you an accurate picture. (Smiles) But he certainly gives you the impression that he is a man who has weathered a lot of storms.'

What about your own strength? Still steadily going up?
'It's the general impression I get that I'm still increasing in strength. But this is all relative. If you're purely looking at age I am now one of the middle-aged participants. A funny situation to be in so quickly after being a prodigy.'

The Queens of Chess

Much has been said and written about the difference or lack of same between male and female chess players. In the absence of scientifically valid research, the theories most often bandied about are the semi-serious ones. A famous theory in Holland is the unshakeable belief of the late Hein Donner, who, in his usual provocative style, propounded that women are superior to men in practically everything. However, in a pursuit like chess they are clearly inferior as they lack something essential, viz. intuition. A man 'feels' in a certain position that the queen sits better on square f6 than on square b6. Not because he has calculated a line, but simply because his intuition tells him so. Obviously, this is a theory that is impossible to prove and the reactions to Donner's provocation were not very illuminating either. One woman angrily wrote him a letter saying that he was a sexist and possibly also a racist. Probably to his mind black people could not play chess either. Calmly Donner retorted that this woman had not understood anything of what he had said. Of course black men could play chess. From what he had said she might have concluded that only black females cannot.

Interestingly, I found some unexpected support for Donner's view at the recent Donner Memorial in Amsterdam. When I told Women's World Champion Xie Jun about Donner's prejudice, she did not protest. Instead she acknowledged that to her mind women are better at details, because their way of thinking tends to be more fragmentary. If you need an overall view, a broader vision, you're better off relying on men. I take it that most Western women do not share this line of thought. While in practice we may still be a galaxy away from truly equal rights for men or women, on the whole we accept that a woman's mental capacities, if properly fed, are essentially identical to those of a man.

In the even less emancipated world of chess this view is not supported with great ardour, there being not too many women chess players anyway. However, the 'gut feeling' of most chess players seems to be that there is a clear difference. Girls are not inferior to boys. On the contrary, at an early age they tend to be more precocious. However, around the age of eighteen they start to lose ground purely for biological reasons. Most chess players I spoke to were convinced that girls lack the right hormones or the purely physical strength once the going gets really tough; in other words, in the final stages of the World Championship cycle.

Going by the interviews I had with male and female chess players, I did see one major difference. The men would talk about their ambitions, their chances to play for the World Championship, or their limitations in this respect. The women would do the same, with one proviso. At one point they would marry and get children, and this would probably be the end of their chess ambitions. Sure, they were going to stay in touch, but from thereon their ambitions would be focussed on their family. Perhaps a most refreshing thing to hear from the two strongest female chess players in the mid-nineties!

Which does not imply that they lack the drive or fanaticism to reach a lot before they will quit. Both Judit Polgar and Xie Jun are fresh, likeable girls, with strong minds and clear convictions. There is no reason to mistake their well-developed social skills for a lack of killer instinct at the board. You only tend to be surprised when they clearly show it.

A couple of years back the Polgar family, without Zsuzsa, visited the New In Chess office in Alkmaar. After we had drunk tea or coffee for a while one of us suggested that Judit and Sofia play a number of blitz games. For our entertainment, of course. After some initial hesitation they consented and sat down to play. A couple of games were played and when Sofia wanted to leave it at that Judit said to me, 'OK, now you play.' I objected that she was much too strong for me and suggested that she took one minute against five for me. Judit did not appreciate my chivalrous gesture, not even when I tried to compromise on three minutes for me and one for her. No, the only format was one minute each. Seeing no escape I gave in and we started to play. Everything went much too quickly for me, but I thought I noticed that she made a slight mistake in the middle game. She lost a pawn and the only compensation she had was the fact that she was her and I was me. Of course she won anyway, but I could see that she was slightly annoyed that I had had the temerity to be better for close to ten seconds. We played two more games. The only thing I remember is that as a punishment I was massacred twice.

Xie Jun's easygoing and innocent air can be even more deceptive. During her stay in Amsterdam for the first Donner Memorial, she showed me what she thought had been the decisive game from her World Championship match against Ioseliani. As she kindly illuminated her moves I thought I misunderstood what she said about one of her last moves. Ioseliani was completely lost and Xie Jun could have forced immediate surrender by capturing her queen. Instead she played another move hoping to prolong her opponent's suffering. Ioseliani had won the previous game and 'come back' from 4½-½ to 4½-1½. Therefore Xie Jun had seen this game as a crucial game. First of all she should not lose. Now that this danger no longer existed she wanted the psychological blow to be as painful as possible.

Both Judit Polgar and Xie Jun know from experience how traumatic a loss to them still is for most men. In a way we are still not used to them. In the two instances I related, the leading ladies of chess demonstrated a drive to win that is seen as a simple, basic requisite for any boy or man. In a girl or woman this drive apparently still surprises me. Perhaps I have no right either to point a finger at the uneducated guys who simply refuse to analyse after they have lost to a woman.

Xie Jun

Baden-Baden, December 1992

'You may think the sky is high, but there is always something higher than the sky'

It is a bit of a sad scene. Right from the start and well into the second week, Women's World Champion Xie Jun had been the stunning sensation of the category 11 Bank Hofmann tournament in Baden-Baden. Now a third consecutive defeat has ruined her chances for first place and a GM-norm. Ye Jiangchuan, China's strongest player, watches stoically as Xie Jun's fingers flitter across the board and push the pieces to squares where they might have had better prospects. Suddenly she flashes a smile at her coach and travel companion and chuckles, 'I'm so lucky'. And at his look of total incomprehension, 'Just imagine how unhappy I would have been now if I were a professional'.

What was one to expect from an interview with a Chinese Women's World Champion? Tight-lipped oriental mysticism clad in mysterious unfathomable smiles? Oblique state-controlled clichés? Or monosyllabic answers in helplessly poor English? As I walked down the deeply carpeted stairs of the stately Badische Hof Hotel on my way to the breakfast room, I was not plagued by such pessimism. The first time I had had the chance to talk to Xie Jun, in Helsinki last September, had been a most pleasant surprise. Without the least trace of arrogance, the twenty-year-old champion engaged in a short but lively conversation that would have wiped away all such prejudices. Shunning no subjects she spoke with engaging directness and openness, and did so in remarkably fluent English.

The only remaining worry might be that she would turn overly diplomatic or shy in the presence of a tape-recorder. Not a worry that was on my mind for long. As I discreetly tried to make my way to some corner table, Xie Jun kindly motioned at me to join her. As I embarked on light breakfast talk I noticed with amusement the enthusiasm with which she had filled her table-for-one with titbits from the buffet; an enthusiasm which more or less led me to show bad manners. Concentrating on our conversation I finished my breakfast without much thought, only to realize that she was still eating. Xie Jun looked slightly uncomfortable and said, as if in apology, 'I'm afraid I took too much. Couldn't you go and get some more breakfast?' Suddenly fully aware of my rudeness I promised that I would, but even before I had the chance to get up she took away her own feelings of unease by quickly pouring me a cup of tea from her pot! Gradually I began to understand why Xie Jun's friends call her 'Baby', which in China also means 'precious one' and is pronounced very much like 'Bobby', but then with a long 'o'. A feeling that did not diminish when we had finished breakfast and decided to deal with some questions.

When I saw you playing in Helsinki it was obvious that you were not feeling at ease. Here you clearly enjoy your games.
'Well, first of all Helsinki was an open tournament and I don't like Opens. If you play an Open in the former Soviet Union there is no problem because they have many strong players and even the weakest player will know how to play chess. This is not so in other countries. If you play one game badly you may be paired to someone who doesn't have a rating. If you travelled all the way from China to play that Open this makes no sense. For a player from Asia it's such a distance. You play nine or eleven games in a tournament and to do so you overcome the time-difference and adjust to the food. This may be no problem at all, but if you end up playing against an unrated player it brings you nothing. Perhaps it meant some promotion for my chess federation, so I had to go to Helsinki.

'Obviously I prefer closed tournaments like this one, although I also liked the Open I recently played in Moscow. At this Alekhine Memorial there was a very strong field and even the weakest player had a rating over 2300. For me the games I played in this tournament were interesting, but even more interesting was to see what happened after the game. Every day after I had finished my game I would be standing there for three hours and watch the strong players analyse. I never had such an opportunity. Even if I hadn't played in this tournament it would have been a useful occasion for me. Can you imagine a player like Zsuzsa Polgar talking like this? They travel very easily. Or like Mr Larsen from Denmark who came to Shanghai with her. He didn't come as her second. When he was asked by journalists from my country why he had come he said that some rich man from your country had told him that he would get some money if Zsuzsa became the challenger. And so he came (laughs). You see? You cannot compare this.'

Before this tournament you were very modest about your expectations. Then you had this fantastic start and boldly hung on to the lead for many rounds.
'When I was asked at the press conference what I expected from this tournament I told the journalists that I just wanted to learn something. I want to practise. I think that category 11 or 12 is just the right category for me. Just a little bit above my own level. In the beginning I played quite OK and I won some games. And I was lucky, because some positions were not that good. But in the middle of the tournament I began to play less well. I was very eager to win the tournament and lost three games. It all started when I drew my game against Mainka from an easily winning

GERARD DE GRAAF

Xie Jun: 'Men are men. Women are women. They're different.'

position. I was thinking for twenty minutes and I could not see how to do it. After this draw I was so sad. That night I analysed the game and could not sleep well. Then the next day, against Bischoff, I thought that I had a nice position and I blundered. Or rather, I saw his move but underestimated the danger.'

Had you become too aggressive?
'I wanted to play for the GM-norm, sure. I have to look ahead. One day I will lose my title and then I will need these norms. It is not an absolute goal, just a logical process. When I became a Candidate I wanted to be the Challenger and when I became the Challenger I wanted to be the World Champion. Right now the master title would pose no problems, so the logical next step is the grandmaster title.'

Has it been a huge disadvantage to live isolated from the international tournament scene?
'I only began to get invitations after I had become World Champion. Many people who had not seen me before came up to me and asked, "How is this possible? We have never met you before. How could you become World Champion?" I would explain that I had no chances to play in tournaments. I now have a coach, Ye Jiang-chuan. He's the best chess player from China. He's maybe rated 2540 or 2545, but he's much stronger. When he was my age, ten years ago, he didn't get the chances I have. In your eyes it may seem that I get very few chances, but for a Chinese player it's quite a lot. It's a dream to play in a western country.'

How could you become World Champion? Without a computer or a lot of information at your disposal?
'Maybe I am overconfident, but I think that if I had had the same opportunities as the Polgar sisters or as other western chess players, I would play much better than I do now. When I was a child I played Chinese chess. I was really talented. At that time there were too many children of my age. There were insufficient schools for

all these children. So, I went to school two years late, when I was eight. Until then I stayed at home. In summer people played chess under the street lights and my father took me to watch them. I found it very interesting. Nobody really taught me to play, but I learned it from just watching. No special training. After some two years I became champion of the children in Beijing. Unfortunately they already had a champion at the Beijing club and that was enough. We don't have team championships in China, only individual championships, so one was enough. At that time she was eighteen years old already and I was only ten, so how could I play her? (laughs) But (mocking malice) I think that I was more talented than her. She now is a business woman and we are good friends. Then a very famous Chinese chess player, who is dead now, discovered that I also had a talent for chess. So, he suggested, if I could not play Chinese chess I should get some training in chess. But we didn't have many good coaches. I only began to learn how to play chess after I became World Champion. Before that time I just played like a child. I didn't know how to play all kinds of positions. I just followed my instinct.'

How did you prepare for your match against Chiburdanidze?
'I didn't go anywhere anymore. I interrupted my studies at Beijing University for three months just to prepare. I worked hard. As hard as I could. And I played training games. It's very fortunate that in my country you don't need a sponsor for such preparation. If the Chess Federation decides that I have to play against him or her, they have to play. We played many openings in these matches and these players told me how I should play certain positions. After I became World Champion I got more and more information about chess. More chess books and more strong tournaments.'

Do you prefer to play in mixed tournaments?
'Of course, I do, because men play stronger. I see a big difference between the Polgars and other women chess players in the way they play chess. If you look at Zsuzsa's games in Shanghai you will see that in some games some moves are not that strong. Yet, they were not exactly weak moves, no blunders. Many women players they simply make blunders. Like I did this time. If you play against very strong players you don't think about these blunders. But if you play against a woman you may think, "What will be her next move? Maybe this or maybe that, or maybe some blunder." You may have made some splendid plan, but she makes a blunder and it's over again. Big deal this plan of yours.'

The Polgars play like men as they are used to play against men?
'You know, I already said this in 1990. One day the Polgars will come back to women's chess. Now they're just training with men. They have sponsors, they will get stronger and then they'll come back. In thirty or fifty years' time women may be able to compete with men. But not now. Not in my time. This even goes for

Judit. She is very talented and for her age she is good enough, but in two or three years' time, you know (laughs shyly). Maybe a girl of twelve can see more than a boy of twelve. Maybe at fourteen she can also see more than a boy. Maybe girls know things earlier than boys. Just like at school. But around eighteen they are overtaken by boys. So, I don't believe that, as they say, Judit will become some top player or even World Champion.'

Is this something mental or something physical?
'Mental. And in a way also something physical. The times are changing. Women play much better than they did twenty years ago. And in twenty years' time they will play much better than they do now. But this is not yet the time for women to compete against men. Even now, if a girl gets married in my country, she'll have to do some housework. She'll have to get a baby, she'll have to take care of her husband and the baby. How can she have a career? Maybe this will change one day.'

This may be different here.
'I think it's similar. In some respects the situation is better than in my country, but still it's similar. For example, Zsuzsa now had her boyfriend with her in Shanghai. Granda (Zuniga), right? I think she had a very good boyfriend. He never said anything or tried to impose his opinions on anyone. But I don't think that if they get married they can continue like this.'

You don't think that women can really compete with men as yet. Is this the reason why there should be women's championships?
'Yes. Men are men. Women are women. They're different. I don't think that in two years' time Judit will be the top player of her age. She'll be eighteen and I think that by then many boys will have grown up. Zsuzsa always said that she only wanted to play against men. And now? She's come back. And one day Judit will come back, too.'

Don't you think that Zsuzsa has only returned for the money?
'Any reason, any beautiful reason. For the money. Because it's the best time for her to play against the women. It doesn't matter. But she's come back.'

Is it annoying to be World Champion while you know that Judit or Zsuzsa Polgar stayed away from the championship?
'You know, even the other day somebody asked me who was the strongest female chess player. I said, "Judit", even though I'm World Champion. I don't mind this, because, you see, we never had equal chances. As for the chances I have got I think that I used them well enough. It's not so important for me. I practise and I want to learn something in chess. The most important thing for me is to improve my chess. I've said this many times, but I don't mind whether I am champion or not. The only

things the title brings me that are important, are invitations. Only by improving my rating can I get invitations when I'm no longer champion and for that I need practice.'

How serious are you about your chess?
'They used to say that as World Champion you have the duty to play chess like the World Champion. However, for me it's different. Even if you let me play against Maya (Chiburdanidze) again, I'm not one hundred per cent sure that I could beat her again. Maybe 55 per cent. Maybe 51 to 49. So, I have to train. I just got the title by luck. Of course, I don't want to lose it. Nobody wants to lose. I want to try my best. But right now I'm studying in university and I don't want to give up my studies. If I only played chess I could not make a living. Maybe I could now, but after five or ten years I may get married and not want to play chess anymore. I cannot save money as western players can. I have to give my money to my federation. Sometimes people tell me, "If this is so, why don't you move to some other country where there is more freedom?" Many Chinese go to other countries. They think they have no future and leave home. I don't think that is the right way. For whatever I do, I could never change my face, I could not change the colour of my hair, of my eyes. I'm Chinese. My mother raised me to become Chinese. Maybe, if I had the chance, I might live in another country for one or two years. But I don't want to leave my country for good. Suppose I could play for some club in Europe. That might be OK for me, but this is unimaginable for a top woman player in my country. They would not let me go. I would have to give up my citizenship and that I don't want to do.'

So, your plans for the future are to play chess for some more years, finish your studies, get married...
'Just follow some natural course. If I can improve my chess I might not want to get married. Because, you see, if you get married in my country... If I do something I want to do it better than other people. If I get married I want to become a very good housewife. And, of course, I will have to work, because in my country both husband and wife have to work to make a living. My husband and my family would be very important. You cannot combine that with chess. Because (starts laughing), just to make a joke, I cannot get married to a chess player from my country, because all the older players already have gotten married. (Laughs louder) We often make that joke. So, if I marry someone else I could not go away for two or three weeks, as it would be impossible for my husband to accompany me. Anyway, chess is not my life. It's very important. And in five or ten years I still will not be old. I have enough time to get married and do everything. But for chess I only have a limited amount of time.'

When you're not playing chess you study English at Beijing University.
'Yes, English and some other subject. I have a special arrangement at the university. The other students have to follow many subjects simultaneously. I can do them one by one and take as much time as I need. English is a very useful language in

China. If you speak English these days you can get a very good job. You can earn more money than I get from playing chess. That's one reason. Another reason was that if you went abroad as a chess player you always needed an interpreter. And this man or woman might not know much about chess, but they would be very proud that they spoke another language. So you could say nothing. The first time I went to Moscow in 1986 for a friendship match with our national team, I only spoke Chinese. I had some pocket money, very little, but this interpreter took it from me. I was so young, didn't know anything. I was just happy that I was travelling. Then I decided that if I ever got the chance I would learn a language. At that time this was still very difficult. The first time I got a chance to learn English was in 1988 or 1989, when they started to broadcast English lessons. And we had some lessons in secondary school. (Starts droning) How are you? How do you do? Things like that. But if you really happened to run into somebody who spoke English you could not say anything else. Nor could you understand what they were saying in reply.'

People from the West know very little about China. Probably the reverse is true as well. What were your impressions when you first came to the West? Was it just as you had expected?
'(Laughs a bit) You see, if my mother had been living in the West and given birth to me in some western country, I would have been luckier. Luckier than I am now. My country is changing. It is getting better and better. This is really true. These changes do not take place as quickly as in the former Soviet Union, but, you see, just one month ago I was in the former Soviet Union, which they now call Russia. They call it a revolution but the actual effect is terrible. The people they get nothing. But in my country, which is gradually getting more open, the people really are getting better and better lives. So, what can I say? I'm Chinese and I couldn't change it. People here don't worry about too much. They don't worry about food, about the basic needs in life. Like electricity. If you leave your house to go out in my country you automatically switch off the light, because you want to save electricity. Maybe you can save a coin. This is something very natural to do. I don't think people do this here.'

In private houses they do.
'No, no, even in private houses they don't turn off all the lights. In our houses we sometimes have three rooms, but when we're sitting in one room, the other rooms must be dark. If they have a chance to save some money the Chinese will save it. Because life is still very hard. People try to save money because more and more things are coming to China. TV, some people begin to dream about having a car. All these things are too expensive for the average Chinese, but he begins to dream about it.'

You say that people begin to dream about these things. Do you feel you're in dreamland when you're walking around here?
'(Gives a short laugh) Sometimes friends of mine go to Europe or to America and the first month they feel so happy that they write letters to their families saying (in

an exaggerated voice), "OK, I came here, very easily found a job, I got a flat and I got a car and everything." If you've never been to any of these countries it sounds like a fairy tale. But when I come here it's just normal. And as for my friends... Let's say, after half a year they begin to feel very lonely. What kind of flat was it anyway? A very small room. And the car may be some very old car. You see, in my country I have to live with my parents. And if I have a brother or a sister we have to share a room. Even at my age. That's why they feel so happy when they get a single room. But after that... And what kind of work do they do in that other country? They wash the dishes or something, whereas they had responsible jobs at home. Abroad they could not get good jobs because they are foreigners. You are a journalist. Can you imagine that you would get the same job when you come to China?'

Do you see a big culture gap between China and the West?
'Here there is more freedom. But in my country some other things are better. The people are more pure. Especially five years ago, when there was no openness yet, they didn't think about money too much. They were living at a low level, but if they had food and some other basic things, they could feel very happy. Because there was nothing to compare their lives with. We lived very close to each other and we didn't know much about other countries. But now they can see this on TV or read about it in the newspapers. Now it's very common for young people to go abroad to find a job. Their parents tend to be very proud, but I think it's funny. I compare things, but I don't want to change everything. Before I went to university I was a student in sports college and learned something about psychology. I don't want to be blinded by outward appearances. I do not simply conclude that people here are living better than in China. I try to learn something from being here and try to change something at home relying on these experiences, but I don't want to look at these things like a child.'

It is often said that Westerners misunderstand Chinese people. For instance, we may not understand why you laugh at certain moments. I do not get the feeling that your laughter differs much from mine.
'You see, one of the good things in my country is that we have five thousand years of history behind us. Over these centuries there have been many thinkers and philosophers, of all kinds of directions, who have left their traces. I think I follow the way of thinking of Kongtse[50]. Many Chinese follow his way of thinking. I am not a staunch follower, but I have taken some of his ideas. Most of them are right. You know, we Chinese do not dream too much. My country is a political country in some way. The people are used to follow the ideas of the leaders. They prefer to do something rather than to dream. For me that's OK. When I'm at home I feel more free and happy than here. Because the people think in a similar manner. You know, in 1989 we had these events in Tianmen square, after which many of our young

---

50 Better known in the West under his latinized name Confucius.

people went abroad. The next year I saw an article on this in a Malaysian newspaper. I had to laugh and made a joke to some friends. I might go abroad for one or two years to study, but to really live there, there could only be one reason. If I loved somebody who was a foreigner. I could not leave my country for any other reason. I feel so happy when I can stay home. I read the article in your magazine about Khalifman. He says, "I can breathe now." Sometimes when I'm at home for a longer period I may feel the lack of freedom to do certain things. But if I have a chance to go and visit some other countries three or four times a year and then come home again, I certainly prefer this to living there all the time.'

Do you dress differently when you're here?
'No, I don't. The situation in China is not as many people in western countries imagine. We are a poor country compared to developed western countries. But as for certain basic things it's OK. We have better food than here and better clothes. People cannot spend a lot of money on food, but they can get it very easily. During the women's Candidates' tournament in Shanghai all the non-Chinese participants would go shopping on their free days. No, not only for silk, also for other dresses. When they arrived they only had one suitcase. They left with three. Some things are very cheap in my country. When I was in Russia I had to spend a certain amount of US dollars a day. But there was nothing to buy. The organizers in Shanghai offered to arrange some sightseeing tours, but these participants said, "No, we want to go shopping." '

What kind of things do you get to know in China? Do you know Michael Jackson and Madonna?
'Yes, but not too well. We know about some things in the West from TV, but not everything because there is censorship. Still we know something. To get music is very easy. Perhaps it is not allowed, but people make many copies from one original tape. But I rather listen to some classical music.'

Do people in China know Bobby Fischer?
'Just the chess players know about him. I myself never had a chance to see him. When Bobby Fischer played the rematch against Spassky our international television channel mentioned it. This news is only ten minutes a day and they only bring very important news. When I played against Maya they also put that on. And also the beginning and the end of the Karpov and Kasparov matches.'

Who is the most popular foreign chess player in China?
'When I was a child there were maybe one or two books on chess. Now they have translated some more. But these don't talk about the chess players themselves. In 1986 or 1987 they published a book about Karpov. It had been given to the publisher in 1984 and he had already lost the title. This is the only book in Chinese on one player. I studied it and liked his style of chess. I think that if he were ten

years younger Kasparov would not be stronger than him. Maybe Kasparov is more talented, but that is not everything. I think that Karpov would be strong enough to fight for the World Championship. Now he's too old. Even I feel that I get older (smiles). Four years ago I could sleep very easily. Maybe even one year ago I still could. Some chess player once told me that the chess player who can sleep well is really lucky. (Laughs loudly) During a tournament I have to sleep twelve hours a day. Yes, like a baby. Now I sleep maybe ten hours a day. When I was young I would lie down in my bed and fall asleep rightaway. Now I first lie thinking a bit. But to return to your question about popular chess players, For the Chinese chess fan every face is a new face. Maybe they have heard the name of Bobby Fischer. Or maybe of Kasparov or Karpov, but they don't know what they look like. (Starts laughing after some hesitation) Maybe I was very popular amongst Chinese chess fans.'

What happened when you became Champion? Could you safely go out in the streets?
'At one moment I couldn't. After I had finished the match with Maya I had to attend banquets and press conferences for about half a month and I really got exhausted. All this time I was staying in a hotel in Beijing, because journalists kept coming to my parents' house to find me. So, I had to hide in a hotel. That's where the Sports Committee put me. After half a month I was so exhausted that I had to go to hospital for a check-up. In the hospital I dressed like a doctor. I would put on a white doctor's coat, but people would still recognize me. They would ask for signatures or just start to talk to me. Last year I was so popular in my country that I was elected Sports Person of the Year. Every year we have a top ten for sports people. I don't think I have a chance to be number one again this year, because we got too many gold medals at the Olympic Games.'

You sound proud of this award. Yet, you keep stressing the relative importance of fame and prizes.
'I think that many chess players, also Kasparov, they want to win too much. This may be good in chess, but in life they should be more friendly. To live on equal terms. No champions, no best players. Sometimes they can be so arrogant. Take this interview, for instance. I might have said that I don't have time, that I have to prepare, that I have to do other things. But if I don't have something else to do, it's OK with me. I don't have to snub at you and say, "You're wasting my time." I don't think you have to do this. One day these arrogant people will lose their title or will get old. Long-lasting friendships and true feelings are more important than some short-lived moment of pride. Some people are very natural. Others are always thinking about their position and may think that they are so important. I think this is just because they are very young. I have talked to and read about many important people and some of them were very wise and friendly. They had come up all these stairs and at a certain point they were proud of themselves. Until they realized that there was always someone one step higher. In China we have a saying that when you think that you are fast, there is always someone faster. You may think the sky is

high, but there is always something higher than the sky. I want to do my very best to keep my title, but I want to stay like I am. Sometimes I have to complain, because I come from China. That's OK, but I should not complain too much. And I don't want to twist things. If somebody says that Judit Polgar is the strongest female chess player, I will say that it's true. Even if I am the World Champion.'

Would you like to play a match against Judit Polgar?
'That's OK with me, but you have to realize that if Judit had played in the Candidates' and become Challenger, I would have had no chance next year. My chances to win would be maybe thirty per cent. Her rating is now close to 2600. My rating maybe about 2500. One hundred Elo-points is too difficult for me to bridge in one year. So, for the moment it's better to learn something. But against Zsuzsa I think I'll have some chances[51]. '

In which country would you like to play the next World Championship match?
'I would prefer to play the match in America or Africa. I come from Asia. If we have the match in Asia, chances would not be equal for Zsuzsa. The food might be slightly different from what I am used to, but still it would be easier for me to adjust than for Zsuzsa. And such a match lasts a month. In Europe chances would not be equal for me. Zsuzsa speaks many languages. For instance, in Spain not everyone speaks English, but Zsuzsa, I think, speaks Spanish. If I had to go there for one month I might get homesick. So, I prefer to play in Africa or America, where chances would be equal. But if Zsuzsa becomes the Challenger I think that we will play in some European country.'

---

51 At this point Xie Jun, like many others, erroneously thought that the Candidates' final between Zsuzsa Polgar and Nana Ioseliani would be a mere formality. That match was tied 4-4 and decided in Ioseliani's favour by a lottery. Xie Jun won the ensuing world title match 8½-2½.

Judit Polgar

Linares, March 1994
Monaco, April 1994
Madrid, May 1994

'I sort of feel that I make some people happy and that's a nice feeling'

'I didn't shoot them, did I?', exclaimed an incredulous Judit Polgar after another bruised victim had rushed off stage without wanting to analyse the game. As she claimed one of her finest victories to date at the Third Comunidad de Madrid tournament the Hungarian Queen of Chess turned a bunch of male opponents into lamentable figures reminiscent of the gloomiest Goya pictures. Twitching at their glasses, blushing or turning deadly pale, they mustered courage to congratulate the girl sitting cross-legged on her chair at the other side of the board. Motionless she sat there, only occasionally throwing back her long auburn hair with a twist of the head. On July 23, Judit Polgar, currently rated 2630, will celebrate her eighteenth birthday. Her male opponents might have gotten used to her by now. 'Yeah', she admits herself, 'But for them losing to me is still like losing to a twelve-year-old girl.'

In 1822 Carl Czerny, the famous piano instructor, took another well-known Hungarian prodigy called Ferenc Liszt to see the great Ludwig van Beethoven. At first the maestro had had no wish to see the boy wonder. Only after Czerny's repeated request did he give in with the words, 'In God's name, then, bring me the young Turk'. Of course, young Ferenc (a.k.a. Franz) came, played and won Beethoven's heart. Yet, in his later years Lizst, too, had an aversion of what he called 'performing dogs'. Apart from the affection they have from the general public, specially talented children are not very popular with the experts in the field where they excel.

Judit Polgar knows all about it. From her first prodigious feats there have been critics to belittle her accomplishments. As she is a spirited attacking player, her style is described as one-sided, and as she is a girl, she is accused of being just that. There is even an uncorroborated rumour that a latter-day Beethoven of chess described her as a 'trained dog'.

Fortunately, this unfair treatment, that she might never have seen, had she been a boy, has not essentially affected Judit herself. If her spontaneous and straight personality is the sad product of her years as a prodigy, then hurrah for prodigies! In fact, I knew only of one major defect in her character when I asked her for an interview. From our first talk in Amsterdam in 1989 I remembered that she tries to keep conversations in front of a microphone as short as possible. So, that's why I suggested three sessions and Judit more or less agreed. Our first talk we had in Linares, over lunch in the company of Zsuzsa Polgar. Referring to the Amsterdam interview Zsuzsa aptly remarked, 'She hasn't changed much, has she?' Well, essentially she was right with her remark that entailed a compliment. Judit is still devoid of any airs or attitudes. On the other hand she has grown into a strong-willed young woman, who will not let herself be pushed about. As she confirmed during our second talk at the Melody Amber tournament in Monaco. And confirmed again in Madrid at the end of one of the happiest moments in her tournament career.

Linares, March 13

When I approached you for this interview, you shot a questioning glance at Zsuzsa. I couldn't believe that someone who is used to being at the centre of attention would not decide this for herself.
'No, I usually decide. But we do things together, you know. I just ask her opinion, but I decide.'

Who decides what in your life?
'My father decides mainly in what tournaments I will play. My schedule. But we also discuss this with the whole family. Well, it's not like at two o'clock there is a family meeting. It can be at any time. An organizer calls, and then we discuss if I want to go. Or for how much I go.'

Do you have the final vote yourself?
'(Laughs) If I don't want to play in a tournament you cannot do anything. When I am really one hundred per cent sure that I don't want to do something, there's nothing you can do.'

If you're alone at a tournament, you quite often phone Sofia. Do you discuss technical matters with her as well?
'Yeah, of course we exchange ideas. I tell her how my game was. Nothing special. I will ask her what opening she thinks I should I play. But that's not asking for advice. It doesn't mean that I will do that.'

You must have quite some telephone bills.
'Some (smiles). But it's worth it.'

Does your father demand any discipline in making international telephone calls?

'No. In the beginning, when we started to play chess it was a problem. Because financially we couldn't afford that. For instance now I won't see Sofia for a month. I go home. Sofia is going to Bled. I'm coming home on the 16th, she's leaving. I go to Monaco, she's coming back.'

Before your game against Anand you wore this nice little white hat in your hair. Is this something you decide on yourself?

'(Laughs in embarrassment)Is that a serious question?'

I'm just trying not to speak about this tournament as we agreed. (Both Judit and Zsuzsa collapse laughing).

Judit Polgar: 'Is that a serious question?'

'Of course, I may discuss this when she is here. But most of the time she is not around. I decide what is comfortable today, what I want to wear. How I should put my hair or anything. This I do myself. Sometimes I feel like wearing jeans and a T-shirt and do my hair loose like this, but when I play in a top tournament I feel that I should dress normally. This also looks much nicer on TV. Potential sponsors may think it is a much more serious event if the players wear suit and tie.'

What kind of requirements should your tournaments meet? Should there be some prestige at stake, or do you prefer fun tournaments like the rapid-blind tournaments in Monaco?

'I like it when it's quiet. No scandals. And I like it when the audience is interested. When you feel this in the air. When the players are quiet, but the audience are really enthusiastic. I am a player who also likes to play for the audience. Not only for myself. For example, when I was dead lost against Kramnik, but didn't resign. There were two queens for him, one for me. I gave some checks and the audience was enthusiastic. Maybe I was winning! Of course I knew what was going on, but at least they got some interesting minutes. If you want chess to be more interesting you have to play for the audience. What I realized, is that for an audience that doesn't play chess, they like it when everything is hanging. Like Shirov, he really plays for the audience.'

In a tournament like the one in Monaco we just touched on there are good prizes, but for the rest there is little at stake. What kind of challenges do you need?
'If there would be only such tournaments, then that would be serious. That's how it is. If you play serious tournaments and then a rapid tournament you feel like, "Oh, I'm relaxing". If there were only half-hour tournaments then it would be the five-minute tournaments that would be relaxing.'

As far as I understand from the latest Fischer rumours you would even be prepared to play shuffle chess?
'Yes. Actually that's also interesting. I only played a couple of games, but the idea is not so bad. Nowadays the audience looks at the game and thinks, "Oh, how interesting", and after the game you find out that it was all book until move 35. It's not really creative anymore.'

Is shuffle chess still enough chess or is it a completely different game with the same pieces?
'I think it's a little bit different. First you should have some tournaments. There can be normal positions. Well, after some moves it can be normal. Especially because all the players will try to get normal positions. Even if it's not good everybody will try to get somewhere where it's familiar.'

The other day you described the restlessness that made you fond of travelling. Do you have a similar enthusiasm when things are changing or something is happening in chess?
'Yeah (laughs). Yeah, that's my personality, I like action. Like my match against Spassky. I enjoyed it very much. Not only because I won the match, but also because the games were interesting and all the audience was thrilled. It was full of people. There were some thousand people in the hall. In Hungary. Incredible.'

Do you have any idea of your popularity in Hungary?
'(With a telling expression) Sometimes I have to complain that it's too much. I go into the street and they recognize me. Sometimes I don't want that recognition. Before they would come up to me and say, "Aren't you Judit Polgar by any chance?" Yes, by chance I am, I would say. Now they only ask me what was my last tournament or where I will go next.'

You may be quite delighted that Peter Leko will take some of the attention now.
'(Vague) Yeah. But I knew that very soon he or some other person would break the record. I knew that already I had so many chances to do it. My first norm was in '89, when I was twelve. And for three years I couldn't do it. But all the time I was missing norms by half a point. So I knew that it could easily be done at an earlier age.'

Has your popularity in Hungary also had any commercial spin-off?
'There is a commercial on TV. We have a sponsor now, a Hungarian bank, OTP. I'm in this commercial together with Tamas Darnyi, a very famous swimmer who won a gold medal at the Olympic Games. It's about thirty seconds, this commercial. I swim and I beat him in swimming. He's playing chess and he gives mate to me. First you have a reporter yelling, "Who's that non-person swimming next to Darnyi?" and they show him as Olympic champion. And when they show us playing chess he yells, "Who's this guy? We've never seen him before." And they have some shots from my match against Spassky. And then they ask, "Who's behind all this?" And the name of the sponsor appears. (Gets very enthusiastic) This has become a slogan in Hungarian. Who's behind this? All our friends are teasing each other with this all the time. On anything they comment (Almost singing), "Who's behind this?"'

Do you promise yourself certain rewards before you go to a tournament? If I win this tournament I will buy this or that?
'Yes, sometimes I do. Once in Hastings I went shopping with Sofia. I think it was before my first game against Bareev. I said to Sofia, "If I win today then I will buy you this jacket and skirt we just saw." Just for fun. But I won and we bought it.'

Did your father make similar promises in the past?
'Yes, sometimes. Not too often.'

This remains an educational dilemma if a child is very talented. Parents run the risk to either spoil you or be too strict.
'I don't know. (Starts laughing) I would be curious to see a perfect parent. Just perfect for everybody. It's very difficult I think. But it's... I'm happy now. Of course, they also made mistakes, but everybody does. Of course we had some difficult times, but so had my parents at the beginning. Many arguments with many people.'

Did you realize when you were small that your parents were choosing for a difficult lifestyle, one that might run into a lot of problems? Did you ever feel the urge to say, 'Please papa, can't I simply go to school?'
'We didn't even know what it was to go to school. No, but I think it was better like this. Maybe sometimes when we played badly... Even though we studied so hard. Oh, then we felt so bad. But after that you had a good result and your mood changed. My parents had the same. Sometimes my father wondered for a short time if it was really good. He suffered a lot. This sometimes happened and then my mother convinced him to continue. We had to fight for fifteen years against almost all Hungary. Maybe against the whole world. It was not easy.'

Would you consider raising children in a similar manner?
'(A bit timid) Well, yeah.'

You agree with your father that a genius can be made?
'Yeah, sort of.'

Are his ideas more widely accepted these days? Are there followers?
'Yeah, a lot of people are doing this. I know some ten people who are doing this. Many people are trying to ask my father's advice. Now there are two little sisters who are also playing chess. Others are coming for advice. Of course it cannot be exactly the same. It is different for people who have financial problems and people who don't. If you can pay a good trainer or not. But in principle, yeah. I don't think I would choose chess for my kids. It can be anything. I don't know yet. But definitely I will teach them many many things at a very early age.'

Monaco, March 27

What were your initial feelings when as a very little girl you entered this male-dominated chess world?
'For me it was quite natural, because Susan and Sofia already played. When I was five it was natural for me to start to play chess among men in tournaments. It came so natural that sometimes when I had to play women (starts laughing) it came as a surprise. That's how I grew up.'

Do you think people gossip a lot about the three of you?
'I think they gossip about everybody. Of course, they gossip about us too, because we are a bit extreme in the chess world. That's an extra reason.'

I heard Zsuzsa explaining to someone in Linares about the book Cathy Forbes wrote about you. She said fifty per cent was true and fifty per cent was not...
'She said that? I think there is more that is not true. She made up many stories. But it doesn't make any sense to discuss this anymore, because she will never write this book again. I just don't want to bother about it anymore, it's such nonsense. Of course, I remember. But I prefer to say my opinion to her face rather than behind somebody's back.'

Which was the most blatant untruth that was ever published about you?
'Oh, one thing I remember particularly. Of course, they wrote many many things in Hungary in the beginning. Which I even didn't read. Only my father. And he would go, "Oh, my god, what's this?" But I remember once this guy from German television, this guy who makes these shows, Thomas Gottschalk I believe. He wanted to get me on his TV show. Something like five years ago. I said that I wanted to think about it. Finally I said "No, sorry, I don't want to do it." They didn't even offer good conditions. Anyway, I happened to be somewhere else. After that he was very upset. How could someone say no to him? And then he wrote an article that I had had a nervous breakdown. Then I was really shocked.'

Were there any cases that you considered to sue somebody?
'My father sued Adorjan. And he won the case. He said certain things on Hungarian radio. I don't know what exactly, but of course in the beginning many people said that my father was destroying the children. That he was crazy and all these things. I don't remember, but he said something really bad. My father was very angry. Adorjan had already done so many times. Then my father said enough is enough and he sued him. And they had to correct these things.'

Do you think that the moment your father started the experiment, the criticism was worse because you were girls?
'Definitely. No question. Most of it was because of this. The first thing was that we didn't go to school. That was one problem. After we got through that the problems we got from the Chess Federation were because of that. They wanted to push us to play against women or girls. And not against men.'

Did you ever have the wish to play in women's competitions to prove something?
'Well, once. When we played in the first Olympiad in Thessaloniki. Then we said, "We are going to win". (Starts laughing) Of course, between the three of us. Before the tournament, still in Budapest, I said to Susan, "I assure you I will make eleven and a half points. That's the minimum. Between eleven and a half and twelve. I promise[52]." I still remember Madl as we were going into the airplane. I said to her, "Yeah, we are going to win. In the worst case we will be second." And she said (imitating a timid voice), "No, no, no, the bronze or the silver is still OK." And of course, the three of us repeated (with bravura), "No, we are going to win." Of course not publicly, but between us. We really wanted to show it.'

How tough are you in these matters? Is your wish to win of male proportions? Or better, do you think that compared to boys, girls of your age have a lesser drive to win?
'No. I think girls can fight very hard. It depends on your personality. And it depends on what you want to achieve in life.'

What do you want to achieve in life?
'Oh, (starts laughing again) I gave you an idea! Of course I want to get further and further. I would like to get into the top ten. But I also regret that I have such bad experiences these days. Like Linares and now here[53]. The top players' behaviour. (Quietly) Sometimes this is not so nice.'

---

52 Judit scored 12½ from 13.

53 Referring to incidents involving Kasparov and Karpov in Linares and Monaco respectively.

In Linares, when Kasparov addressed you in the restaurant after your loss against Karpov you felt insulted by his tone.

'Yeah. Probably many people felt this. I felt that he spoke with me because I am a girl. Somebody told me this was his way of talking because he is from Baku. This is the way they talk. And I said, "I don't care". Suppose I had already known him for a couple of years, we had had dinner sometimes, and we were friends. Then you can allow yourself such things. But when you try to have a conversation for the first time in your life. Then you're not shouting, are you? Sort of the main point is that you're a big patzer. He said like, "You never heard of black squares?" And he named another move and said, "Why didn't you play this?" The next day he found out himself and came up to our room and said, "Oh yeah, this what I said is losing immediately. The other move is better." And I felt he didn't care about me or my game. He just cared because I lost to Karpov. I just don't understand. All chess players allow him to speak with them like...'

How did you react?

'I was just shocked. First of all I lost to him the day before. Then I lose against Karpov. No chance at all. Then he comes in when I am having a friendly conversation with Gelfand, Anand and some other people. In the middle of this conversation he starts talking to me. After that I was just shocked and said to these people, "Who is he to talk to me like I'm a five-year-old kid?" I was so shocked that I just couldn't believe it. Nobody should treat people like they don't know how to play chess. That there is such a big difference. I don't like it when they treat me differently because I am good. It happens in Hungary for example. I go to the theatre and I go to the buffet and I ask, "Do you have mineral water?" And they say no. Then they look up, recognize me and say, "Oh yes, of course." I don't like that. They have mineral water or they don't. It's not good that they have it if you're a chess player or whatever. I think some chess players maybe think they are special and they need special treatment, you know.'

As for the women's competitions, did you ever consider to take the women's title, let's say, in passing?

'(Calmly) No. (Explains) No, because I think our father educated us like that. All the time we heard that women's chess is unfortunately at a very low level. Because of that you play between men, and try to go for the men's titles. To go as far as you can. That's the main point and just forget about women's chess. It was so natural for us. Even at one point my father said, "Maybe you should play in the women's Olympiad", and I said, "I am sorry. You educated me like this. You always told me there was a different level." And I got the point (laughs). I believed in these things. So, I won't go back.'

You never thought when Zsuzsa was trying her luck in the women's cycle that in the end you might have a spectacular supermatch with her?

'Well, sometimes yeah. The main problem is that I don't feel the excitement of the women's World Championship match. There are many things that are exciting and make sense to me. There's nothing to prove for myself. If I win I would think, "OK I was better anyway". I cannot win so much for myself.'

What did you think when Xie Jun said that one day the Polgars will return to women's chess?
'Well, she thinks like this, I think differently. Of course, anything can happen, but why should I want a World Championship match where there are twenty people watching.'

Madrid, May 13

It must have been quite some time ago that you were as happy as you are now after winning this tournament? Any idea when this was?
'I was incredibly happy when I won the Hungarian championship in 1991. It was important that I showed a great result in Hungary and of course it was a strong tournament. Everyone was playing except for Ribli and Pinter. I cannot even compare this win here to the Olympiad. This result is something special.'

Is it also something special because it comes at the right moment? You had some lesser results and some people might even have started to forget about you.
'First of all this kind of result always comes at the right time (laughs loudly). Secondly in my last few tournaments I didn't play very well and my results were quite bad and I lost some rating as well. But I just kept on fighting. I knew that I was going away for two months to play four tournaments and I knew that if I do badly in the first one I have to fight in the next one and third one. If I went home I would just be sad and think about it. Just like in this tournament when I had four and a half out of five I could not say, "Nice score, but I am sorry, I am so tired."'

Did you feel tired?
'No, I just don't want to think about it. Yesterday I was tired but this was sort of because it was finished and I won the tournament. I could not allow this with two rounds to go when I still needed one point or something to win the tournament.'

Several of your opponents felt unable to have a post-mortem. You're no longer twelve and you're an over 2600 GM. Shouldn't they have gotten used to you by now?
'I don't know why this is. For them to lose to me is still almost as bad as to lose to a twelve-year-old girl. Before every big achievement of me or my sisters nobody believed it. At least most of the people or most of the chess players didn't. OK, they are nice girls, they laugh a lot, but come on, you're not serious, you don't think they can...'

And they just play well in certain positions because they play a lot of blitz games...
'And people cannot play against them because they are girls. It's all kinds of things. Of course it's different for them, because I'm the only girl who is playing in such

high-level tournaments. Unfortunately. I thought that they would get used to it after a while, but it's still not completely like that.'

Do you just shrugg it off or does it also disturb you?
'It's sort of annoying and disturbing. Why can't he smile or why can't he analyse after the game? Why is it something special to lose against me? On the other hand I don't care. If this is the way they react then it's their problem. I'm not going to force them to analyse. I didn't do anything. I didn't shoot them. I just played a game and I won.'

Of course you came close to shooting them.
'(Laughs) Yeah, maybe at that moment they felt like being shot.

So far you've had a very smooth career. You had marvellous results and became a grandmaster at a very young age. Now you're approaching your eighteenth birthday. A crucial age. For biological reasons it is often argued that in a sport like chess that combines intellect with physical strain girls are at a disadvantage from that age onward.
'I don't know. I don't think that in principle it's boys or girls. It's just a different attitude which has existed for many many years. Each year that a boy becomes older he starts to worry about earning money more. Fifteen, sixteen, seventeen years, he should look for a job. He has to study and has to earn money. On the other hand girls when they become sixteen maybe begin to think that they should start looking for a husband and have children and so on. But I think that nowadays this is getting different. Women are also enthusiastic and want to show results as men do.'

Did it ever bother you that it might be biological? That at a certain point you would find out that you are at a disadvantage compared to boys of your age?
'No, I don't think so. Of course men and women are different. But it's not a matter of being worse. Some things women can do better and some things men can do better. Or they are simply different. Like a man cannot give birth to a child. These are things that keep the world moving. I think it remains a matter of attitude. At eighteen a man cannot say, well now I want to get married and have children. That would sound quite stupid. But for women that's quite normal. Or was quite normal. So, if women say they want to have nice results and go here and there I don't see why they should not do this. In principle everybody has his or her problems. Happy days and bad days. Men can have their problems, too. They can play worse because of private problems too. That has nothing to do with men or women.'

Is it improper to ask what are your own plans in this respect? Do you have any idea till when you intend to play chess?
'In principle I definitely want to stay with chess. I don't know till when I am going to play professionally, in tournaments. Later on I probably will do some

teaching or promote chess. I think there are very good things you can do in chess. Nowadays there is some nice money in chess, but they are not arranging it in the right way (laughs a bit in embarrassment).'

Which 'they' do you mean?
'Well, I don't know. I think that in principle whenever you have a big amount of money you should really think for some time and then use it in the right way. To organize good tournaments with good conditions.'

Are you referring to the PCA?
'(Starts laughing loudly) Well, I don't want to say anything about the PCA or anything. I just want to say that there are many ways to spend money, but you need the right persons to do it. People who are enthusiastic about chess and do this full-time. Nothing else. Wherever they go they promote chess. They talk with kids and try to convince them that chess is a nice game. Someone who really believes in it himself and does not only do it for money. You just have to find the right way to present chess. Like here or in Immopar, with commentators. Everything can be shown in an interesting way. But it should be done in a professional way.'

Somehow it sounds as if you don't find the PCA professional enough?
'(Hesitates) Yeah, in a way, if you want to hear it. I don't feel that they are really professional. I don't think it's good for everybody. They really go for the American way, where number one is getting this big amount of money. I don't think it is all that important. I win this tournament but I don't know how much is the first prize. In principle I think it's better to organize a ten players' tournament like here with nice conditions, a nice playing hall, and everybody is happy. Take for example the World Championship in London. They put up, I heard, a couple of million of pounds, and most of the people were not happy. I have no problem with some people making millions of dollars, I have no problem with that. I just think that with such an amount of money you can arrange many many things to make many people happy.'

As for your future plans, how much do you get affected by leading grandmasters who don't tire of saying that you don't stand a chance to ever become World Champion?
'I don't care. First of all, I don't think that you can say of any person that he or she cannot be World Champion. Especially when they are young. Nowadays you can see that some players you never heard of are suddenly on 2650 in one year. You can never know.'

As you started to play chess very early you have been pestered by this World Championship question for many years. Do you see a development in the answers you have been giving over the years?
'When I was little I probably said "yeah" most of the time, but this is also because kids don't think about what they say in such cases. I mean, to be World Champion.

Even when you say it, you don't know what it is. Now I always say that I try my best, but that you can never know. You should play well and on top of that you need luck. It's impossible to tell how far you can go. It is also important how your life is going, your private life, your family. Some people say I am a future World Champion, others say I have no talent at all. Nowadays it's impossible to say who will be World Champion. I would have no idea who would be World Champion if we had no Kasparov and Karpov.'

Could you imagine yourself as some ambassador of chess after your active career?
'I think so, I think so. I sort of am now. Many people are happy when I play, and I am very happy when I see the audience enthusiastic. Like two days ago some gentleman came up to me and said, "Thank you very much, thank you for your game." And sometimes I feel that they are really honest about this. I sort of think that I make some people happy and that's a nice feeling. If I am no longer as good as I am now, or later when I am older and have kids, I definitely will want to stay with chess.'

Finding Bobby Fischer

When one day I remarked to Anatoly Karpov that it must have been tough on him that he always had to live with the ghost of Bobby Fischer hovering in the background, Karpov answered, 'Yes, but Fischer was always behind us. Behind Kasparov, behind me. What can you do?' Indeed, as he had been for me. No matter how many grandmasters or living legends I interviewed, the recurring question from family and friends would be, 'What about this Fischer, is he still around?' For quite a while I could honestly reply that he was not on my mind. As it had become blatantly clear to me that chances ever to talk to the Ghost from Pasadena were virtually zero, I persistently tried to ignore his very existence. There was only one problem. In almost every interview I had, Fischer would crop up. I once told Tim Krabbé about a letter we got from a reader asking to ban Fischer from the pages of New In Chess. I had no such intention, but I felt what this reader meant. Why evoke that yearning for his comeback time and again, when he was not going to come back anyway? Krabbé did not agree and flatly stated that every bit of information about Fischer was worth recording.

Of course, sometimes I did give it some thought and imagined all kinds of unrealistic adventures. Why did I not give it a try and travel to the United States to find Bobby Fischer? Wouldn't it be wonderful if I managed to convince him of my good intentions and my wish to let him tell his story after all the fabrications and lies that had been spread about him so lavishly? To begin with we shared a love for the history of chess. Had not Frank Brady's description of Fischer's library in *Profile of a Prodigy* given me a good insight into his catholic taste? And had not Kurt Rattmann, the chess book dealer from Hamburg, told me that Fischer had ordered a couple of Steinitz books from him in the seventies?

But of course, nothing happened. Until I flew back to Amsterdam from the Munich SKA tournament in the spring of 1990. Still not fully recovered from the closing ceremony, I accepted a Dutch newspaper which I do not normally read. A small article on the front page had me wide awake at once. 'Bobby Fischer pops up in Brussels', it said. Immediately I drew my conclusions. He must have been staying at Bessel Kok's, a close friend of Jan Timman's. Jan Timman was the editor-in-chief of New In Chess, so perhaps... For more than half an hour I sat staring at the words 'Bobby Fischer pops up in Brussels.' From that moment on I no longer thought of meeting Bobby Fischer as a pipe-dream.

Initially nothing much happened. The closest I got to Fischer was when I visited Bessel Kok's home to interview him on Kasparov's resignation as GMA President. Having been invited to stay for dinner I was given the choice where to sit at the table. My answer was unambiguous, 'On Bobby's chair.' After this visit I cherished good hopes that perhaps Bessel Kok might arrange Fischer's return to chess, but the gradual disintegration of the GMA and Kok's reduced interest in chess as a result soon overshadowed these hopes.

As we all know, the *deus ex machina* happened two years later, when the mysterious Mr Vasiljevic created the weird backdrop against which Fischer was prepared to defend his world title. In what follows, you find an account of why and how I travelled to Sveti Stefan. What I did not describe is that on the eve of my departure I phoned Rob Verhoeven, who unfortunately did no longer work at the Van der Linde-Niemeijeriana collection. I happened to recall that he owned a hardcover copy of Fischer's *My Sixty Memorable Games*. My humble request was if he would sell it to me so I could take it to Sveti Stefan. Rob saw no objections and handed it to me with the memorable words, 'Chances look slim, but if there is one person who will get to Fischer, it will be you.' He was right, and what is more, Fischer signed my newly acquired copy. When I was sitting in the press room of the Fischer-Spassky match on the day after my visit to the Howard Hughes of chess, a Dutch journalist who was working on an article on the Yugoslav press in wartime, interviewed me about my scoop. Carried away a bit by my elation I confessed that I felt I had done all that had to be done. What more could I wish for? I might as well quit.

This was not true. Immediately after my return from Sveti Stefan I left for Helsinki, where Garry Kasparov was to attend the opening ceremony of a big Open organized by his Chess Players Union. Naturally I wanted the World Champion's views on the return of our idol. Kasparov's reaction was dignified and well-balanced. Still, I will not easily forget the look of relief in Kasparov's eyes when he welcomed me and immediately asked, 'Did you see the games? Well, what did you think about the level?'

Bobby Fischer

Sveti Stefan, September 1992

'I'm not going to give you an interview'

While roaming the streets of Budapest, an inevitable stopover en route from Sveti Stefan to Amsterdam, I suddenly recalled a remark that Lajos Portisch made over lunch at the Linares tournament a few years back. He had noted that you have to be careful what one says in the company of journalists. When I replied that he knew that there was no need to worry he had a good laugh and reassured me with a friendly, 'Yes, but you're not a journalist!' Now, in his city, it occurred to me that I must have proven myself a journalist in his eyes after all, and I wasn't so sure whether I liked it. I had visited a well-known grandmaster and, without telling him, had written down what I had seen and heard for publication. Was I tormented by compunction and remorse? No, not really. The name of the chess player happened to be Bobby Fischer.

Part of the shock that came with Bobby Fischer's stupendous return to chess after twenty years of voluntary exile was caused by the announcement that on the eve of the first match game the Howard Hughes of chess would answer any and all questions at a press conference. Was Fischer really going to talk to the press? The scum of the earth, from whose prying curiosity he had managed to stay clear for a record two decades? Most certainly he was, but those attending his first public appearance soon found out that he only wanted to play by his own rules. Fischer chose the questions he deigned to answer and lost no time making clear that his personality had not changed materially during his public absence. Nor could there be any misunderstanding about his customary inaccessibility. He stayed in a heavily guarded and secluded apartment on Sveti Stefan, and whenever he left the island he was shielded by an impressive number of no-nonsense body guards. Chances to speak to him or even get anywhere near him seemed zero.

    The one journalist I met on the spot who had had the incredible good fortune of exchanging a few words with the living legend was bound to a solemn promise not to write about them. Most other journalists I spoke to had not even bothered to consider the possibility. One of them went as far as to confide that he could write objectively better articles if he did not get to speak to Fischer. Why hurt your ego if there is no need to? So much was clear, only an overdose of good luck and

unpredictable circumstances could make the ultimate dream of every chess journalist come true: finding Bobby Fischer and seeing for yourself what the enigma
was like.

My luck started on August 30 at 9.19 pm when the New In Chess office received
a fax from Sveti Stefan. Its contents, a request to send Mr Fischer all available Spassky games, would have been enough to create a commotion. As it was it filled the
office with Fischer Fever. It was not clear who had written the request, but at the
bottom of the page there was an authentic-looking 'sincerely Bobby Fischer'. Even
two days before the start of the match, the news about the reprise of 1972 had
failed to overly excite the New In Chess staff. There certainly was a buzz, but the
prevailing sentiment was, 'We'll believe it when we see it. Let them play some
moves first'. Even the fax could not dispel this feeling completely, but we quickly
agreed that if there was going to be a match we might have a chance to actually get
in touch with Fischer. Wouldn't it be great if he would work with NICBase? And
wouldn't it be an undreamt-of opportunity to approach him for an interview if I
were to bring him the requested articles personally?

Inevitably there were a couple of other questions to be answered as well. How
safe was it to travel there? And was it morally reprehensible to attend a match in
a country that had been internationally condemned for starting a gruesome civil
war? On the question of safety I received mainly reassuring answers. With hindsight I know that this information, while largely correct, was also simplistically
overoptimistic. Travelling through Yugoslavia was mainly time-consuming, but
both there and (especially) in the border district of Hungary you stood an excellent chance of being robbed.

The moral question I decided to dodge for various reasons. First, because I
simply did not want to miss this theoretical possibility to meet Bobby Fischer.
Secondly, because I was secretly curious to visit a country that I had last seen in
peacetime and hoped to get a better understanding of by talking to people there.
Thirdly, because I sincerely mistrusted the motives of the people whose moral
objections I heard or read about. Most of them, I was convinced, were either afraid
to go to a country at war (a very good reason), or knew that from a professional
point of view there was little use in going there, because there was absolutely no
chance that they were going to speak to Fischer or, indeed, Spassky, anyway (also a
good reason, but not so easy to admit).

Another risk to be considered was the fact that this troublesome and perhaps
even hazardous journey through a strife-torn country might, in the end, not yield
more than a close-up view of the muscle-bound chest of one of Fischer's gorillas.
So, when I arrived in Sveti Stefan around noon on Wednesday September 9th after
26 hours of travel (from Amsterdam to Budapest by plane, then on to Belgrade by
bus, and then to the coast of Montenegro by plane again), I decided to proceed
cautiously. Not that there was another option, of course, but my first impressions
in situ only reinforced my misgivings. Just before half past three in the afternoon,

ROSA DE LAS NIEVES

**Bobby Fischer at the press conference before the match
against Boris Spassky in Sveti Stefan in 1992.**

while being kept safely away by armed guards some of them trying to be friendly, most of them trying to look grim, I first set eyes on Fischer as he emerged from a black limousine to play the fifth match game. The haste with which he vanished and the scurrying people around him vividly reminded me of a picture in Frank Brady's *Profile of a Prodigy*, showing Fischer on his arrival for the first game in Reykjavik. The main differences were that Fischer had grown twenty years older, that here there were only two interested onlookers, and that, in marked contrast to the evidence from the Icelandic photograph, pointing a camera here was asking for serious trouble. Nor did the situation in the playing hall create the impression that Fischer had started mingling with mere mortals. Even from the best seats in the spectator section Fischer and Spassky were two distant figures at the far end of the players' section. Following Fischer's complaint that he was still disturbed by the noises made by people who were sitting at least 35 metres away from him, the big hole in the wall separating the two sections would even be closed off by glass partitions and a glass door after Game 6.

Now, at the beginning of the fifth game my view is not yet obstructed by this further whim of Fischer, but tiny persons they remain. Having watched the opening moves of the game I withdraw to a quiet room next to the press room to write a letter in which I inform Fischer about my arrival. Of course, any time is convenient for me to be received by him and to hand over the material he has asked for. In the meantime it does not look as if this day is going to be a convenient one for Fischer. A bad mistake ('a lemon', as he called it himself immediately after the game) has handed over the initiative to Spassky and it is clear that the white position is rapidly going downhill. Nevertheless I see no reason to put things off and approach Fischer's second, Eugene Torre, who promises to give the letter to Fischer after the game.

The only thing I can do now is wait. Two hours later Fischer resigns and I go to have dinner. On the terrace of a restaurant across the street I bathe in the balmy evening air, watch the peaceful Adriatic Sea below and have only one question on my mind. Have I written a letter, a copy of which deserves to be framed on my return to Holland or will I regret my choice of words for the rest of my life? The beer that accompanies my thoughts makes me drowsy and as it is highly unlikely that Fischer would like to see anybody after his second consecutive defeat I go to bed early. Just as I am about to turn off the light the telephone rings and the familiar voice of Svetozar Gligoric speaks the words that have me wide awake in one split second. 'Mr Fischer was very pleased by your letter and wants to meet you now or at some other time.' Temporarily befuddled by the ease with which the invitation has been obtained I hear myself suggest that tomorrow at lunchtime might be a suitable moment. Then, quickly regaining my senses I tell Gligoric that I will be down in the lobby as soon as possible. Downstairs Gligoric once again apologizes for the late disturbance and takes me to a car that has been waiting for us. The following scenes are pure Hollywood. Servile guards nod meekly and lift barriers as they recognize Gligoric's private driver. Smoothly he steers his limousine along the winding road that lead to Sveti Stefan. The causeway linking the rocky and heavily protected fairy island to the mainland we have to cross on foot. Climbing the cobblestones inside and greeting more guards Gligoric explains that this former fishermen's island was transformed into a holiday resort under Tito. In the meantime I try to get across that I have not only come to bring Fischer the Spassky files, but have also the vague expectation of attaining the impossible, an interview with him. Gligoric is afraid that this is indeed impossible, but gives me a glimmer of hope. He had sent Fischer the interview I had with him in Antwerp a couple of years ago, and Fischer had liked it. He might introduce me as the young man who had done that interview, but right now it was more important to install the NICBase program into Fischer's laptop.

For that purpose we first go to Fischer's computer expert, who also lives on the island. While he is installing the program Gligoric leaves the apartment to go to Fischer's place. On returning he urges me rather nervously not to broach the subject of an interview under any condition. He had brought up the interview with himself and this had obviously spoiled the American's mood. Neither Gligoric nor I can remember the passage, but Fischer had complained that when Gligoric spoke about his chess level when they played a couple of offhand games a few years ago, he had not been appreciative enough.

So far everything has gone swimmingly, but this slight setback makes me feel a tinge of nervousness. Nevertheless I feel miraculously neutral when we finally leave for Fischer's apartment. As if someone wants to introduce me to an acquaintance of his. No more, no less. (Curiously enough, there was a strong delayed reaction the next day, when lying on my bed and playing my walkman I suddenly got very nervous.) A castiron gate and another guard are the last obstacles separating us from Fischer. The guard nods, opens the gate and proceeds to ignore us as we enter the wide-open door which, a bit surprisingly, leads us straight into the sparsely lit living-room. Seated around a big square table are three persons. Eugene Torre, Zita Rajcsanyi, Fischer's Hungarian girlfriend, and, yes indeed, Bobby Fischer. Fischer gets up, tall, overweight, and slightly clumsy. He tries to fulfil the duties of the host and shakes hands, but his nervously darting eyes betray his unease with the situation. This is not a man accustomed to receiving visitors. Gligoric informs him that the computer expert is installing the program and the Spassky games in his computer, but that right now he does not have enough memory for the 50,000 games package that I brought as well. Fischer repeats, almost mechanically, that he does not have enough memory. For a moment I think he is joking, but his abstract stare and toneless voice show that he most certainly isn't. Gligoric, who has already urged me to take a seat next to Fischer, now encourages me to give him the presents I have brought. First I take a stack of paper from my bag, the printouts of the Spassky files. One containing some 1500 games classified by opening, the other containing the same games in chronological order. Gligoric notes that the oldest game dates back to 1948. 'When you were five years old'. Fischer smiles and repeats, '1948'. He is highly pleased with the printouts: 'Nice print, very clear'. He delves into them like a hungry adolescent about to wolf down a Big Mac. Suddenly there is a problem. He looks helplessly around him and notes that the pages have not been numbered. True, they have not. His voice is really loud. He repeats that they have not been numbered, observes that they should be and wonders whether the numbers should be at the bottom or the top of the page. Everyone is ready to help him. Like an understanding father Torre gets up, looks at the prints and points out that there is more space at the bottom of the page. Fischer agrees and, obsessed by this practical problem he drones, 'Yes, we should number them at the bottom of the page. Yes, maybe you can do that.' There is general relief, until another aspect of the problem crops up. 'But what colour pen?' Several solutions are suggested. I propose a contrasting colour, but he quickly agrees with Gligoric that black is best, because the print is black too.

This short scene has not exactly boosted my hopes of having a normal conversation with Fischer and I am racking my brains trying to find the best approach to get him to talk. Fortunately I am given some respite when Gligoric prompts me to present my other gifts. Fischer is most pleased by the magazines and the latest Yearbook. As he starts leafing through one of the magazines, Gligoric asks him if he is willing to sign my copy of *My Sixty Memorable Games*. Without any hesitation he obliges and opens the book. 'It's the English edition[54]', he notes. My reply is slightly off the point. 'Yes, it's the English edition, not the American first edition.' Briefly browsing through the book he repeats that it is the English edition. His autograph he enters with such concentration that he does not hear Gligoric's suggestion to add my name. When he has finished I tell him that we will only be too happy to send him the New In Chess products. He only has to tell us where to send them. 'Wait, I'll give you my address right away.' As he rummages in his pockets, I try to find a slip of paper. Until a much better idea pops up. 'Here, you can write it in the directory of my diary. Just put it under F.' Entering his address he wonders about the number of his post office box and for the first and only time he looks at and speaks to Zita. She smilingly confirms that the number he had in mind was the right one and returns to the book she is reading.

High time to ask Fischer whether he knows New In Chess. 'O, yeah, sure.' His reaction shows that he appreciates the magazine. It is a good magazine. There is only one but. 'It's too pro-Soviet.' 'Too pro-Soviet?' 'Yeah, definitely.' He feels no urge to explain what he does and does not like in the magazine. It's just too pro-Soviet. 'Well, I remember one good piece, in which Kasparov accuses Karpov of fixing games.' Sooner than I had expected we have reached one of his favourite subjects. The never-ending Soviet conspiracy, which, together with the worldwide Jewish conspiracy, as Fischer never tires of repeating, has had such a damaging effect on his personal life and consequently the chess world in general.

Fischer is on home ground now and the hesitant attitude of the first ten minutes is gone completely. As if actually wanting to warn me of a peril of which I am unaware, he looks into my eyes and says, emphasising every word, 'You have no idea what crooks these Soviets are. All of them.' And then he bursts into a bitter diatribe. 'All matches between Kasparov and Karpov have been prearranged. Move by move. If I have time after this match I will write a book and demonstrate that all games were prearranged. I will prove it in my book. Adorjan has written in a book that he played a game with Kasparov that they had prepared completely.' Fischer confirms that he means Adorjan's *Quo Vadis, Garry?*, at which Gligoric asks him whether he knows what 'Quo vadis' means. With the shy smile

---

54 At this point I did not know that Fischer was very unhappy about the English Faber & Faber edition and that it was a small miracle that he signed it.

of a schoolboy who doesn't, but would gladly be told Fischer guesses wrong and Gligoric tells him.

But I have no wish to discuss Adorjan's writings and bring up his accusation made at the press conference that Kortchnoi, too, had fixed his matches with Karpov. That did not sound very logical. 'All Soviets are incredible cheats. They all cheat. Kortchnoi too. Even Boris.' I suggest that he must have told Spassky and that most likely he liked the allegation, but Fischer does not react. This is not the moment to make jokes.

To keep the conversation going I make a concession. Turning to Torre I remind him of the Brussels 1987 World Cup tournament in which he participated. Many grandmasters had the feeling that Tal tried to make it sufficiently clear that he had lost the crucial last-round game against Kasparov on purpose. Torre confirms the story and Fischer draws his own conclusion. 'He admitted that the game had been fixed? That's what he said? You see, everything prearranged.'

But is it not extremely difficult, if not impossible, to prove such suspicions unless one of the players involved acknowledges such deals? 'That is just gossip, which you don't need. In my book I will prove move by move how Kasparov and Karpov did it. In a scientific manner. It took me one and a half years before I saw how they did it. When I was playing through one of their games I suddenly saw how they did it.' But what about the blunders and mistakes I dare to object. No chance. 'Even the blunders were staged to give the match a facade of reality.'

These were the same accusations he made at the press conference. Perhaps it is time to give some examples. 'No, I will not give you any examples. I will write them in my book. I'm not going to give you an interview.' Calmly I inform him that this is not an interview as I have no tape-recorder with me. For understandable reasons I do not tell him that I intend to write down our conversation as literally as possible from memory as soon as I will get back to the hotel. To divert his attention I remark that it was only in the New York/Lyon match that some people began to accuse Kasparov and Karpov of having fixed their games, but he thinks that they started this business as early as 1984. Gligoric praises my agile mind and laughingly says, 'Well, you catch on quickly.' This was the comic relief I was hoping for and enthusiastically I join him and Torre in their laughter. Even Fischer shows a faint smile.

The fun does not last long. Imperturbably Fischer continues, 'Timman is in on it as well. He's been throwing games to the Soviets.' He's talking about the World against the USSR match. 'In that match he lost against Kasparov on purpose.' My objections are ignored. In fact, I do not try too hard. I suddenly remember a remark of Timman before I left for Sveti Stefan. When I asked him how he rated my chances to get to Fischer he joked, 'You just have to hope that he doesn't think your name too Jewish.'

Gligoric is about to suggest our departure, when he sees that Fischer suddenly changes his mind. 'Okay, I will give you an example.' With agitated movements he starts banging out moves on the chess board in front of him. It is the 24th game of the match Kasparov and Karpov started in 1984. Having reached the position after Black's 16th move he looks at me and continues with an expression as if the following conclusion is blindingly obvious if one has eyes to see. 'This position Kasparov reached when he was 4-0 down. (With emphatic irony) Coincidentally this position was already known from a Yugoslav game between (...)[55] and Gligoric in which White got an advantage with 17.♖b1. (Behind me Gligoric admits that he had difficulty to make a draw, with Fischer drawing out every word as he continues) Now Kasparov thought for forty minutes, played the whimpish c4 and offered a draw.' With disgust Fischer plays the pawn to c4 and wonders, 'If that is no proof?' And there is another example he would like to show me. Energetically Fischer gets up and goes upstairs to fetch a book to corroborate his theory. Now he wants to show an endgame position that Kasparov and Karpov had deliberately aimed for. It is the sixth game from the same match. As it says in the book, the same position, albeit with colours reversed, had already appeared in a game and been analysed in depth by Ftacnik. Fischer looks at the position as if he still does not believe it. 'Chances that you get this same position are zilch. Yet, they managed to reach it by playing very badly. Kasparov even had to play the ridiculous 41.♖h5 to provoke h6. That's why he quickly played this before adjourning, because otherwise it would have been too obvious.'

I return to the fact that he keeps accusing all the 'Soviets'. Does he really also include young players like Ivanchuk ? Fischer is getting a bit tired of my incredulity. With a weary gesture of his hand he dismisses my question and murmurs, 'All of them, all of them.'

Despite Fischer's overzealous attacks the atmosphere is still relaxed and I have the feeling that I would not outstay my welcome if we talked for another hour. However, Gligoric is really tired and rightly points out that Fischer also should get some rest before tomorrow's game. Fischer and I get up from our chairs to shake hands and only then do I notice the strange shoes he is wearing. Big, black laceless rubber clogs, which combined with his somewhat clumsy way of moving about and his tall, thickset figure strengthen the impression of some sort of monster of Frankenstein. An essentially kind and innocent person, who can suddenly lash out when he is overcome by his monomaniacal obsession. But who can also be endearingly friendly and engaging. As he is now, when we take our leave.

Slightly stooping forward he stands in front of me and with genuine interest he suddenly starts asking me all kinds of questions. Whether I play chess myself ('Are

---

55 Probably he referred to the game Cvetkovic-Gligoric, played in the Lugano Open in 1983, which saw 17.♖ab1. However, according to the databases, that game also ended there and then in a draw!

you a master or only a chess writer?') and how long I will stay in Sveti Stefan? He is all smiles as he listens to my answers and even gives a short laugh when I tell him that in 1972 there was 'this American guy named Fischer' who was to blame for my chess addiction. Then suddenly he frowns again and becomes contemplative. As if he wants to give me some food for thought for the road. 'The problem with chess these days is that it is all cheating. They should change the rules to prevent them from preparing that far.' But how can you avoid that? 'You can shuffle the position of the pieces by computer before the game.' Capablanca's idea? Maybe he did not hear my question. Fischer still seems lost in his thoughts when I ask him if he is not afraid that such a new rule might destroy the chess heritage. Again he says nothing, but the wry smile he produces is a mixture of 'why' and 'oh well, we'll see'. One final time I shake his hand, not knowing which of the Bobby Fischers I have seen will stick in my mind. As I walk down the sloping path that leads from Sveti Stefan to the parking lot I feel pleasantly sentimental. Gligoric accompanies me to the limousine that will take me back to the hotel and once again apologizes for having disturbed me at such a late hour.

Garry Kasparov

Helsinki, September 1992

'It's just very sad that such a great player is living in such mental misery'

'One of my worries is the destruction of the Fischer legend. It hasn't disappeared for me and I hope that it didn't disappear for you, but it may disappear for young players like Kramnik and Lautier.' Garry Kasparov, the man whom Fischer called 'a pathological liar', reacts mildly and with compassion on the boisterous return of the eleventh World Champion. He wouldn't even rule out a match with his childhood hero, although he treats the question as a hypothetical one. 'Fischer doesn't belong to our world. He's an alien.'

'During the past fifteen years we heard so many times that Fischer was coming back, venues were announced, and nothing happened. That's why it was very hard to believe that it would happen this time. But the information we got in July from the sources around him showed that he had this intention to come back. He wanted a big audience for his views on Jews and on how Kasparov and Karpov prearranged their matches. And there was a woman, which is always a good driving force. Plus the money and the political climate in Serbia which perfectly fitted Fischer's mentality. A pariah state fighting against the rest of the world community.

'Another reason why I believed that he would play was Spassky. If Fischer was going to play it would be Spassky. Fischer would not be confident to take on anyone else.

'I spoke to many players and everyone wanted to believe that he was going to play great chess. To a certain extent we were dealing and are still dealing with people's expectations to see a big fight for the World Championship. I hope that Timman and Short will not be displeased by what I am saying, but the world does not believe that a match between me and either one of them is a full strength World Championship match. OK, maybe I see this wrong, because the World Championship match remains the World Championship match, but the general public wants a bigger event. And suddenly there was this chance. Suddenly there was Fischer. The legend replaced all sense of reality as to what was actually happening. I spoke to some very pragmatic chess players and although they understood in their minds what would really happen, they wanted to believe in something great.

'And then there was this press conference. I knew what he was going to say, because I knew his political convictions from people who had met him. What I was interested in was the reaction of the world. I think that the general reactions were quite amusing, because people pretended just not to hear. His views were not immediately rejected because of the great expectations about his performance. If he was still a great player we might see his greatness as an excuse for his ideas and convictions. Now that the miracle has not taken place you can see that the attitude of the press is changing. I didn't think this was important, because I didn't consider him to be a normal person. It's just very sad that such a great player is living in such mental misery.'

'Yes, the first game was a good game, although it gave me mixed feelings. Spassky has been playing this line for many, many years and then not take on c3 after eight minutes of thinking? That's very, very unusual. OK, Gufeld is telling everyone that the match is fixed and that Spassky is supposed to lose. I don't want to follow Fischer's example, but the first game made this impression on many people. When I saw the second game I thought that something was wrong with Fischer. The win in this ending was too simple to be missed. The second game proved for me that Fischer would have severe problems if he has to overcome very tough resistance. I don't know if anyone is analysing the games seriously, but in my opinion there were many ups and downs in this game. The worst thing about the games they played is the enormous number of moves dramatically changing the position.'

'The things he has been accusing me of and the names he has been calling me do not affect me. I am much more concerned about the other statements. His anti-Semitic remarks and his political statements. Which may create a long-term danger for chess. Being actively involved in the promotion of chess I understand that there are many places, the United States of America first and foremost, where people are going to ask, "You are promoting chess and want our children to play chess. Now just one question. The greatest known star of the West has become a neo-nazi and an anti-Semite. How can you claim that our kids will benefit from playing chess?" That is an important question and I think we have to prepare ourselves to deal with this problem.

'One of my worries is the destruction of the Fischer legend. It hasn't disappeared for me and I hope it didn't disappear for you, but it may disappear for young players like Kramnik and Lautier, who will say, "What kind of chess is this? 1972? Was this a great player?" Because he is now playing the same as he was twenty years ago. The same kind of chess. Old-fashioned chess. Like Borg playing tennis with a wooden racket. I would have preferred if they had presented Fischer with this amount of money for what he has given to chess. But not to let him play chess (laughs). Two generations have passed. He may know all the games that have been played in the meantime, but he has not been growing with this chess. I belong to this world, Ivanchuk belongs to this world, even Karpov belongs to this world. Fischer doesn't belong to this world. He thinks he is the World Champion, which is an absolutely correct statement. To my mind ex-World Champion doesn't sound right. He is the eleventh World Champion. And he's the undefeated champion of 1972. Let me ask my favourite question. How many of today's first one hundred players ever played Fischer? (Holding up four triumphant fingers when I guess wrong) Kortchnoi and Portisch, they played many games. And Polugaevsky and Hübner, who played one game each. Now that's a different world. It's not his fault. Such is life.[56]

'I think it's a hypothetical question, but I might play a match against him. However, there are several conditions that would have to be met. Conditions number one and two are connected. The match should take place in a country that belongs to civilized society, not in Yugoslavia. And there should be legitimate corporate sponsorship. I don't think that the money with which this match is paid comes from a legitimate source. People are talking about arms deals, connections with the Yugoslav government, communist money. I don't know, but it smells. People say that five million dollars is a huge amount of money. Fine. I think that if we were to play in Baghdad, we could get more than ten million. We could go and play in Medellin and they would pay us twenty million. This is not the money we are looking for. Chess cannot be linked with criminal activities. I will not accuse Mr Vasiljevic. Maybe he's a great person. But I have serious doubts. I think this is a political game supported by the Serbian government.

'The third condition if this match were to be is that he should behave himself at least a little bit. Under the pressure of the world opinion I might play with him, even if I don't care about it. But I believe that we are talking about a hypothetical question. I don't think that he will play any other serious games after this match. And, to be fair, I think that Fischer should play somebody else first. I would even support the idea of a match with Karpov. Make Karpov happy. But I don't think he'll play again. He may have been the greatest player of all time. He was perhaps ten years ahead of his time. Now he's someone from the past. He doesn't belong to our world. He's an alien.'

---

56 Jan Timman pointed out that Fischer played an exhibition game against Ulf Andersson organized by the Swedish newspaper *Expressen* immediately after the Siegen Olympiad in 1970. A closer look at the Elo-list and the index of Christiaan Bijl's *Die gesammelten Partien von Robert J. Fischer* helped me add five more names. Henrique Mecking (Buenos Aires 1970 and Palma de Mallorca 1970), Bogdan Kurajica (Rovinj/Zagreb 1970), Vladimir Tukmakov (Buenos Aires 1970), Vlastimil Hort (Vinkovci 1968, Rovinj/Zagreb 1970, Siegen 1970, Palma de Mallorca 1970) and, of course, Bent Larsen (fourteen games between Bad Portoroz 1958 and Denver 1971).

Name Index